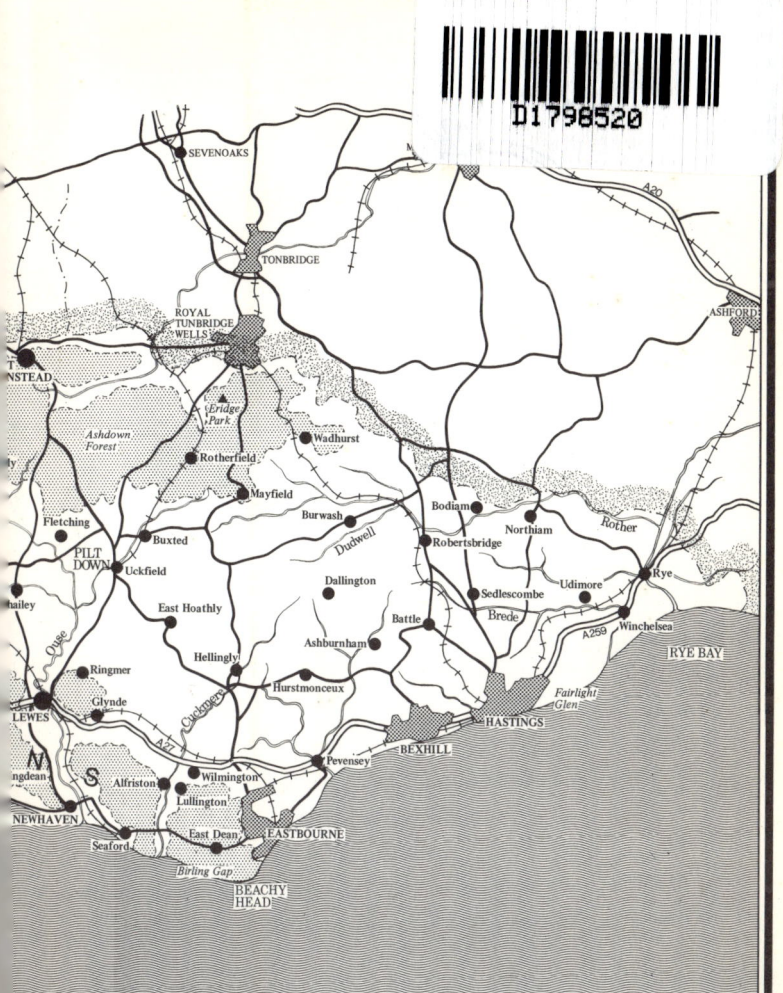

SEVENOAKS

TONBRIDGE

ROYAL
TUNBRIDGE
WELLS

ASHFORD

NSTEAD

*Eridge
Park*

*Ashdown
Forest*

Wadhurst

Rotherfield

Mayfield

Burwash

Bodiam

Northiam

Rother

Fletching

PILT
DOWN

Buxted

Dudwell

Robertsbridge

Uckfield

Dallington

Udimore

Rye

hailey

East Hoathly

Sedlescombe

Brede

Winchelsea

A259

Battle

Ashburnham

RYE BAY

Ringmer

Hellingly

Hurstmonceux

*Fairlight
Glen*

Ouse

Glynde

Cuckmere

A27

LEWES

HASTINGS

ngdean

N

S

Wilmington

Pevensey

BEXHILL

Alfriston

NEWHAVEN

Lullington

East Dean

EASTBOURNE

Seaford

Birling Gap

BEACHY
HEAD

SUSSEX

0   MILES   10

GDM

COMPANION INTO SUSSEX

Spurbooks Companion Series

Bodiam Castle and Moat

COMPANION INTO
SUSSEX

By NORMAN WYMER

*WITH PHOTOGRAPHS AND
ENDPAPER MAP*

SPURBOOKS LIMITED

Originally published by Methuen & Co. Ltd.

This edition, with revised photographs and endpaper map, by
SPURBOOKS LTD.
1 Station Road, Bourne End, Bucks
1972

Reprinted offset litho by
Biddles Ltd., Guildford, Surrey

SBN 0902875 17 5

ACKNOWLEDGMENTS

THE natives of any county are inevitably the best companions of all. For a large part of my life I have lived among the proud folk of Sussex, during which time I have visited them at work on the beaches, in the woods, and in their little village workshops, and it is from their lips that I have learnt much of what I now write. They have been my companions as I am now to be yours, and my one regret is that space does not allow me to say more about this loveliest of counties which for so long was virtually a kingdom unto itself.

Indeed, I might parody Mr. Churchill by saying that seldom has one man owed so much to so many as I do to the people of Sussex. First and foremost I would like to thank Mr. R. J. Sharp of Chichester for many kindnesses. A native who has done much to keep alive some of the old songs of the county and such traditional features as the Tipteer plays, his knowledge of Sussex generally is probably unsurpassed. Besides reading the whole book in MS. form he has also provided me with a great deal of most unusual information such as is not generally known, and the trouble he has taken on my account has been almost as great as if he had been writing the book himself.

Next, I am extremely indebted to Mr. Walter H. Godfrey, the well-known architect, for correcting various details regarding Herstmonceux Castle (which he himself restored) and many other notable Sussex buildings with which he is more than ordinarily familiar.

To single out individuals when so many have shown me kindnesses is perhaps invidious, but I cannot close without mentioning the help afforded me by the Rev. W. R. Lloyd, Rector of Stopham and Hardham, the Rev. D. L. Couper,

Rector of Crawley, Mr. Leslie Burt of Steyning, Mr. C. G. Browne of Brighton, Miss Ethel Gerard, until recently Head Librarian and Curator at Worthing, Capt. L. A. Vidler and Messrs. Edwin Dawes and W. F. McCoy, all of Rye, and Mr. R. W. Brown of Lewes. Here I may add that the officials of the various local government bodies, both urban and rural, have also been extremely helpful.

Finally, I must thank the Editor of *Country Life* for permission to reprint from various articles of mine which have appeared from time to time in that paper.

NORMAN WYMER

Eastergate,
Nr. Chichester.

CONTENTS

ILLUSTRATIONS

Reprinted with the permission of 'Sussex Life.'

The illustrations, except where otherwise acknowledged, are from photographs by the Author

CHAPTER ONE: *Sussex and Her People*

NO one can know Sussex who, on his wanderings through the countryside, does not pause now and again to chat with the men and women who are her sons and daughters: with the countrymen who set about their daily work on Down or Weald, by marsh or coppice, and return home of an evening to the villages which their forefathers built centuries ago and which succeeding generations have watched grow up from youth to old age. For, just as the natives have tilled the fields and built the towns and villages, and thus combined with Nature to give Sussex her individual charm, so, in turn, have the peculiarities of her soil and settings, and her history, helped to mould the character of the people.

A little dour—perhaps even a trifle ' stand-offish '—our Sussex folk may appear upon first acquaintance. Yet, really, that apparent suspicion of strangers is nothing more than a cloak with which to hide a natural reticence that has been born of centuries: behind it all they are as staunch and true as the most outwardly courteous of countrymen, and certainly every bit as wise, genial and interesting. Many factors have combined to bring about this reticence. To start with, Sussex, along with her eastern neighbour, Kent, has been in the forefront of our island defences to a greater extent than any other county, and has the distinction of being the only one of all the forty to be divided into ' rapes '; a system perfected by the Normans from a Saxon origin, very largely for the purpose of affording the most effective resistance to the would-be conquerors who so frequently cast longing eyes upon the coast of Sussex.

Altogether there were six rapes—Chichester, Arundel, Bramber, Lewes, Pevensey and Hastings—and each stretched from the sea right inland to the county's northern border and boasted a castle or strongpoint occupying a commanding position in its capital town; that is, the town after which the rape was named. With the strips running parallel to one another the whole coastline was thus covered, and where possible the castles were built at some strategic point along a river. Thus, while Arundel Castle was built on the River Arun, Bramber's castle commanded the Adur, and that of Lewes the Ouse, all three rivers providing easy access through the South Downs into the Weald beyond.

For two thousand years now—maybe even longer—the men of Sussex have been on their guard. Romans, Saxons, Danes and Normans, all have landed on her coast in their time, and, scattered here and there throughout the county, we may still come upon material reminders of their life in Sussex—as also we shall find links with a people far older than they; men and women who inhabited the downland country two thousand years and more before Christ was born.

Generation after generation have been called to the beaches to stand at arms since that day in 1066 when the tide of English history was turned on Sussex soil at the Battle of Hastings. 'Look ye well to the defence of Sussex' rang out Drake's Armada warning, and the volunteers stood-to with their pikes and lit their downland warning beacons whenever danger seemed imminent; but the cry went out afresh when Napoleon was ravaging the Continent, and this time the Sussex folk turned out with their muskets, and built their Martello towers on the beaches. . . . And the dangers have only increased with the advancing years. Twice in our own lifetime they have been called again to stand where their forefathers stood to answer the threats of first the Kaiser and then Hitler.

Memories have not been dimmed by the passing generations. In Sussex history has almost literally repeated itself. Old documents and letters have been passed down the line from father to son to prove that those who, in 1914 and again in 1940, stood ready with their emergency rations and clothing awaiting an order to evacuate, were taking just the same precautions as their ancestors had taken in the days of Queen Elizabeth and of Napoleon. Moreover, many who joined the Home Guard and other Civil Defence organizations in the last war could claim to be defending the very same villages as their forefathers had watched over during those earlier scares; and those who manned Pevensey Castle were doing as other Sussex men had done nearly nine hundred years ago when they had stood at this same spot scanning the horizon for the coming of the Conqueror.

Declared enemies have not proved the only source of trouble. Down the centuries the coast lay in the shadow of another ever-present menace: the menace of French raiders, who, in retaliation for the capture of their shipping, would land by night, or in daytime when the menfolk were away at work or attending the inland fairs and markets, and plunder, sack and burn whole villages. These pirates proved so great a trial that the inhabitants were often granted special privileges by the reigning monarch, and in one or two places—Tarring, in the Borough of Worthing, for instance—those rights are still maintained.

These things in themselves have done much to bring about this native reticence. But there have been other factors at work to accentuate it. The coast that proved so great a draw to our enemies was, at the same time, a haven for the smugglers who were once so active there. Every little inlet from west to east, from east to west, was a landing-ground for contraband of some kind, be it spirits, tobacco, tea or lace; every river a waterway along which to take the illicit goods to a safe inland hide-out, either to the cellar of some old cottage, to a little-known underground tunnel in the park of a stately home, to the hollow tomb of a country churchyard, or perhaps to downland caves such as those in Brandy Hole Lane, to the north-west of Chichester, whose whereabouts were only recently discovered when a number of modern houses, built on land above them, began to settle. Those who risked their lives to land their casks often enjoyed the support of the local gentry, who would leave their stable doors unfastened at night, and, in return, find a keg of spirits by their borrowed horses next morning. In Sussex, smuggling, or 'the Trade', was never regarded as dishonest but rather as work carried out in answer to the introduction by an unpopular government of taxes which, though modest as judged by modern standards, were then considered to be an infringement of liberty. Even those who did not openly throw in their lot with the smugglers usually sided with them secretly, so that, from childhood, all were brought up to see and hear as little as possible of what was going on around them and on no account to open their mouths to strangers lest they might, unwittingly, pass on useful information such as would later find its way to the ears of the Preventive Men. As Rudyard Kipling, who lived in the heart of the smuggling country, wrote, the policy, whenever a 'run' was contemplated, was to 'watch the wall, my darling, while the gentlemen go by'.

The coast, and all that it has stood for, was not the only physical feature to cause these Sussex folk to close in upon themselves, however. The dense forest of the Weald to the north of the county, together with its sticky clay—that forest wherein the finest oaks (known to this day as 'Sussex Weed') were grown for the shipwrights, and iron was smelted before the North and Midlands rose to prosperity; where the gangs of charcoal burners would be busy from morn till night providing the fuel for smelting, and where the best gunpowder in the world was once made—the Wealden forest so effectively cut off Sussex from the rest of England that, right down to the eighteenth century, when the Prince Regent turned the little fishing village of Brighthelmstone into the fashionable town of Brighton, Sussex remained much the same kingdom of the South Saxons as Aella had founded in 477, still devoid of any sizeable towns.

So sticky—or 'slubby', as they say in Sussex—was the clay

that produced those fine-quality trees and iron that it sometimes took as long as two years to transport a load of pig-iron to London from the Wealden foundries, while even in the driest summer some of the larger trees had to be taken to the River Medway on specially constructed carts, or ' tugs ', drawn by no less than twenty oxen. Even then it was often more than the beasts could do to move them. Sometimes, when they had scarcely started on their journey, the carts themselves sank so deeply into the clay that they had to be abandoned, and might be left to block the tracks for years. The oxen—employed until quite recent times for ploughing the fields—were certainly kept busy in these parts: Daniel Defoe told how, every Sunday, the wife of a certain squire had to be drawn to church by a team!

The roads of Sussex became as notorious for their shocking surface as those of Cornwall. To be bogged in the mire was an experience which all contemplating a journey had to anticipate; but it was one which those without preferred to leave to those within, with the result that Sussex remained a remote land.

The face of Sussex has changed a deal since then as it has grown in the last two centuries from one of the least known of the Southern counties into perhaps the most popular. Yet, as the native has failed to shake off his reticence in the changing years, so to this day he continues to reveal his Saxon origin not only in his flaxen hair and bright blue eyes—two features most noticeable in rural Sussex—but also in his daily speech; in such words as ' geat ' for gate, ' bleat ' for cold, ' hog-pound ' for pig-sty, ' drythe ' for drought, ' do's ' for does, ' bide ' for remain, and ' bettermost ' for something really out of the ordinary. But perhaps the best example is to be heard in the way the carter still calls ' muther-wut ' to his horse when he wishes it to turn to the right. . . .

Not that he is entirely Saxon. In many parts, though particularly around Rye, Winchelsea and Hastings, words that are unmistakably French in origin may still be heard—' frap ' for hit, 'boco' for very much, 'peter grievous' for irritable, 'dishabil' for untidy, and 'valiant' for stout: words to remind one of the Norman conquerors, of the French merchants of the Middle Ages with whom the natives of these parts carried on an illicit traffic in the export of wool, and of those unhappy Huguenot refugees who, driven from their homeland by the Catholic persecutions of the seventeenth century, sailed into these Sussex ports to seek shelter. Their French descent is so pronounced in these parts that some believe that the East Sussex folk song, *The Old Sow*, now so familiar for its grunt, snort, whistle and chorus, was originally introduced from France by one of these refugees or merchants.

Whether Saxon or French, these Sussex folk sometimes have a most unusual way of putting things. If, when you inquire at the village shop for old Maister Brown, who will be 84 come Michaelmas, his daughter shakes her head and laments that he is 'nohow' or 'out of kilter', it will be her way of stating that he is far from well. On the other hand, should she reply 'about as common' she will mean that at least he is enjoying reasonable health.

Fail to close the door behind you when you step into the comfort of some Sussex homestead, and the cottager will ask, in his dry, good-natured way, whether you were born at Yapton; just as, if you call in upon the village saddler and stand in his light while he is trying to work, he may challenge you to deny that your father was a glazier! And should you, while in his workshop, flatter the craftsman for his work rather more than he considers he deserves, he will almost certainly turn round and tell you to 'butter me no parsnips'. For these clannish people cannot abide anything savouring of the insincere, since they themselves are so very straight and downright.

Words that would have no meaning elsewhere are everyday parlance in rural Sussex; words like 'scrouging' for pushing, 'dentical' for weak or feeble, 'shruck' for shrieked, 'ampery' for rotten, 'budge' for serious or solemn, 'beazled' for weary, ' ackle ' for fit, and a hundred others every bit as unusual. Yet of the whole Sussex vocabulary none is heard more frequently than ' sure*leye* '; a word with which the native will end all sentences to which he wishes to give special emphasis.

This raises a most important point: the place names of Sussex are mostly pronounced entirely differently from the way one might expect, and those who fail to master the strange county lore are dubbed at once as ' furriners ', or ' up from the Shires '. Unnatural though it may sound,

> If true Sussex you would be,
> Say sure*leye*, not surely.
> In names of places stress should dwell
> Upon the final syllable.
> Thus, Arding*leye* doth well accord
> With South*wick*, Ber*wick* and Sea*ford*.

So too it should strictly be East Hoath*leye*, Helling*leye* and Chidding*leye*. The trouble is, though, that even where the emphasis is laid upon the first syllable matters are not entirely simplified; for instance, while Easebourne (near Midhurst) becomes ' Ezbourne ', Halnaker turns into ' Hannaker ' and Cuckfield into ' Cookfield '; worse still, Burwash, to the local inhabitants, is always ' Burrish '; as, for that matter, is Horsham ' Horse-ham ', and Alfriston ' *Orl*friston '. So that, really, there is little to guide one, and the best thing to do is to listen attentively to the native and just hope for the best!

Behind that crust of suspicion, our Sussex folk will be found to possess an unusually entertaining dry sense of humour. The Brighton fishermen, for instance, say of the Hastings fishermen that when it is time to get up in the morning, they first hold a lighted candle out of the window. If the flame blows out they will shake their heads and declare: ' 'Tain't safe to go out for there be a gale blowing ', and at once return to bed; on the other hand, if the candle stays alight it will be: ' 'Tain't no good going off, for there bain't no wind! ' Then, too, there was the smuggler who so tied up an Excise man with his subtle witticisms that he was successful in getting the latter to carry his cask of contraband spirits and then hand it back to him at the end of a long and weary trek! Best of all was the time when Lord Leconfield, a former Lord Lieutenant, lost so many sheep on his estate at Petworth that a C.I.D. detective was sent down from Scotland Yard. In the course of his inquiries he called in at the ' local ' where ' Old Garge ', fully aware of the latter's mission, even though the detective endeavoured to keep this secret, implied that he knew the whereabouts of the sheep. As was intended, the detective sidled up to him and stood him a drink; and so it went on. At last the detective revealed his identity and prevailed upon the countryman to name the thief. Whereupon ' Garge ', promising to tell all he knew if he had but one more beer, gulped down the last dregs, licked his lips, and said dryly: ' Well, Lord Leconfield had 'em, but he ain't got 'em now, 'as he! "

They can certainly be stubborn—even cussed—too, as George IV discovered to his cost when the bell-ringers of Burwash flatly refused to ring the bells as the king passed through the village on his return to Brighton because the latter had stupidly forgotten to order them beer on his outward journey. Their county motto always is ' We wunt be druv ', and they are even less likely to forget this than the Christmas plays of their Tipteers or the old songs and dances of their fair countryside, many of which still mean much to them—*The Sussex Mummers' Carol, Bonny Breast Knot, Over the Sticks, The Triumph, The Sussex Sheep-Shearing Song*, the remarkable gipsy carol, *King Pharim*, and, of course, *Sussex-by-the-Sea* which, though comparatively modern and certainly not traditional, has become more or less the ' county anthem '.

Though, here and there, the jerry-builder has cut deep inroads into much that was once beautiful in our countryside, the old-time Sussex countryman, at heart, has really changed but little. Up by the Surrey border, as on the green at Battle, he still plays marbles on Good Friday as his forefathers have done for close on three centuries; on Bonfire Night at Lewes he yet displays his 'No Popery' slogans with as much feeling as if it had been *his* friends who had been burnt at the stake; at Ebernoe, too, when times are normal, he will roast his sheep in the open as did the medieval peasants at their Boon Day feasts. His father's son, he remains as faithful as ever to those old beliefs and superstitions to which his father and his grandfather pinned such confidence and which he himself has found no occasion to discredit. To this day there are some who have not quite shaken off their belief in the fairies—or, rather, ' Pharisees '—of the woods and downs! True, they may take rather more finding than of old, but on Downs and Weald alike they are with us still, ready to talk to those who will go off the beaten track to seek them out . . . the countryman with appetite enough for steak and kidney pudding fried for breakfast, if only he could get it, and with happy memories of the ' pond ' and eel puddings, the bullace cheeses, flead cakes and ' lardy Johns ', and the wheatear pies, made from that particularly succulent downland bird which they used to pot and send to London—not to mention the myriad home-made wines, all of whose recipes have been handed down from one generation to the next through the centuries . . . the countryman whose ancestors have stood up since time immemorial to the old gibe of their neighbours, ' Silly Sussex '.

When things have gone wrong—as, for instance, when the sign painter mistakenly painted Sir John Flagstaff ·for Sir John Falstaff, outside the village pub—and news has filtered through to Kent, Surrey or Hampshire, the wits beyond the border have invariably made fun of them. But the Sussex folk will never be ' druv ' . . . For silly, they know, comes from the Saxon ' selig ', meaning happy or holy, which presents a very different picture, especially when one remembers that in an ancient carol Christ is referred to as the ' Silly Child '.

Certainly the people of Sussex could never be called silly in

the sense of stupid. They have given too much to the world
by their skill and enterprise for that. It is, to a large extent,
upon the famous South Down sheep that the great sheep
industries of both Australia and New Zealand have been
founded; upon the Sussex red bulls that the South African and
Argentine herds have long depended. It was in Sussex that
the glass-house industry found its birth; from the pips of a
Sussex vineyard that the first Californian seedless raisins were
raised. While the Light Sussex poultry are as popular on the
Continent as is our downland Bob-tail sheep dog.

Retiring and perhaps a little quiet then, strong-willed, yet at
all times amusing and wise too, these men and women of
Sussex must always be the true companions for those who
would see the county in all her moods and tenses. The ploughman on the downland furrow, the hurdle-maker in the woods,
the village blacksmith and the wheelwright, the fishermen of
the coast, these and many other sons of the soil and sea give
life to the Sussex scene as do the quail of the Pevensey Marshes,
the wild duck of the Manhood, the tern of the Cuckmere
Valley, the scoters of Rye Bay or the herons of Parham Park.
. . . They are an indivisible part of Sussex, like the chalk and
flint and marble, the clay and sandstone that combine to give
this land such rich variety, leaving their mark on town and
village architecture—on home and church alike—as upon the
fields themselves.

And how very varied this land of Sussex is—this land so
long and wide that it is divided into two separate administra-
tive areas with capitals at Lewes and Chichester, and may soon
be split into three—with her harbours, creeks and marshes, her
plains, rivers and heather-clad moors, her copses and forests,
and, above all, her downs—those glorious whale-back South
Downs that roll on and on for something like eighty miles
from Hampshire right down to Eastbourne; those downs,
barren to the east of the Adur and wooded to the west, whose
springy, almost velvet, grass is still clipped short in parts by the

tender mouths of sheep, even though their numbers have dwindled terribly in the last decade or two; those downs that are still dotted, here and there, with windmills, many of which once provided the power not only for grinding the corn but also for working the great bellows of the Wealden iron furnaces. . . . Very varied; very lovely.

CHAPTER TWO: *The Manhood and Chichester Harbour*

I. THE HUNDRED OF MANHOOD

I

SINCE it was at Selsey that, virtually, Christianity was introduced into Sussex there can be no more appropriate point at which to start our explorations than in that flat peninsula to the extreme west upon whose southernmost tip Selsey stands —that peninsula to the south of Chichester known as the Hundred of Manhood.

It was in 680, or thereabouts, that St. Wilfrid, the exiled Archbishop of York, landed at Selsey to found the monastery that was later to become the seat of a new diocese of Selsey, and, ultimately, of Chichester, and the tales they tell of his arrival are many. Once, before his exile—in the hour of his glory—he nearly set foot here accidentally. He was sailing home up the English Channel, after his consecration by twelve bishops at Compiègne, when a storm drove his ship towards the peninsula and left him stranded on the sands. His reception was anything but courteous, and it must have been a terrifying experience for St. Wilfrid and his small body of companions to see the Sussex ' savages ' descending upon them in overwhelming numbers, uttering curses that would have pleased even Balaam as they went. All efforts to appease them —either by kindly word or with offers of money—proved in vain. Yet, where saints trod, miracles sometimes occurred, and just at the moment when things appeared at their blackest one of St. Wilfrid's companions slung a stone at the ' chief magician ' with such uncanny accuracy that it penetrated his brain; and then the prayers of the Saint himself were answered when the sea returned as quickly and unexpectedly as it had gone out, to set their ship afloat once more.

When St. Wilfrid arrived in 680 his fortunes had changed; he had been deprived of his bishopric and banished from the North of England. But those who greeted him were likewise in a different mood. For three years now there had been drought—or ' drythe '—in this heathen country: the land was parched, and the people dying daily of thirst and famine. Indeed, it is said that, rather than await the inevitable end, many even chose to drown themselves in the sea, going down to the water with joined hands to give themselves courage.

Thus, it was a crowd of weary and ravenous people who watched this second landing, and there is a local tradition to the effect that St. Wilfrid gained his first converts by making nets and teaching the people how to fish where hitherto they had known only how to clasp their hands together and take eels from the ponds. And as he held his first public baptism here the rains came for the first time in those three long years; ' soft and plentiful showers ' that brought the land back to heart and gave the people hope once more.

It was a miracle, but it brought Christianity to Sussex. King Edelwalch himself soon granted him lands around the tip of the peninsula; and when, some five years later, Edelwalch was slain by Caedwalla, and St. Wilfrid achieved the seemingly impossible by converting the new king, the latter, in gratitude, not only confirmed the earlier grant, but also added further lands.

So it was that, with the whole Manhood, together with the parishes of Aldingbourne, Lidsey, Eastergate, Mundham and one or two widely separated places now in his possession, St. Wilfrid, already much beloved of the people, set up his monastery at Selsey and appointed the four priests who accompanied him on his expedition secular canons.

II

Right down until 1081, when William the Conqueror ordered the removal of all cathedrals from villages to cities and work began on the building of a new edifice at Chichester, the See of Selsey flourished. To what stately proportions St. Wilfrid's Cathedral, built by the greatest of all builders among bishops, may have arisen will never be known, however, for the only relics left to us are a holy water stoup, now in the chapel of Arundel Castle, and two carved stones—one of Lazarus and the other of Christ with Mary and Martha—both of which may be seen in Chichester Cathedral.

Selsey was then a very different place. The sea has since eaten deep into this western end of Sussex with the result that the cathedral, together with the ' Park ' where St. Wilfrid and the twenty-one bishops who followed him kept their deer, now lie several miles out beneath the coastal waters . . . unseen, but neither forgotten nor, it seems, unheard. For there are some who still declare that they can hear the muffled toll of the old bell below the tidal waters when the wind is still; just as to this day the fishermen talk of going to fish ' in the Park ', even though both have been under the water at least since Elizabethan times.

Selsey was then so nearly an island that there is a tradition to the effect that it gains its very name from ' Seal Island ' or the ' Island of Seals '. This once popular belief has become the subject of much controversy in the Manhood in recent years, however, for many, remembering St. Wilfrid, prefer to think that ' Selsey ' is but a corruption of ' Selig ', the Saxon word for holy. Again, some point out that ' sel ' was the word the Saxons used to signify fertile soil, while others think always of the little town as the ' Island of Willows ' (' sallow ' being a local alternative to willow), in the same way as they picture Thorney Island, a little farther to the north-west in Chichester Harbour, as the ' Island of Thorns '.

Which of these theories is the correct one is, of course, impossible to say. Though it is doubtful whether seals really frequented these shores, the whole Manhood is acknowledged to be among the most fertile farming lands in Southern England, with willows abounding in the marshes. Nor could anyone deny that Selsey has the right to be considered holy in the face of such age-old traditions.

Not that the morals of its inhabitants have always been beyond reproach, it seems. Until a vicar ordered its burial some years ago, an old gravestone in Selsey churchyard revealed a somewhat opposite outlook :

> Here lies ——'s daughter, Charlotte,
> Who was born a virgin and died a harlot.
> For fifteen years she kept her virginity,
> Not a bad record for this vicinity.

III

Except for a few attractive Tudor and Georgian houses and cottages and the chancel of the original church, now known as St. Wilfrid's Chapel, Selsey has grown into a place of little charm whose magnificent stretch of sands—where, as on those of Bognor Regis to the east, racehorses can be seen at exercise from time to time—has caused the once quiet village to develop into a miniature holiday resort.

Nevertheless, Selsey has another side to its character. As the old ' town crier ', dressed in frock coat and top hat, still trundles around the district on his tricycle, calling all to attention by his handbell, so in the fishermen's quarters from East Beach down to the Bill are men who will always be a part of Sussex; the descendants, maybe, of those whom St. Wilfrid taught and converted.

To watch these sturdy veterans of the sea landing their mackerel, which they then hawk around the Manhood in carts, calling, as they go, their old familiar cry : ' Mackerel, mackerel;

fresh Selsey mackerel '; to see them gathering in their cockles; or, perhaps more important still, to watch them setting off in their ' crabbers '—smart little craft of the cutter type—in search of crabs and lobsters, often lowering several hundred ' pots ' at a time into the water, is a joy which no one with a love of the sea should miss.

Fish caught off the shores of the Manhood has long been renowned for its succulence. The fishermen take a particular pride in both the lobsters and the crabs, and always make their own ' pots ', cutting their willow rods in the marshes, and then peeling them and weaving them on their circular frames either on the open beach or in a shed in their cottage gardens.

In the fishermen of Selsey we may meet with men as staunch as any, who man the lifeboat and brave all weathers to go to the rescue of ships in distress in the shoals and sandbanks off this part of the coast, and who can spin many a good and exciting yarn; men who knew what it was to be machine-gunned by Nazi airmen in the last war and yet never flinched from fulfilling their task of bringing in the fish.

Entertaining folk, they have many a tale to tell of the keepers of Owers Lightship, some five miles off the Bill, who flash their warning signals to shipping to keep clear of the shoals between the lightship and the Bill, and who, in the past, would wile away their time making waterproof straw hats which became so popular that they were soon widely sought; of the mouse-trap industry where the womenfolk would help to turn out a thousand traps a week which were exported all over the world and, in fact, were the cause of the old tramway being laid down to link Selsey with Chichester. . . .

IV

Throughout the centuries men have waged relentless war against the waves, not only around the Manhood, but along the entire coastline. Tragic stories have been recorded at different periods of houses being washed away overnight and whole families lost, and how great the cost in Sussex soil has been can be judged by the fact that where once the coast between Selsey Bill to the west and Beachy Head to the east was straight, it is now an immense bay. It is the strong Atlantic tides of the Channel, coupled with the prevailing south-westerly winds, that have caused the havoc. Together they drive the shingle eastwards, which explains not only why the groynes on the beaches are set with a slight westerly tilt, but also why the coast to the west of each of these headlands slopes gently, whereas to the east it shelves abruptly.

Part of the Manhood to suffer particularly badly from these inundations is Pagham Harbour, known until comparatively recent years as Selsey Haven. It was round about 1345 that the sea first devastated something like 2,700 acres of rich loam land here to cut an estuary a mile wide that stretched for an even greater distance as far inland as Sidlesham. Yet more than once since then the sea has receded, only to return again. Not even the artificial shingle banks which a previous owner of Norton Priory laid across the harbour between the rocky little inlet of Church Norton, a little to the north of Selsey's fishing quarters, and what is now the Pagham Beach Estate, have been able to stem the tides.

Few inlets can have alternated between farmland and port quite so frequently. Where in the Middle Ages men once tilled the soil, at the time of the Napoleonic scares Nelson was able to sail up to the tide mill which Woodroffe Drinkwater, a Chichester corn merchant, erected at Sidlesham in 1755 to load his ships with grain, while the smugglers landed their contraband here at dead of night. Yet long before the nineteenth century was out, 750 acres had been reclaimed and men were driving the plough once more, until, in 1910, the seas came yet again to give us back the harbour we see to-day. But it is a very different harbour from the one that Nelson knew: the mellow old tide mill, boasting three water-wheels and eight pairs of stones, and capable of grinding a load of corn in an hour, has departed, and the water is too shallow to-day to beach anything larger than a skiff at Sidlesham, let alone a frigate! Still, the harbour is deepening almost year by year, and sand is spreading over the bottom, driving away the cockles.

v

Once known as Pagenham, the whole of this parish into which the harbour has been cut was transferred from the See of Selsey to that of Canterbury, whose archbishops made the district one of their temporary abodes until, finally, Cranmer ceded the land to Henry VIII. Thomas à Becket, accompanied by a large retinue, often stayed in the palace here, and it is to him that Pagham's church—which, it is thought, may well have been built by one of the archbishops—is dedicated; indeed, it is a popular belief that it was a dispute concerning the manor of South Mundham in this same lordship that caused the friction between Thomas à Becket and Henry II which ultimately led to the former's martyrdom in Canterbury Cathedral.

As a place, Pagham, like Selsey, is disappointing. Sidlesham, a sprawling village if ever there was one, is rather more attractive. It is a village of two moods. The corner by the harbour, swept by strong sea breezes, with a few small dinghies moored near the spot where the old mill stood, provides a remarkable contrast to the farmlands clustered around the church, a mile away, with the cows mooing, the wood-pigeons cooing and the tractors purring, and, behind it all, the square and unusually pleasing tower of the church looking down benignly from above the tree-tops upon all that is going on. Sidlesham is by far the largest village in the Manhood, and with the Sussex farmhands and the Land Settlement workers from the North of England working in adjacent fields, is as varied in its character and make-up as it is widespread. Here, as in a great many of the scattered hamlets all over the peninsula, are many beautiful Georgian farm-houses and cottages, a great number of them having been built by the merchants of the eighteenth century when Chichester was an important corn exchange; but, alas, there are also homes that are far from beautiful.

VI

There are not really many villages in the Manhood. Except for the three already mentioned and the two Witterings—East and West—by Bracklesham Bay, whose shore is renowned for its fossils, it is almost entirely composed of scattered hamlets— pleasing little hamlets like Earnley with its windmill, two sails of which are made of canvas, and Highleigh with its haunted house in which the sound of crockery falling to the floor is sometimes heard—with perhaps an inn or ale-house, a farm-house or two and a few odd cottages, some of them perhaps three miles from the nearest bus stop.

It is that kind of country—agricultural, pure and simple: Peter Scott country, studded with marshes in which the willow and rushes prosper, and in parts so crossed and criss-crossed with rifes and ditches that only those with a knowledge of the terrain may walk any distance across the fields without finding their way cut off by water. . . . The kind of country that one dislikes for its flatness or loves for its sunsets and its wild life all about. It is the birds that make the Manhood— the whimbrel and the oyster-catcher, the guillemot and the bittern, and the myriad other sea birds that call from Pagham Harbour, one of the last breeding-places of the common tern; the pheasants that nest in so many of the cottage gardens; the wild duck and other sea fowl which, though lessening in numbers, still cause the sportsman to bring out his gun; and, above all, the wild swans swooping low over the hedges to join the cattle in the fields by the ditches as the reddening sun sinks steadily lower in the western sky to silhouette those passing clouds in a way that can be fully appreciated only when one has unbroken distance as in the Manhood.

VII

Two farm-houses of special interest are Carthagena Farm, a little to the north of Somerley, some of whose timbers are said to have been taken from the Spanish galleon of the same name that was grounded off Bracklesham Bay at the time of the Armada; and Cakeham Manor, in the parish of West Wittering. The latter was once the palace of the bishops of Chichester, one of whom, Bishop Sherburne, built the tower, and you can still see their little private chapel, which is so old that many believe that it may well have been used when the see was still at Selsey. In the churchyard at West Wittering is the tomb of a boy bishop; one of only two such tombs in the country, the other being at Salisbury. In the Middle Ages every cathedral city appointed its boy bishop who would be elected on St. Nicholas's Day from among the choristers, the rest of whom were likewise each granted the temporary rank of a church dignitary. He held office until December 28, during which time he was allowed to wear episcopal vestments and had the power to dispose of any prebends that might fall vacant during his term. One of his duties was to preach a sermon at Childermass, though this boy did not live long enough to undertake this particular task. As he died during his term it is surprising that he was not buried in the cathedral itself, since this was one of the rights pertaining to the exalted rank of a serving boy bishop.

In some respects West Wittering is as interesting historically as Selsey—perhaps even more so. For tradition has it that it was at a point near here—at a spot known as Ella Nore—that Aella landed with his three sons in 477 to found the kingdom of the South Saxons, though this claim is challenged by Selsey folk who believe the landing to have taken place in their vicinity, perhaps at the very spot where now rides Owers Lightship. But West Wittering has another and far older link with the past. Through the narrow and extremely tricky entrance between here and Hampshire's Hayling Island the Romans sailed into Chichester Harbour to found the great city of Regnum, and it was here, they say, that their general, Vespasian, landed on mud so squelchy that many of his elephants became bogged!

2. CHICHESTER HARBOUR

I

For those who love the sea Chichester Harbour, into which the Romans sailed over nine hundred years ago, must ever hold special appeal, and there are few more enjoyable experiences than to follow its whole jagged and devious coastline round from, say, Itchenor, almost due north of West Wittering, to Prinsted, by the Hampshire border (only more perfect is to sail upon the waters themselves). Haven of yachtsmen young and old, good and bad, this harbour can have changed but little through the ages. It is a waterway that brings sportsmen from the far corners of the world to compete in the international sailing contests that are staged here from time to time. No less than four channels—the Chichester Channel, Bosham Channel, Thorney Channel and Emsworth Channel—have eaten into the mainland so deeply as to give us three great headlands in which may be found a series of quiet little creeks. Though no longer a great commercial highway, in summertime it is as busy as ever—pleasurably busy in a most refreshing way. For what more refreshing than to stand by the quayside of any one of these creeks and watch the twelve- and fourteen-foot International dinghies sharing these inland waters with the Fireflies, Merlins and Sharpies, each yacht constructed to the design of the harbour club whose pennant she bears; or, if it be on a Sunday between early May and mid-September, to watch the hoisting of the Blue Peter and see the members of one of these clubs—of Itchenor, Bosham, Birdham or Dell Quay in Sussex, or of Emsworth, Langstone or Hayling Island in Hampshire, all of which enjoy rights that are centuries old— lining up their yachts for their weekly races?

II

Since the water lies deepest off Itchenor, the starting-point for our harbour explorations, and Bosham, both these places enjoy a rather greater popularity than the other creeks, and at each may be found some of the better known racers and cruising yachts. In fact, so ideal in many respects are the conditions at Itchenor that some enterprising Georgian gentle- man once attempted to develop it into an important ship- building centre which he hoped might soon rival Southampton itself. The scheme came to an abrupt end, however, when a serious accident occurred at the first launching, so that the beauty of Itchenor, with its row of Georgian houses—prim little houses of the larger cottage type as the Georgian ones so often are—leading down to the wide open channel, has been left undisturbed.

Our first call after leaving Itchenor will be Birdham, and a few miles farther on towards Chichester we come to Dell Quay, one of the most enchanting corners of Southern England. These two—Birdham and Dell Quay—have a great deal in common in that it was they who handled the traffic when the Chichester Channel formed so important a commercial high- way. While the Romans made Dell Quay their port for Chichester (a proud position which this Sussex hamlet enjoyed until the early years of the nineteenth century), in 1824, with a view to improving transport communications with inland

Sussex, a canal was cut from Birdham to link the harbour with the River Arun at Ford. A tremendous volume of traffic once passed to and fro along this Chichester Channel, and as we stand by the water's edge at either of these spots to-day we can think of the coasters moving seawards with their many and various cargoes of which perhaps none were more important than the flour for the West Country, the malt for Ireland, and the timber —that home-grown ' Sussex Weed ', felled by Sussex men— that would be sent to the dockyards of Portsmouth and Devonport to be fashioned into the ' wooden walls of England '. Nor was it only a one-way procession. From the sea itself other vessels made their way for Dell Quay or Birdham with the much-needed supplies of Norfolk barley, Newcastle coals, sundry provisions from Ireland, and matured wines from Portugal.

Though the channel has been used for commercial traffic in quite recent years, with the coming of the railway the greater part of the canal has long fallen into disuse, while such of it as is left is largely choked with rushes and is less navigable than when Turner painted the scene. Still, this section may come into its own again, for there has been some talk in recent months of clearing it and stocking it with fish, thus making it a resort for anglers and an inland boating centre.

Birdham is steadily rising in importance once more. In the last few years considerable alterations and extensions have been made to this part of the canal with a view to turning it into a miniature boat-building centre, and a number of quite sizeable craft have already been constructed here.

It is only to be hoped that this latest enterprise will not spoil the delightful old-world charm of this yacht basin with its lock and pleasing little green, its scattered cottages and its tide mill, which, though no longer used as such, is still haunted by the ghost of ' Old Stevens ', a former miller.

Birdham has other memories than those of shipping, though. Fred Lillywhite, the ' Nonpareil bowler ', who was born at

Westhampnett, a mile or two to the east of Chichester, used to play cricket in a field that is now one of the mill ponds, while on June 8, 1824, Birdham was the scene of a notable prize-fight when Tom Spring, champion of England, fought Jack Langan, champion of Ireland, for £500 aside. The contest was fought on a wooden platform and 53 farm wagons, ranged around the arena, provided accommodation for the spectators. The contest went to 77 rounds, at the end of which both combatants were so exhausted that the fight ended by Spring simply pushing Langan over!

III

Enchanting as Birdham is in many ways, Dell Quay is perhaps even more so. To stand upon the little jetty here and look out at the sailing boats as they pass between the wooded banks of ' Old Park ' towards those glorious South Downs that stand out so majestically in the distance, is to gaze upon a waterscape the like of which is seldom seen outside Cornwall. Yet to return to the jetty of a summer's evening, when the sun is setting over Bosham, and, by way of contrast, to face southwards to watch the swans coming up the water, may well bring ecstasy to any man.

Dell Quay has been described as the smallest port in England, and this may well be true. Certainly, there can be none with fewer houses. Yet once it ranked as the ninth port in England. It sent two ships to fight the Armada, and when Queen Elizabeth visited Chichester she granted special harbour rights ' as far as the sound of a horn blown from Dell Quay could be heard '.

In a district so closely associated with the Romans it is not surprising to find relics of their time, and about three-quarters of a mile south of Dell Quay there are a number of Roman flanged roofing tiles lying about under the trees. Since these appear by an outcrop of mottled red clay, which forms the local subsoil, it is possible that they may mark the site of a Roman brickworks or pottery.

IV

Dell Quay comes into the parish of Appledram, whose fine Early English church, containing a squint, is thought to have been rebuilt by the monks who once had a monastery at Bosham. They say that this church was built on the site of a Saxon burial mound, and particularly interesting features are the beautifully carved door and an old dial on the inside of a window by which, in the days when clocks were unknown, the sexton could roughly tell the time in the morning by studying the position of the shadows cast onto the sill. Originally this church was a Chapel of Ease for Bosham College, and at one time William of Wykeham was a prebendary here.

Just by the church is an old farm-house—known as 'Ryman's Towers'—containing a tower-like structure which is the object of much controversy. While some believe it to be the remains of a fortified manor, others hold that it was simply a country house, part of which contained three storeys. It was built in the fifteenth century by the Rymans, and tradition has it that one of the family, anxious to fortify his home with a tower, imported stone from Ventnor and Bembridge, in the Isle of Wight. At that time the Bishop of Chichester was anxious to build a bell tower for the cathedral, but was experiencing difficulty in obtaining suitable materials at a reasonable cost. Seeing in Ryman's enterprise his opportunity, he waited until the latter had accumulated sufficient stone for his (the bishop's) needs, and then advised the king that one of his subjects was undertaking a work that, in the sovereign's own interest, should at once be quashed. When the king agreed, the bishop was able to persuade Ryman to hand his precious stone to the masons of the cathedral; and that is why the bell tower is still known as 'Ryman's Tower'!

V

Appledram—alternatively spelt Apuldram—was once a salt-producing centre. At one time there were something like three hundred salt-pans in Sussex, and a prosperous trade was carried on with the French and Dutch. Indeed, its past importance lingers not only in the names of some of the houses round about but also in the highway, known as Salt Hill, that still leads from the salt mill at Fishbourne inland to Funtington and the downs beyond.

To collect the salt, shallow pans were constructed of well-beaten clay, and into these the sea-water was drawn to a depth of perhaps three or four inches. Here it was left for as long as four or five years until sufficient of the water had evaporated to leave a strong brine, which was then transferred to shallow iron pans and subjected to a lengthy process of boiling. This boiling caused the salt to crystallize on the surface of the liquid, and after a time the crystals grew to such size that their own weight carried them to the bottom of the pan. So that, when the boiling was over, all that was necessary was to rake them out and set them to drain and dry. It is an interesting fact that one of the methods used to this day in the great salt-producing county of Cheshire is based entirely upon those employed by the Romans at Appledram and elsewhere.

VI

At Appledram we are almost at the head of the Chichester Channel, and from here we shall move westwards to Bosham, which commands the second channel beyond the first of those tongues of land I mentioned earlier. On the way we shall pass through the main-road village of Fishbourne—also noted for its salt-pans—where a number of Roman discoveries have been made from time to time, including part of a villa, with a bath and a tessellated pavement. Though not much to look at from the road, there are, nevertheless, some surprisingly pleasant peeps in the meadows to the south, with the mill and the church, in which may be seen a beautiful fragment of stained glass portraying ' the Body of Christ '—all that is left of a window ruthlessly smashed by the Cromwellians.

Bosham—pronounced always as ' Bozzum '—is a perfect corner of old England, with its little green leading down to the water-front, its harbour and fascinating lanes, its mill-house and manor, its eighteenth-century house looking proudly down upon the moat in which, tradition has it, Canute's infant daughter was drowned, and its high-spired partially Saxon church where she now lies buried. ' Happy Bosham ' we in Sussex call it.

And what coming and going this little village has seen! It was here that King Canute commanded the waves to recede, and the local inhabitants have a most acceptable explanation of how this well-worn story may have come about. Once rich corn and pasture land, the fields of Bosham, it seems, were menaced by the sea when Canute, who lived in a palace where now stands the early seventeenth-century gabled and moated manor-house, and who was keenly aware of the dangers, conceived the idea of building earthworks upon the foreshore with which to keep the sea at bay. Since such earthworks became known as ' chairs ', it is doubtless that what may well be fact has been turned into what would seem to be fiction.

Canute was not the only ruler to tread the soil of the village. Here, it is believed, came Vespasian himself to build a Roman villa; here, too, as the Bayeux Tapestry shows, came the luckless King Harold, mounted on horseback, his hounds before him and his hawk upon his wrist, to set sail for France for his fateful meeting with the Duke of Normandy: a meeting that was to lead to his defeat and death at the other end of Sussex.

A highly prized manor in its time, and once a great ecclesiastical centre, Bosham can claim links with many famous people —the Venerable Bede, William the Conqueror, Earl Godwin and William of Wykeham, founder of Winchester College, to name but a few.

Occupying a strategic position with extensive views to sea, Bosham may well have served as a look-out post at least since the time of the Saxons. Indeed, its importance in this respect at the time of Armada was so considerable that Queen Elizabeth granted a special charter under the terms of which the lord of the manor still holds the right to his own coroner and chamberlain. At one time he was also granted his own admiral, whose duty it was to see that this stretch was kept free from the menace of raiding parties.

This monarch was not the only one to grant a charter; at Bosham to-day they still tell how their ancestors saved the citizens of Chichester from starvation and death at the time of the Plague, and how certain rights were granted to them in recognition of their work for humanity.

When some lone traveller brought the dreaded disease to the cathedral city, the gates of the ancient Roman town were closed at once. Days passed. From end to end men, women and children became stricken in ever-increasing numbers with the fearful purple spots. Torchlight burials in the common pit in the churchyard of St. Pancras became a nightly occurrence. Weeks passed. Food stocks ran so low that even those not actually afflicted were in danger of dying of starvation. At last it was decided to set up notices upon the city gates proclaiming the pitiable state of affairs within, and appealing for help from without.

The first to read one of these notices was a Bosham villager who had been tending his cattle in a field near the walls. Trekking the four miles home again, he collected together a few of his companions and returned soon afterwards with cartloads of meat, fish, grain, poultry and sundry other edibles. Then, signalling to the pickets by the West Gate that they had brought relief, the little group placed their produce upon a pile of stones near by, together with their bill of account, giving instructions at the same time for the money to be left in a water-trough so that they could pick it up on their next journey, for, of course, all contact was out of the question.

Day after day, for weeks on end, the men of Bosham continued their errands of mercy until, at last, the city of Chichester was free and clean once more. To this day the 'Boshamers' hold the right to sell fish in any market in England without paying tolls, besides holding the rights to free mooring, wild-fowling and fishing within the waters of their own harbour, and they will tell you that it is by virtue of the several parts their forefathers played that they enjoy these privileges to-day.

In fact, many of their rights are far older than they would have one believe, James I having excused them the payment of tolls ' for the carriage and passage of goods ' and exempting them from giving service and one or two other irksome duties.

Old beliefs die hard in this quiet corner of Sussex. Strangest of them is the legend built up round the village church. In the days of Canute, the story goes, a fleet of Norsemen sailed up Bosham Channel, bent on plundering the village. They landed, sacked the place, and were making off with the tenor bell when the monks, who had been somewhat neglectful of their duties, having pleaded in vain with the pirates, ran to the church tower to ring a peal in gratitude that at least their lives had been spared. As the joyful peal from the remaining bells echoed across the water, the tenor bell at once moved in sympathy, causing such a rocking that it fell through the bottom of the boat without, however, allowing a single drop of water to enter the hold.

The monks at once prayed to St. Nicholas to give them his aid in recovering their precious treasure, but their prayers remained unanswered. Finally, they decided to purchase a new bell rope and to employ a team of pure white heifers (the suggestion of a witch, no doubt) in one big salvage operation. All went well for a time. Indeed, the bell was actually brought to the surface and was about to be landed when, at the critical moment, someone noticed that one of the wretched beasts harboured a single black hair in its tail! Whereupon the rope snapped, and the bell plunged deeper than ever into the mud below, where it remains to this day.

There are people in Bosham who declare that, on a still day, they can hear the muffled toll of the old bell, below the tidal waters. Lest any should forget this legend, a red bell on a white background is the chosen burgee of the Bosham Sailing Club.

When one has explored Bosham one has really seen everything on the first of these headlands. The rest is all farmland, cut up into something like eight independent farms. The second headland is even less populous, with sleepy Chidham, set in the midst of further farms, the sole village, and boasting nothing more than an Early English church with a Saxon font, one or two houses of the ' old vicarage ' type, a few odd cottages, a school, and a triangular green that is lined with trees. Little more than a hamlet, Chidham has nevertheless left its mark upon Sussex life as a place notable both for its red ochre beds and for its ' white ', or ' hedge ', wheat, whose seeds have been eagerly sought by farmers all over Southern England and the Home Counties.

This wheat first rose to popularity when a certain Mr. Woods, strolling across his fields here in the closing years of the eighteenth century, noticed a patch of self-sown wheat growing in the hedgerow, and discovered that its thirty ears contained no less than 1,400 corns. These he sowed the following year with most satisfactory results. Not only was the yield quite remarkable, but Arthur Young tells us that it was also so wonderfully long in the straw that, even in the wettest of summers, it would stand to a full six feet. Though

Chidham wheat is, naturally, no longer grown only in the village whose name it bears, the seeds sown in many a Sussex cornfield to-day owe their origin to that chance discovery by Mr. Woods.

Unless it be just to call in on Prinsted, which nestles so pertly at the head of the third channel of Thorney, and Hermitage —where more than one car driver of my acquaintance has been surprised at seeing a phantom coach drawn by four luminous horses drive across his path into the carriage-way of a house on the south side of the road!—I do not think that we can do better now than to rejoin the main road and retrace our steps to Chichester. For the third headland of Thorney Island, in many ways once the most fascinating of all, is now an air-field. The droning engines of the aircraft have taken the place of the songs of the many, and rare, birds that once frequented this little islet, and all that is left is the manor-house, a few cottages, and the church, the latter containing the oldest inscribed bell in the county.

CHAPTER THREE: *Chichester*

I. THE CITY

I

EVER since, some 2,000 years ago, the Regni tribe moved from their hill-top position on the Trundle, by Goodwood, to establish a dwelling-place on the rich, fertile plain below, men and women have lived in the compact and dignified cathedral city of Chichester. A lovely old market town, its Corporation, which may well have grown out of the Saxon Guild Merchant, still preserves the charter which King Stephen first granted them and which five later sovereigns confirmed.

Though Chichester was inhabited for a century or more before the arrival of Vespasian, it was the Romans who laid the foundations of the city we know to-day. When they built the walls of Regnum and appointed Cogidubnus, the disloyal Regni chieftain, its ruler, they made this their first town in Sussex and their second in all England. Many buildings have since arisen, only to fall into decay in the passing centuries: the Plague has taken its toll, and fire and civil war have ravaged the streets . . . and yet, in plan and lay-out, Chichester, with its two main streets stretching to the four points of the compass and intersecting each other by Bishop Story's magnificent market cross to divide the city into four distinct sections, is still unmistakably Roman.

The Roman influence is not confined to the lay-out. Though the four gates have long disappeared, their work is still noticeable in the medieval walls of flint that to this day enclose part of the original city area; while the famous Stane Street still leads through Halnaker to the South Downs, reminding us that, in about A.D. 70, the Romans laid this great highway to London. At intervals of about twelve miles, a rest house, complete with sleeping accommodation, cart sheds and stables, was provided where—as at Hardham and Alfoldean—the weary travellers could rest, and give drink and sustenance to their hard-pressed beasts of burden.

Many Roman relics have been brought to light at various times in Chichester, including, besides numerous coins, the foundations of buildings, fragments of tessellated pavements, the remains of a hypocaust in South Pallant, and an amphitheatre near the site of East Gate where the Romans engaged in their baitings and sundry other sports.

The most unusual discoveries, though, were three stones of the first century containing carved dedications to the Emperor Nero, who was regarded as a god, to Neptune and Minerva, and to 'Jupiter, Most Excellent'. The first of these has been lost. Of the other two, one is preserved in the Guildhall and the other in a glass case in the wall of the fine colonnaded Council House. It is the latter that has aroused the greatest interest. Discovered under the foundations of a building at the corner of North Street and Lion Street, it is thought to have formed part of a heathen temple, and its Latin inscription tells us that Pudens granted the site and that the local craftsmen dedicated it to Neptune and Minerva 'by the authority of Tiberius Claudius Cogidubnus'.

The discovery of this last stone has led to a somewhat flimsy tradition that St. Paul himself visited Chichester.

Perhaps, in the years to come, Chichester may yield further secrets, for where bombs have levelled buildings to the ground archaeologists now dig deep.

II

The Romans are not the only people to figure in Chichester's scrapbook of history. By 516 one of Aella's three sons, Cissa, had been appointed governor, and Regnum, first Sussex capital of the Romans, became, likewise, first capital of the South Saxons, changing its name to Cisseter in respect for its new ruler.

As the pages of this scrapbook turn, we think of Athelstan, and Edgar after him, establishing their mints here; of Chichester thrice attacked by the Danes; of Roger de Montgomerie, commander of William the Conqueror's central army at Hastings, being granted the whole rape, and building the castle in Priory Park, which King John later seized and Henry III, who came to Chichester in person, destroyed so ruthlessly as to leave only that small mound which to-day spectators find so convenient a spot from which to watch the cricket matches that are staged on the green sward below. . . . We think of the carpenters and masons building and rebuilding the cathedral, and picture the arrival in the early years of the thirteenth century first of the Franciscans—the choir of whose church still stands in Priory Park—and then of the Dominicans.

The years roll by; it is now 1541, and the Earl of Scarbrough is busily preparing to entertain Queen Elizabeth in that magnificent medieval structure, now known as the Old Punch House, whose superb Italian ceiling may still be seen. This is her second visit to the city, and all is gay. In another fifty years or so, however, civil war was to cast a gloom over the Sussex countryside, and Chichester, largely Puritan in its sympathies, fell to the Parliamentarians after an eight-days' siege by Sir William Waller, who had already captured Arundel Castle. Then came the Plague. Yet Chichester's darkest hour was soon to be followed by the bright dawn of the eighteenth century which was to see the town arise in its present beauty.

III

Though still Roman in plan, Chichester to-day is essentially Georgian; an eighteenth-century town where architectural styles, from late Stuart or Queen Anne to Regency, executed in mellow red brick, are seen to the best advantage. With the exception of Bath, Chichester may well rank as the most perfect example of the period now left to us. Though I have travelled England far and wide to write of each one of our forty counties, I have yet to meet a town or city (except for Bath) that can surpass the glory of Chichester, and it always surprises me that the fineness of its architecture appears to have been so little recognized by earlier writers. Doubtless this is because it boasts no mineral springs and so never became a fashion centre like Bath, Cheltenham or Tunbridge Wells: even though the sacred concerts in the cathedral, and the dances and social gatherings in the Assembly Rooms were both to gain more than local fame before the eighteenth century was out.

Though, admittedly, some of Chichester's outskirts are far from attractive, as a whole it is splendid. West Street, leading down to West Gate, is particularly charming with the cathedral standing in such dignity on the southern side opposite the long, low Georgian coaching-house, the *Dolphin and Anchor*, that once was two inns of serious rivalry, the one patronized by the Whigs and the other by the Tories. The whole street is lined on either side with really beautiful Georgian fronts, boasting a rich assortment of ornamental stack-heads, porticoes and fanlights. And, as a dividing line between the larger houses of West Street and the smaller ones of West Gate, stands Westgate House, now the home of the county library, which is rather dubiously attributed to Wren.

Nearly every street possesses a wealth of lovely architecture, the most notable individual buildings being the eighteenth-century Council offices with interior stucco reliefs of 1800;

the twin-bayed house of 1760 just outside North Gate; *The Ship*, with its magnificent Adam staircase; the Council Chamber, erected in 1731 by public subscription, and behind it the Assembly Room built in 1780 by James Wyatt; the churches of St. Olave and St. Peter The Less; the Market House by Thomas Nash; St. Mary's Hospital, founded in 1229 on the site of a nunnery, once the home of the Grey Friars and now an almshouse; and the old Corn Exchange. . . . But where so many buildings are lovely it is almost invidious to single out any particular one.

Naturally divided by its four intersecting roads into four more or less independent squares, Chichester is a town of unending surprises. Little London, East Row, and St. Martin's Square, where stands St. Mary's Hospital, are but three streets of unsuspected charm, while the Pallants—so called because the Archbishops of Canterbury were once its possessors, and were empowered to hold palatine jurisdiction over the area—is, in its plan, a miniature of the city itself, intersected by two roads, and containing many charming houses, including the red-brick Pallant House, known as the ' Dodo House ' for its strange ostriches on the gate posts.

A pleasing feature about Chichester is that its harmony is not being disturbed by the incursion of modern buildings. The new Post Office, built in 1937, under Georgian influence, is already on the best of terms with the *Dolphin and Anchor* next door, while the County Hall, opened but two years before, affords an excellent example of how even the largest structure can be made to tone in with old surroundings.

IV

The development of the corn exchange, together with the rise of Goodwood, was the main factor in bringing about Chichester's prosperity and architectural glory. Though the surrounding farmlands had long been renowned for their corn, hitherto the farmers had been content to sell their goods at stalls. In the eighteenth century, however, a number of local moneyed gentry decided to build a range of granaries and start an exchange in Chichester where farmers could be certain of selling all their produce at an agreed figure. At the same time they made provision whereby the corn could be milled on the spot and exported direct to London by sea. Naturally, the farmers were delighted to avail themselves of this new opportunity, so that in a comparatively short time Chichester became the principal granary of the South, the rapid development being speeded up by the introduction of more up-to-date farming methods. As, year by year, the profits increased, so the merchants extended their Exchange, and built more and more houses—those for themselves large and perhaps even elaborate; those for their workpeople small and often inconvenient; yet all of them dignified and tasteful.

Not only Chichester but many of the surrounding villages owe the best of their architecture to those merchants, and it is pleasing to think that a Wednesday corn market is still held within the shades of the old Exchange, even though the imposing pillared building itself now serves as a cinema. Moreover, the market is still regarded as one of the most important south of London, attracting merchants from London and farmers from all over Sussex, Surrey and Hampshire.

v

That is one of the delights of Chichester: it is not merely a place of charm, content, as is so often the case, to fall asleep in the shade of its cathedral and merely dream about the past, but a flourishing market town, vivacious and happy, and as much the centre of country life for miles around as it has been for centuries.

As the Old Year gives way to the New they still join hands to sing *Auld Lang Syne* and dance to the midnight chimes around that floodlit market cross—a perfect cross of eight arches with flying buttresses rising to a central finial (acknowledged to be the finest in England) which Bishop Story built in 1500. No longer do the womenfolk of the outlying villages rise betimes to sell their produce within the shelter of this cross, yet on alternate Wednesdays, mindful of the time when Chichester's was second only to that of Smithfield, a cattle market (occupying eight acres, and still one of the best equipped in Southern England) is staged, when farmers from all over the South and Midlands enter their cattle, sheep and pigs. At these fortnightly markets as many as 3,000 store sheep, 1,000 fat sheep, 500 fat and store pigs, 150 dairy cows, 100 fat beasts, and 400 to 500 cattle—not to mention poultry, rabbits and dogs —may come under the hammer.

True centre of country life, in Chichester you will meet not only farmers, but men and women who, like their forefathers, still ply trades that are closely connected with agriculture—family concerns whose names have been household words in the city for a century or more: firms like Sadler's, who, until their mill was burnt out recently, had processed flour for more than a century, and who, to-day, are famous for their dog biscuits and their cattle cakes; Bartholomew's who, though younger, supply the local farmers with much of their cattle, pig and poultry food; Henty and Constable, who buy enormous quantities of home-grown barley for the brewing of their 'Chichester Ales', and commission artists to paint inn signs that really are works of art; Shippam's, who, of local pigs and fish, cook their delicious pastes in steam-jacketed cooking-pans, thus maintaining an industry that was first started in the eighteenth century. You will meet, too, harness-makers and those who devote their entire lives to the care and maintenance of the all-important implements of husbandry; men to whom the ploughshare is, rightly, of greater moment than the most luxurious of cars and to whom the only thing that matters is that the farmer's work shall never be halted.

Chichester Cathedral from the Meadows

Old Bosham

Chichester Cross

VI

Oldest of all Chichester's craftsmen are the tanners, whose trade has flourished in the city since Domesday. It is interesting to see the skill with which the craftsmen at the factory in West Street turn the hides of cows and horses into leather for boots and shoes and farm saddlery.

It takes anything up to a year to tan a hide. After being rough cleaned, the hides are placed in chemicals or lime baths for about a fortnight to loosen the hair and fill up the pores of the skin in a way that will prevent shrinkage. Next they are 'unhaired' on a scraping machine, after which comes the most skilled part of all—'scudding'. This operation is now done by machinery, but until quite recently it was the practice for a craftsman to place his hide over a kind of sloping 'horse' and remove the surface fats from the grain by means of a long, curved blade—a highly delicate operation since one false stroke could damage the hide and reduce its value.

The skins are then 'rounded'—that is, the edges are cut away with a sharp knife, and it is not until the hides have been given a thorough washing that the actual tanning begins. The liquid used for this is obtained from the bark of oak trees, which is stripped in April or May, when the sap is rising, and then ground down by means of an antiquated-looking grinding machine, and left for days to soak in cold water.

This liquid is pumped, in varying strengths, into a series of baths, and into each of these in turn—starting with the weakest and ending with the strongest—the hides are suspended in an upright position by means of wooden slats, which, attached to one end of the skin, overlap the edges of the bath. After several weeks in these baths the hides are placed in a revolving drum to be treated with a mild dressing solution as a preventative against oxidization. Finally, they are oiled by hand, hung in an airing room to dry, and rolled.

These tanners, like the saddlers, are the survivors of a great craft community for which Chichester was once famous. Even in the late Middle Ages, when its streets were mean and dirty and were frequented by vagabonds, the skill of its linen-makers and spinners and weavers, who made the kerseys and broadcloths, was known afar. Indeed, in the fourteenth century Chichester became the staple port for the export of wool; and it is said that Sir Richard Whittington, the famous Lord Mayor of London, was among the merchants to export wool from here in the time of Henry IV. Chichester had button-makers too, and nowhere were sharper or better needles made than here, until the Civil War threatened and the ' needlers ', uncomfortably situated in St. Pancras, just outside the East Gate, took fright and fled to Redditch in Worcestershire.

VII

From quite early times the St. Pancras district has liked to be independent of the rest of the city, and still boasts its own ' Mayor and Corporation ', complete with mace, chain of office and staffs. It all began at the time of William of Orange, it seems, when those who dwelt outside the city walls were constantly at loggerheads with those who lived inside. And vice versa. The landing of Dutch William brought matters to a head, and ever since 1689 it has been customary for the citizens of St. Pancras to meet to elect their mayor, who then appoints his town clerk, recorder, surveyor, treasurer, macebearer, engineer, sanitary inspector and chaplain. As might be expected, the elections are made the occasion for a dinner at the ' local '; a jocular affair that may last until midnight when by tradition the various ' dignitaries ' are taken home in wheelbarrows.

In its long history this civic body has never once paid the slightest attention to civic matters. Yet, they meet regularly every Friday or pay a fine of sixpence a head in default. These meetings are not entirely frivolous, for 'the Corporation' are the custodians of the old ladies who live in Dear's Alms-houses, a charity started about the same time, and their object is to provide funds for their 'god-children' and give them an annual Christmas dinner at the *Unicorn*, when brandy, port and old beer quench the thirst of those aged throats, and chicken, pork, plum pudding and mince pies satisfy the appetite.

Chichester boasts another interesting charity. Something like one-seventh of the ratepayers still benefit to the tune of a threepenny rate under a bequest of nearly £23,000 left by a tobacconist, John Hardham, who became famous for his snuff, which was eagerly bought by the Georgian dandies. Though Hardham's shop was in London, and though it is mainly the multiple firms who now benefit by this charity, the name of John Hardham is remembered as affectionately as two of Chichester's own sons—the Lord High Treasurer, William Juxon, who spoke such comforting words to Charles I as he stood by the scaffold, and who, on the restoration of the second Charles, became Archbishop of Canterbury; and the poet son of a hatter, William Collins, who took to writing only when pronounced 'too indolent even for the army', yet managed to gain lasting fame for his odes before succumbing to a mental disease.

The oldest and best known of Chichester's traditions, though, is the Sloe Fair which is held in Oaklands Park on the twentieth day of each October, the season of the year when the country folk make their 'sloe gin'. Though now a thing of hurdy-gurdies, 'dodgems', merry-go-rounds, and all the other paraphernalia calculated to cause fun, merriment and noise, its origin dates back to the twelfth century when Henry I granted Bishop de Luffa the right to hold a fair. For centuries merchants from miles around used to converge upon the sloe tree that stood by the North Gate, their pack-horses loaded down with their wares, while the Bishop's gavelmen were required to bring straw—daily if necessary—from the Manor of Cakeham.

2. THE CATHEDRAL AND PRECINCTS

I

The south-western of the four distinct squares formed by the old cross-roads is dominated by the cathedral and its precincts, and the Prebendal School which Bishop Story also founded.

There is something very majestic in the way Chichester Cathedral—a landmark at sea, the second broadest in England (surpassed only by York Minster), and boasting a unique detached bell tower which was built separately to relieve the strain on the central tower—is set in the very heart of the town. Admittedly, its interior, though interesting, has neither the brilliance of Canterbury nor the fine detail of, say, York or Lincoln; it lacks, too, the fresh, inviting atmosphere of Wells and Norwich, yet its setting is only a little less delightful than that of Salisbury. From whichever angle we view this building, whether from the meadows to the south or from the high ground to the north, whether from close-up or afar, it is imposing.

As for the precincts, they are as peaceful as any. Only the gardens at Wells can be more beautiful than those of the Bishop's Palace, which are still enclosed in part by a section of the South Walls, and boast a rare Ginka tree, of which there are no less than three specimens in Chichester; while the graceful palace contains a timber ceiling painted by Bernardi and a kitchen with unusual hammer beams. Graceful is perhaps the best description for the whole of the precincts with their Georgian houses, some quite large, others small, the twelfth-century chapel in which is the mural painting of The Virgin and Child, famous as the 'Chichester Roundel', and the quiet

St. Richard's Walk leading the way from the dean's house to
the cathedral cloisters.

It is perhaps surprising that the atmosphere should be so
peaceful, for ever since Bishop Stigand transferred the see
from Selsey the cathedral has been subjected to one misfortune
after another. Ralph de Luffa—who was consecrated in 1091,
and now lies buried in the Lady Chapel—had not long dedicated the first Norman church when the entire upper part was
destroyed by fire, and building had to begin afresh. By 1184
the masons—who, to give relief to their Quarr (Isle of Wight)
stone, introduced Purbeck marble and a special stone from
Caen, most of which they imported in exchange for Sussex
wheat—had laid down their trowels for the second time, and
the cathedral was dedicated anew, only, however, to meet a
similar fate but two years later. And so the builders were
brought back yet again.

Fire was not the only enemy. The altars, stained glass and
ornaments suffered badly at the hands of Henry VIII's
despoilers, while the Cromwellians caused even worse havoc.
And, as if that were not enough, in 1861 the spire itself, which
had been set on inadequate Norman foundations, suddenly
collapsed, like a child's plaything, leaving its finely carved
stones to meet an ignominious end as rubble with which to
fill in Chichester's disused wells and build garden rockeries,
some of which may be seen to this day.

The cathedral we see to-day, then, is something of a hybrid;
a building where Norman, Transitional, Early English,
Decorated and Perpendicular all join hands; one in which
craftsmen of all ages have left their mark, from (it is believed)
the medieval workmen who were trained at Canterbury under
William of Sens and William the Englishman to those who,
under the guidance of Sir Gilbert Scott, so skilfully rebuilt the
spire, largely to Wren's design. Though of exquisite proportions throughout and boasting, in addition to the panels from
Selsey already referred to, no less than eight Flaxman sculp-

tures, its fine stone work is inclined to lose much of its splendour in the fact that it is neither pleasantly ornate nor impressively severe, and so needs rather more careful examination than usual to be appreciated. It is said, unkindly, that the Master Craftsman built Salisbury, but left Chichester to the Apprentice!

II

The most beautiful part of the cathedral is the retro-choir with its graceful triforium arches, its clustered pillars and arcaded entrance to the Lady Chapel. On the little altar here a sanctuary lamp is kept burning to the memory of the county's best loved saint—to Chichester's bishop, Richard de la Wych, who in life scorned riches that he might succour the poor, and who in death was canonized, his body being translated in 1276 in the presence of Edward I from the north aisle of the nave to the spot where this altar now stands.

Though just on seven centuries have passed since St. Richard breathed his last, his name is still hallowed throughout his diocese as a man of understanding and kindly virtues. When his parents died and fortunes failed, he served as a common labourer on his brother's farm, ' working now with the plough and now with the cart, and enduring many kinds of hard and humble toil patiently and modestly '. His life alternated between the enjoyment of high office and low, yet it always seemed that he would have been content to remain a parish priest, and that his success was forced upon him by his personality and strength of character.

Many beautiful stories are told of St. Richard and the miracles he performed in the Sussex countryside—miracles of which, in his modesty, he never believed himself to be capable. Once he happened upon a group of fishermen near Lewes who had toiled all day and caught nothing. On learning of their plight he gave them his blessing and bade them try again;

whereupon they cast their nets afresh, and were rewarded with four fine mullet. On another occasion he performed a miracle reminiscent of that of the 'loaves and fishes' when, at a time of great famine, he blessed the inadequate supply of beans which his servants were cooking for the hungry at his manor at Cakeham and thereby rendered more than sufficient to satisfy all.

A disciple of St. Edmund, he once cured a cripple boy by bidding him drink from the cup which the saint had left him in his will; while it is said that he even caused a blackbird to sing again after its tongue had been cut out by a cruel youth.

The power of St. Richard was acclaimed so widely that when they built a shrine above his tomb in the retro-choir, men women and children of all walks of life came from near and far to pay homage to his name and offer their gifts. Indeed, though the shrine was one of the cathedral treasures to be destroyed by Henry VIII's despoilers, and though the saint's body too has vanished, St. Richard of Chichester still brings pilgrims to the great church over which he once presided, when, every year upon the Feast of his Translation (June 16), the bishop leads a procession to his altar where, on a pavement strewn with rose petals, the congregation join with him in special prayers to his memory.

III

Several interesting old festivals are staged in Chichester Cathedral in the course of the year. Every Epiphany the children of West Sussex take part in a ceremony that is as old as Christianity, when the 'Three Kings', each dressed in Eastern costume and bearing gifts of gold, frankincense and myrrh, lead a long procession through the building to the High Altar, attended by their candle-bearers. Behind the 'kings' the choir follow with their candles, and behind them members of the Dolmetsch family playing on recorders; finally comes the main body of the procession. There is something very stirring, almost ethereal, in the way those boys and girls of such tender years, some of them so young that they could never be trusted with a candle if it were not for the fact that they have an elder brother or sister to walk beside them, progress so slowly, and yet so solemnly, to the altar for the staging of their Nativity tableau.

Of all the religious festivals in the diocese none are more important than the four whose roots are bedded deep in the land —Plough Sunday (changed for convenience sake from the traditional Monday) when the bishop blesses the plough of the Young Farmers' Clubs by the choir screen; Rogation-Tide, when special prayers are asked, and in the fields the blessing of God is sought for the growing crops, the weather, and all young life; Lammas-Tide, when the first sheaf of corn and the first loaf of bread made from the new and tender crops are brought to the cathedral as in the days of the Anglo-Saxons; and, of course, Harvest Festival.

IV

These traditional ceremonies are by no means confined to the cathedral city. In parish churches throughout Sussex, in cornfields and in market squares, town and country parsons now bless the land and the fruits of the good earth at the appointed seasons. From time to time the bishop, too, journeys round to the various markets. Those at Horsham, Steyning, Heathfield and Haywards Heath have all been blessed by him at different times, while at Chichester the ceremony even has a place in the auctioneers' catalogue. In some ways the blessing of Chichester market is the most impressive, for whereas in other towns the bishop is often accompanied by a crossbearer and robed choir and clergy, here he mounts the rostrum entirely alone, dressed, simply, in a purple cassock and carrying a shepherd's crook as his pastoral staff, and the solemnity of the occasion is only accentuated by the lowing of the calves that are to be auctioned at the end of his prayers.

To help bring about this great revival of a tradition of centuries the Bishop of Chichester, together with the Suffragan Bishop of Lewes and representatives of the Free Churches and the Roman Catholic Church, inaugurated a few years ago the West Sussex Church and Countryside Association—a move which was followed almost immediately by the formation of a similar body in East Sussex.

How successful the efforts of this interdenominational body have been can be seen in the fact that four special festival services have been written by the Rev. D. L. Couper (former Bishop's Chaplain) for use by the various Young Farmers' Clubs, many of whom now boast their own surpliced choirs, and in their sincere enthusiasm have rekindled in their parish churches a spirit whose light once shone so brightly until, with the coming of industrialism, so many mistakenly forsook the land for the factory.

It is not only the youth who are being directed towards a better appreciation of Mother Earth under the guidance of this body. As the parson of old was in every way the shepherd of his flock, so to-day he is encouraged to study at first hand the ways and needs of the land workers, and bring them into fellowship with his other parishioners. In short, the diocese of Chichester has given a magnificent lead such as is already bringing about a re-birth of the old community spirit where all lived and worked for the good of all, looking towards the Church as their spiritual head and to the land as the core of their existence, as did the squires and yeomen, craftsmen and peasants, in previous centuries.

3. THE DISTRICT AROUND

Unlike many of our cathedral cities, which stand out as jewels in an otherwise uninteresting countryside, Chichester is surrounded by a host of pleasing villages. Besides affording the obvious centre from which to explore the harbour creeks and Manhood to the south, many appealing spots separate it from Goodwood and those glorious South Downs to the north.

To the east, along Stane Street, is Halnaker, with its ruined manor-house and old mill on the hill-top, and, near by, Boxgrove. Here, in addition to the fine priory church, with its interesting murals and vaulting, are the ruins of one of the richest monasteries in Sussex—a monastery whose prior, alas, Bishop of Sherburne of Chichester once found it necessary to reprimand for engaging in archery contests upon the Sabbath!

Until the outbreak of the last war they still performed their Tipteer plays at Boxgrove, and it is to be hoped that they may soon do so again. Counterpart of the Mummers' plays of other counties, the principal characters are the Turkish Knight, St. George, Father Christmas, the Valiant Soldier (Bon Slasher), the Prince of Peace, the Doctor, and Little Jolly Jack, the last carrying dolls on his back, in representation, it is thought, of the flight of the Holy Family into Egypt. Like the Mummers, the Tipteers brightened the winter evenings in the county's stately homes in the days when the country folk made their own entertainment instead of seeking it in the towns, and the farmhands found in these performances a means of alleviating their hardships at the season when work on the land was more or less at a standstill. Except at hay-making, hoeing and harvest, when they were able to earn overtime pay, the labourers had to rely on a wage of perhaps ten shillings a week, so that the few pence they could pick up here and there by their plays were most welcome in that long interval between harvest and ' haying '.

Westwards from Boxgrove we come to Westhampnett (birth-place of Frederick Lillywhite) whose church contains a certain amount of Roman brickwork. Proceeding up country from here and then bearing westwards again, we pass next a string of pleasing villages or hamlets in the Lavants (Mid and East), East Ashling, West Ashling and Funtington. At the last of these there is a charming old farm-house with a Flemish gable porch into whose stonework has been introduced an old insur-ance sign portraying Chichester Cathedral. This sign dates back to the days when only the wisest insured and all who paid their premiums were rewarded by having their houses marked with the symbol of the company which covered their risk. These companies maintained their own fire-brigades, and in the event of fire breaking out in the district, invariably turned out to safeguard any property that bore their sign.

A little to the north of Funtington, in the direction of Stoughton, is Kingley Vale, with its grove of ancient yew trees terminating in Bow Hill, site of a British earthwork. For centuries these massive trees have stood in their splendour. Some believe that they were planted by the Druids; others that they were placed there to guide the way to Canterbury, the yew tree being one of the few to stand out in its dark greenery in times of snow.

Here we are on the edge of Stanstead Park, seat of Lord Bessborough, where the Stanstead Players used to stage their notable productions in his lordship's private theatre, until it was gutted, and where the head gardener gained fame as an expert on dahlias and for the fine quality of his ' Stanstead Park Lettuces '.

Well wooded and very lovely, this countryside which borders Hampshire has, of necessity, a certain romance about it. Charles II came here on his historic flight after the Battle of Worcester to meet Colonel George Gounter at Stanstead House, and by the little shingle-spired church of Racton—in which may be seen the tombs of some of the Gounters—is the black-and-white cottage, once the rectory, where the Merry Monarch found shelter. Charles had perhaps more reason to be thankful for his visit to Racton than to any other house, since it was Colonel Gounter who arranged for Captain Tattersall to ship the king from Shoreham to France.

But Racton has also earned notoriety for another event whose story is recalled in the strange ruined folly tower on the hill-top above the church. This tower, it is said, was built at a cost of £10,000 by a previous Lord Halifax, who lived in the long-departed manor-house near by. Though many believe that he erected it as a place from which to admire the view, the native of these parts will shake his head in his emphatic Sussex way, and declare that, on the contrary, it was as a place in which to entertain the Excise men of an evening that the Earl—who, incidentally, was later hanged—raised those walls of stone. Here he used to prime them with goodly food and wine until all were in a stupor, whereupon he would mount the steps to the top of the tower and light flares as a signal to the smugglers out at sea that the coast was now clear for them to make their ' run '!

CHAPTER FOUR: *The West Sussex Downs*

I

TO the north of these villages neighbouring Chichester the South Downs roll in from Hampshire to stretch in noble folds along the greater length of the county, thereby forming a natural barrier between the coast on one side and the Weald on the other, whose long continuity is broken only by the river valleys, or 'gaps', of the Arun, the Adur, the Cuckmere and the Ouse, and by the dry valleys, or 'denes'.

More wooded than the rest, this stretch to the west of Arun, which is studded with long barrows and tumuli and with the camps and earthworks of primitive man, is perhaps the most beautiful of all the Sussex downland. Though the characteristic tender green sheep-grazed slopes, speckled in parts with furze and stunted junipers and an occasional woodland clump, are in evidence, trees flourish on this ridge. The beech is perhaps the most prolific, but the furze is golden for so long that it is said hereabouts that ' when the furze is out of blossom, kissing's out of season '. While to the east of the Arun the downs are often as barren as those of Wiltshire, the range between Harting Hill and Duncton Hill in this western sector comprises an almost unbroken stretch of woodland with Hill Lands Wood, Winden Wood, Linchball Wood, Westdean Woods, Venue Wood, Hacking Copse, Wellhanger Copse, Singleton Forest, Charlton Forest, and Eastdean Wood merging nearly into one. And beyond Duncton is Houghton Forest.

Though seldom rising to more than 800 feet above sea-level, there is an indefinable majesty in the rounded contour of these downs and the way they stand out from the Weald to north and the coastal plain to south as a landmark for miles in all directions. I know of nothing more soothing than to laze on these slopes on a hot summer's afternoon, and breathe the scent of the wild thyme, when the heat is tempered by a breeze off the sea, and the stillness broken perchance by the song of the lark, the drone of the bees gathering their nectar from the aromatic wild thyme, or perhaps by the far-away barking of a sheep dog driving a flock of sheep to be folded.

There is nothing quite like these downs with their myriad wild flowers—the blue field scabious, knapweed, rare rampion, cowslips, and autumn gentian, lady's bed-straw, primroses, hare-bell, marjoram and wild orchids; their deep combes and chalk-pits; their ' hangers ' of beeches and their ' holts ' of oak, ash and hazel, the last supplying the hurdle-makers with their raw material; their dewponds and their giant ' fairy rings ', or ' hag tracks ', of deep green grass, formed by an edible fungus, which some still believe mark the spots where the fairies dance of a night-time.

Not every one takes kindly to these downs at first; yet there are few who do not grow to love them as they know them better. For they cannot be seen in a day, a week or even a month. They must be visited at all seasons—in autumn when there is a nip in the air and the overhanging mists dampen the grass to bring out the snails, which, eaten by the sheep, improve the quality of the Southdown mutton, the shepherds say; in winter when the snow lies deep, or a hard frost causes the grass to sparkle; in springtime when the wind-driven clouds cast their long undulating shadows over the velvet turf, and, of course, in summer. . . . They must be seen in every mood, by downland track and lowland roadway. To admire them from the villages at their foot is not sufficient; one should also mount the various ' borstals ' and wander in complete solitude along their brow, looking down upon mile after mile of open country to see a great patchwork of hedged-in fields of green, yellow and gold, with here and there the shingled spire of some Saxon or Norman church rising out of the foreground to indicate a village or hamlet tucked away in one of the folds of the hills.

II

From Racton our nearest downland villages are Compton and the four Mardens—East, West, Up and North—which together form a half-circle round a Neolithic long barrow, known after some local giant as ' Bevis's Thumb '. Set in the midst of a series of woods and copses, these villages provide a perfect introduction to the serenity of the downs, and from them we may zigzag our way from village to village, by road and by-lane, round this entire western sector without once departing from pleasing country.

Passing eastwards along the southern side of the downs, we come in quick succession upon four hamlets; Chilgrove, West Dean, Singleton and East Dean, where, for more than 200 years now, the womenfolk have engaged in cricket matches against one another. By tradition the women of Chilgrove and West Dean always side against those of Singleton and East Dean, and the enthusiasm is so pronounced that the matches are often umpired by former county cricketers.

Though the main road from Chichester to London passes through Singleton on its journey over the downs to Midhurst, the old-world beauty of the village's flint cottages remains surprisingly undisturbed, while the by-road that forks right to East Dean, and on to the old Saxon burial ground of Upwaltham, where Cardinal Manning was once curate, cutting a way between Singleton Forest and the haunted Charlton Forest to the north and the Goodwood country to the south, is as quiet as any. All this was once important hunting country. Charles Lennox, first Duke of Richmond, and natural son of Charles II, frequently rode with the Charlton pack, then the most famous hunt in England, and at Singleton may be seen the monument which he erected to the memory of his hunts-

man, Thomas Johnson; a fine ducal tribute ending with the
lines:

> Here Johnson lies, what Hunter can deny
> Old Honest Tom the tribute of a sigh?
> Deaf is that ear which caught the op'ning sound,
> Dumb is that tongue which cheered the hills around,
> Unpleasant truth—Death hunts us from our birth,
> In view, and men, like foxes, take to earth.

III

Bought by the first duke as a hunting-box, this rich forest
land still forms part of the Goodwood estate, which now
extends to something like 12,000 acres.

Although there is reason to believe that he occupied the
mansion and hunted the Charlton country for many years
before, it was not until 1720, when he was close on fifty, that
the duke came into the possession of Goodwood House, which,
since the early Middle Ages, had passed from one family of
noblemen to another and had twice become the property of the
Crown.

One of his first acts was to pull down the original Gothic
building and erect in its place an altogether smaller home in
tone with the style of the period. Yet the Palladian building
we see to-day, built to three sides of an octagon in beautiful
parkland at the foot of the hills, is not so much the work
of the first duke as of the third, who was also christened
Charles.

In the latter part of the eighteenth century this third duke,
who had already devoted considerable attention to the lay-out
of the estate, decided to make extensive additions to the house
itself, and entrusted the work first to Sir William Chambers,
who designed the fine range of stables and then, upon his
death, to James Wyatt, who likewise is credited with having
built the kennels.

Arundel Castle in the Spring

Horsham, a View of the Causeway

Using downland flint, these two, between them, developed what was probably little more than a modest-sized country house into a great mansion with a front of 166 feet and boasting two wings of 106 feet each, both of which were set, as we may see, at a slight angle to the main building and were terminated at either end by circular towers surmounted by somewhat unattractive green copper domed roofs.

Architecturally, Goodwood House does not rank very high, and probably the most pleasing feature is the entrance colonnade with its portico of six Doric pillars supporting a like number of Ionic ones. It is the setting that makes Goodwood. Nevertheless the house contains a remarkably fine collection of old masters. Titian, Vandyke, Romney, Kneller, Rembrandt, Reynolds, Rubens, Hogarth, Lely, Gainsborough and Lawrence are represented, and there are also a number of unusual treasures such as the magnificent tapestry in the main drawing-room, the tapestries of the seasons in the state bedroom, marble busts of Claudius, Trajan, Hadrian and George III, a collection of silver plate that once belonged to Napoleon, a French standard captured by Wellington, and a shirt worn by Charles I.

Some of the portraits are particularly interesting in that they bring to life so vividly the royal ancestry of this romantic dukedom of Richmond and Gordon. While Charles I, in his full robes of State, and his Consort, Henriétta Maria, are both portrayed by Vandyke, the three that tell the story of the love match between a king and his mistress that was to bring about the rise of modern Goodwood are Lely's portrait of Charles II and Sir Godfrey Kneller's two paintings of Louisa de Querouaille, Duchess of Portsmouth, and of Charles Lennox, the first duke.

As we gaze upon these three we think of the intrigue that first brought the Merry Monarch and the duchess together, when, anxious to cement a friendship between England and France, Louis XIV persuaded Charles's sister, the Duchess of

Orleans, to take Louisa with her on a visit to the king at Dover in the hope that she might be able to woo him by her charm and thus exert a French influence over the English court. How fully Louis XIV's efforts to bring about an intimacy between the two were realized we recall in the fact that though the ' baby-faced ' Breton became known and detested throughout the land as ' Madam Carwell ' (so called because no one could pronounce her name), she nevertheless exercised so great an influence over Charles that when, in 1672, he created her Duchess of Portsmouth the French king also awarded her considerable lands in France, providing at the same time that, at her death, these should pass to any sons she might bear to the Merry Monarch.

It was on July 29th, 1672, that Charles Lennox, the only son of this subtle scheming, was born. As a dutiful father, Charles attended his christening, and in the first year of his life made him Earl of March, Duke of Richmond and Baron Settrington; three titles to which were added in 1675 those of Duke of Lennox, Earl of Darnley, and Baron Methuen of Torbolton. (The present additional title of Duke of Gordon was inherited in 1836.) When he was still but a boy of nine, Charles II created him a Knight Companion of the Garter, and later appointed him his Master of Horse.

Though Charles II died when the first duke was in his middle teens, the link with royalty was not to be severed, for William III appointed Charles Lennox a personal aide-de-camp, and George I a Lord of the Bedchamber. Possibly it was round about the time of his holding the first of these two appointments that Kneller painted his portrait, and we see him as a swarthy, clean-shaven, handsome young man with a wealth of black hair and heavy eyebrows, who, from this likeness, might well pass for his royal father in his youth.

Kneller has also left us a painting of the first duke's wife, Anne, daughter of Francis Lord Brudenel, whom he married at the age of twenty, and among the many other interesting portraits of the dukes and their wives is one by Sir Joshua Reynolds of Charles, third duke, who, as already mentioned, enlarged the mansion.

IV

Interesting as they are, it is impossible to study these fine paintings without experiencing a certain feeling of sadness that the splendour of Goodwood, whose dukes were hosts to the nobility and gentry and benefactors to the country folk, should so largely passed away.

As we look upon the likenesses of these Dukes of Richmond the pageant of Goodwood unfolds . . . the stag hunts in the forest lands when perhaps three hundred guests might be invited to dine in a parkland setting that would be lit by several thousand candles . . . the special dinners for the estate tenants . . . the first meet in 1802 on the hill-top of the local hunt and the local militia that was soon to see the establishment of a private racecourse and the rise of ' Glorious Goodwood ' . . . the great meetings of Victorian days when, in race week, the larger houses round about might be let for £100 a week; when water-carts would be sent by the various Sussex towns to lay the dust of the flint roads whereon the carriages of the gentry made their way to the course, and when, for days after the last of the carriages had departed, the surplus dripping from Goodwood House, and all the other large homes in the district, would be sold in the shops of Chichester.

In those days Goodwood House was a stately home. Death duties on the estate of the eighth Duke of Richmond and Gordon proved so burdensome, however, that in 1938 his heir, Frederick Gordon-Lennox, the present duke, was obliged to form the Goodwood Estate Company, having already sold 70,000 trees as standing timber for £45,000 to help meet his tremendous expenses. So that to-day the duke and his duchess occupy only a suite of the great house, the rest of the building being assigned to purposes connected with the management of the estate. Where the bewigged and powdered lords and ladies once danced in the gilt and scarlet ballroom, typewriters now click; where kings once slept in the oak-panelled suit, darts now zing and quiver against the walls, while beer barrels are lined up on the bath-tub in the royal bathroom. So, too, it is the staff who to-day use the billiard-room whose walls are still hung with paintings of famous horses by equally famous artists.

The atmosphere of modern Goodwood is as democratic as is the management of the estate enterprising. The business is by no means confined to the conduct of the racecourse. The estate's vast acreage of timber is marketed with care, and the cleared areas replanted. Even the odd branches for which the manager of the sawmill can find no use are put to good account: with the aid of lathes and other machinery local hands now turn these into broom handles and heads, axe handles and spigots for beer barrels. For some years now it has been necessary to run the gardens on a commercial basis— even to the extent of sending holly to Covent Garden market at Christmas time—while the estate farms are of more consequence than ever.

Yet the duke is always at pains to see that the beauty of the park is in no way spoilt. Though but thirty of the original thousand cedars, which the third duke planted in 1760, now remain, Goodwood is still renowned for its trees, of which there are no less than 400 different kinds, including one or two cork trees, many beautiful chestnuts, fine beeches, thirty types of oak, and tall slender birches. Around the lovely ' Birdless Grove ' of beeches many a legend is woven. Apart from the cedars, these are probably the oldest inhabitants of Goodwood Forest, and they say that no birds will ever sing in this dark majestic avenue. Even the keepers on the estate declare that it is impossible to introduce a newly captured bird to the grove. Yet really, it is merely the lower parts they scorn, and that only because there are not sufficient insects and they dislike the shady atmosphere caused by the prolific foliage at the top of those long barren trunks; from the uppermost branches the birds sing as merrily as anywhere.

v

In this Goodwood country is one of the most interesting of all the prehistoric downland sites. Three thousand years before William the Conqueror compiled his *Domesday Book*, referring to Goodwood as ' Godinwood ', men and women lived on the hill-top close by the racecourse. A local legend says that the Golden Calf lies buried in the Trundle, and within the great rampart and ditch with which the men of the Iron Age enclosed their fortified city are the traces of a causewayed camp where Neolithic man dwelt, perhaps 4,000 years ago.

Though the earlier settlement has been all but obliterated by the later one, aerial photography revealed what the human eye could never have seen and thus enabled Dr. E. Cecil Curwen to carry out his interesting excavations which not only brought to light a number of Stone Age relics in the form of pieces of pottery and flint tools, but also gave us an indication of the lay-out of the camp and the lives led by those early downland dwellers.

This camp, it seems, comprised two distinct rings with a spiral of pits between the two. The innermost one, some seven feet high to the north and containing a main entrance to the south, enclosed something like three acres, and is believed to have been used as a cattle enclosure. The outer one, on the other hand, took in eighteen acres, and, since a number of shallow post holes were discovered to suggest that these may have been used for roofing timbers, it is thought equally likely that this area constituted the dwelling quarters : in which case the pits would have served as houses, and were probably roofed with a thatch of grass. For men hollowed out their homes before they caused them to rise from the ground.

Here in these pits the Neolithic folk led their self-supporting lives, gathering flint from their near-by mines with which to fashion such tools and implements as they required, tending their beasts and crudely curing their hides to provide covering material for their bodies and perhaps even for their homes, making their earthenware cooking utensils and pots on a turn-table composed of sodden leaves, and weaving their cloths on upright looms whose warp they kept taut with weights of downland chalk.

The Iron Age city whose rampart and ditch we see to-day was an altogether more important place. On the ground that the Trundle is situated between two waterways—the Lavant Course and the River Arun—it is thought that this may have served as the headquarters of a small tribal district. Occupied from the fifth to the first centuries B.C., the plan appears to have been modified from time to time to afford greater protection. Here gates were erected at the entrances to the passage between the ramparts, and Dr. Curwen tells us that at one phase two were ranged, one behind the other, at the eastern entrance to form a kind of barbican such as is found in medieval castles.

In this city the people dwelt in huts of wattle-and-daub, and besides fashioning flint, spinning and weaving, and making pottery, also wrought tools of iron. Unlike the people of the Stone Age, they kept no beasts, but bartered their goods with the inhabitants of the more low-lying districts in exchange for corn, milk, meat and other produce. Thus, the Trundle served as a kind of market town. . . . But it was also a fortress, and when danger loomed the herdsmen around would drive their beasts to the hill-top, confident that shelter awaited them behind the ramparts.

VI

The views from these Goodwood hills are magnificent. Southwards the whole countryside in which the story of Sussex

began is spread out like a map at our feet. Selsey Bill, where
St. Wilfrid landed, and the whole Hundred of Manhood that
witnessed the arrival of Aella; Chichester Harbour up whose
easternmost channel the Romans sailed to found the city of
Regnum; Chichester itself with its slender spire rising out of
the middle distance to pinpoint the spot where the Belgae
settled when at last the Trundle was abandoned; all are there.
And beyond, on a clear day, the Isle of Wight is plainly visible
behind the sparkling sunlit waters of the English Channel.

In all directions the countryside is lovely, and it is small
wonder that the poet and essayist, William Hayley, saw the
hamlet of Eartham, but a few miles to the east of Goodwood,
beyond Halnaker, as ' the little Paradise '. Nestling at the foot
of the hills with its inn and few odd houses, it remains as
supremely peaceful as the day when William Hayley, having
inherited the estate which his father had bought here in 1743,
proceeded to enlarge the villa and plant out the grounds in a
way that commanded the finest vistas of the surrounding
countryside. Though Hayley, who was born at Chichester,
devoted the greater part of his time at Eartham to writing, he
was also a moderately gifted artist, and it was his enthusiasm
in this direction that governed much of his planning, prompting him to build a studio in the grounds and arrange seats at
all the points whence the best views could be obtained.

When inflammation of the eyes caused him to abandon this
side of his calling, he decided to offer the studio to his friend
George Romney, whose poor health appears to have proved a
constant worry to him, and so wrote to the great portrait
painter imploring him to ' exchange, for a short time, the busy
scenes and noxious air of London ' for the tranquillity of
Sussex.

' Here,' he wrote, ' are three divinities, Health, Gaiety
and Friendship, that invite you very eagerly to this pleasant
retreat.'

One of Hayley's reasons for inviting Romney was that he

was anxious for him to paint a number of life-size portraits of his friends to hang in the various rooms of his home. Romney readily accepted the commission, and soon was paying the first of the many visits to Eartham that were to be repeated at almost annual intervals for the next twenty-five years. Some of these visits stretched over many months, during which time the two, the poet and the artist, would chat long hours together in their ' chace of ideas ', Romney taking up his pen to make a rough sketch whenever some point in their conversation struck him as lending itself to the development of an imaginative master-piece.

To Romney, Eartham became a second home, and at various times Hayley invited many famous people here to meet him. Edward Gibbon, John Flaxman, William Cowper, and the novelist Charlotte Smith, who lived at Brighton, all received invitations to Hayley's house-parties, and in his studio Romney painted each, while, in turn, Flaxman made a small bust of Romney.

It was in this Sussex studio that Romney worked on the first sketch of his canvas illustrating a scene from Shakespeare's *The Tempest*; here that he was introduced to the Duke of Richmond, who may personally have commissioned him to paint some of the portraits that hang in Goodwood House to-day. Certainly it was as a direct result of these holidays at Eartham that he was asked to execute the works now to be seen at Petworth House. Some of these he painted in Hayley's studio, some at Petworth, whither he would ride across the downs each morning.

Not all the time was given up to work, however. In company with Hayley he was able to enjoy the countryside for its own sake, and would often go bathing in the sea or rambling over the downs, filling his lungs with ' the fine balsamic air of Sussex '.

VII

One of the many ' social walks ' that Romney and Hayley may have enjoyed together is that along the quiet lane at the foot of the downs to the neighbouring village of Slindon, birthplace of Richard Newland, father of modern cricket who, before Lord's rose to fame, taught many of the Hambledon players the ' gentle art ', among them his nephew, Richard Nyren, celebrated host of *The Bat and Ball*. Slindon was an important stronghold of cricket in those early days when Sussex, Kent and Hampshire were the leading counties, and Romney and Hayley may well have found time to saunter over to watch the villagers at play.

Slindon has memories other than those of cricket. Archbishop Stephen Langton, who was largely instrumental in forcing King John to sign the *Magna Carta*, died in the thirteenth-century residence of the Archbishops of Canterbury which stood on the site of Slindon House. When Slindon was alienated from Canterbury, the estate passed to the Kempes, and it seems probable that the fine wooden effigy (the only one in Sussex) in the parish church of the recumbent knight in armour may be the figure of Sir Anthony Kempe to whom Queen Elizabeth conferred the manor.

Like the lovely Fairmile Bottom, with its beech-clad Rewell Wood, which mounts the downs to the east of Slindon, the whole of this estate is now to be preserved for the nation. Some years ago the Earl of Hardwick presented Fairmile Bottom and the surrounding woodlands to the Society of Sussex Downsmen; now, under the will of the late F. J. Wootton Isaacson, the Slindon property has been left to the National Trust. So that between the two, mile upon mile of beautiful country is to be preserved unbroken.

Altogether the latter estate takes in some 3,600 acres of some of the grandest Sussex scenery, including part of the pretty village of Slindon itself, two miles of the downland section of

Stane Street, more than 1,000 acres of farmland, Nore Hill, and over 1,500 acres of beech woods, some of which are almost sensationally beautiful. Set on a slope, the estate stretches as far northwards as Bignor Hill, where it reaches the crest of the downs, and from here, at a height of about 700 feet, it is possible, on a clear day, to pick out such widely separated landmarks as Chichester Cathedral to the south-west and Blackdown and Leith Hill to the north and north-east.

VIII

The village of Bignor, whose Tudor grocer's shop of half-timber and thatch is set on fifteenth-century foundations so high that they have to be mounted by steps, nestles in a hollow to the north with the famous Roman villa, a little farther to the east, near the by-road leading past West Burton, where in 1740 the bones of a number of elephants were found nine feet below ground, to Bury.

Bignor villa marked the tenth mile along Stane Street's route from Chichester to London, and was the palace of the Governor of Regnum. In this noble pillared building, which boasted perhaps sixty-five rooms for himself and his entourage, together with baths, hypocausts, barns and granaries, as well as separate quarters for the slaves, the immensely rich governor lived a life of luxury, enjoying every modern convenience then known.

Though the palace must have numbered among the most magnificent of all the stately Doric homes erected by the Romans in this country, nevertheless for several centuries after their departure not a vestige remained for the eye to see. In 1811, however, a ploughman, employed by a farmer named Tupper, turned the soil rather deeper than usual, and so brought to light the first traces of a number of fine, tessellated pavements, which, happily, Mr. Tupper recognized and so carefully preserved under thatched huts.

Other than a few fragments of pillars and water-flues and a general outline of part of the ground plan, there is still little enough to show, yet these pavements afford a splendid example of the superb degree of craftsmanship reached by the Romans. The skill with which they fashioned their tiny cubes of white chalk, red brick, blue-green limestone, and even glass, is matched only by their artistry in piecing them together to form those readily understandable symbolic mosaics.

On the floor of what was once the triclinium, or principal dining-hall, we see, framed in one circle, the young Ganymede, in cloak of red and holding his shepherd's crook, being carried away by an eagle as he stands guardian over his father's flocks; and in a second, the figures of girls dancing round what, probably, once was a fountain. A second pavement shows the head of Medusa from which issue fourteen snakes; a third, Venus, surrounded by long-tailed pheasants, looking down upon three panels in which a number of Cupids are seen playing as gladiators, some of them armed with shield and crested helmet, some with net and trident, others, simply, with rods.

A homely touch is given to one of these pavements by the presence of the footmark of some Roman dog, which, presumably, must have trodden on the mortar before it had set.

How soon after the departure of the Romans this great villa fell to decay no one can say, but it is believed that part of Bignor's Early English church—unusual for its fifteenth-century oaken Easter Sepulchre with cinquefoiled tracery panels, buttresses and battlemented cornice—was built of its materials.

IX

Westwards from Bignor a quiet road, that alternately climbs and drops and twists and turns all the way, leads us back along the Wealden side of the downs to a string of delightful little villages and hamlets—Sutton, with its timbered medieval priest-house, built of mud bricks and now the rectory, with its memories of the rector, Aquilo Cruso, who, accused of Popish sympathies, cunningly prepared his case in Hebrew, and, since nobody could justly dispute it, won the day; Duncton, also the site of a Roman villa, nestling at the bottom of its steep hill— so steep that it also had to be made unusually wide in order to ease the strain on the horses by enabling them to 'quarter' as they climbed—below the 837 feet high beech-studded Duncton Down where, in the past, some of the most vicious of the downland cock-fights were staged; East Lavington, home of a famous stud whose horses—among them the Derby winners Captain Cuttle (1922) and Coronach (1926)—have long been trained on near-by Woolavington Down; and Graffham, memorable alike for its red ochre beds and for its associations with Cardinal Manning.

At Graffham we are but a short distance from Heyshott, where Manning preached his last sermon before changing his faith, and not far off is Dunford House which the great nineteenth-century free-trader, Richard Cobden, who was born in a farm-house in the village, built for himself out of the £80,000 awarded to him by a grateful nation. In the hands of the Dunford House Memorial Association—a body whose object is to foster goodwill between nations—his home remains much as he left it, with his family portraits hanging on the walls and his school books still preserved in a cabinet, while in the church the font in which he was christened and the pew from which he worshipped may still be seen. Though the grave of his brother is here, Cobden, surprisingly, was buried at West Lavington, just south of Midhurst, whose church Manning restored.

Heyshott lies to the north of the Charlton Forest, and at Cocking—whose partially Norman church contains two piscinae, an aumbry, a canopied tomb and the remains of some wall paintings—we recross the main road that leads over the downs from Singleton and pass along the foot of a lovely down-land stretch past Bepton, for Didling, Treyford and Elsted.

All three of these places are quite enchanting. Tucked away up a quiet lane under the downs, surrounded by fields and all but hidden by its great yew tree, Didling's tiny church, with its thirteenth-century oak benches and altar rails, is rendered the more interesting on account of its ' phantom choir boy '. A former rector of Elsted, into whose parish Didling falls, told me that at various times the melodious treble voice of a boy has been heard accompanying an all-male congregation of farm-hands in their hymn singing. The voice is heard only at widely separated intervals. Sometimes as many as ten, or even twenty, years have passed between two of its chantings, and all the well-known theories like ' bats in the belfry ' and ' owls in the churchyard ' have been tested in the hope of finding a solution. . . . But the voice remains a mystery.

Four churches—the one at Didling, another at Elsted, and two at Treyford—are now included in the parish of Elsted. Alas, two of them are in a sorry state. While that of Elsted—a fine example of Saxon work containing some of the most perfect herring-bone masonry in England—has long lost its roof and has its floor carpeted with grass, Treyford's original church is so badly ruined that the few fragments of stone that are left are mostly buried under bushes and fallen trees. This need never have been. When these two buildings first began to show signs of serious decay a certain rich woman in the district was approached on the question of providing the neces-sary funds for their repair. Unhappily, she appears to have had little appreciation of old and beautiful things, and, rather than restore what was old, preferred to build a new and altogether larger church. And so Treyford's second church arose; an ugly Victorian edifice that is all too big and so out of keeping with its surroundings that it is referred to locally as the ' white elephant '.

But the story is to have a happy sequel. Treyford's new

church, built in 1849 of chalk and 'clunch', is showing signs of crumbling, and as I write there is a plan afoot to raise a subscription of £10,000 for the purpose of restoring Elsted's church. If this is put into effect Treyford's 'white elephant' would be demolished, and the materials sold for building purposes.

Close to Treyford's ruined church is a fine manor-house, notable for its brickwork, bearing the date 1621, and in the centre of the village is a most unusual road sign, carved in wood and finely painted, depicting St. Christopher, the patron saint of travellers who was held in the highest esteem in the Middle Ages, bearing the Christ Child on his shoulder. Below are written the words: 'Who carried Christ; speed thee to-day and lift thy heart up all the way.' With one hand St. Christopher points the way back to Bepton, and with his staff to Harting, our last village in this circuit of the Western Downs.

x

A valley village, with the coppered spire of its great church—one of two in Sussex to be known as 'the Cathedral of the Downs'—standing out from the many roof levels of its old houses and cottages, South Harting is one of the 'show villages' of Sussex, if only for its spacious lay-out. It is also one with a number of interesting associations.

For more than forty years Gilbert White owned various properties round here, inheriting them from a great-uncle, while Anthony Trollope, whose grave is in the churchyard, spent the last two years of his life at Harting Grange, whither he moved from London in 1880 in the hope that the fresh downland air might give relief to his asthma. Here he was visited several times by Millais, and wrote his last four works, *An Old Man's Love*, *Kept in the Dark*, *The Fixed Period*, and *Mr. Scarborough's Family*, and began his unfinished Irish novel, *The Landleaguers*. Alexander Pope, too, had ties with South

Harting when his friend John Caryll—who inspired the poet to write *The Rape of the Lock*—owned Lady Holt Park, by West Harting Down.

Perhaps the most interesting associations, though, are to be found in Uppark, a mile or two to the south of the village, which has been the seat of the Fetherstonhaugh family—many of whom are remembered in the church—ever since Sir Matthew Fetherstonhaugh bought the property in 1745 from the Earl of Tankerville, grandson of the first earl of this name who built the mansion in the reign of Charles II. To this gracious building, designed by Talmar, pupil of Inigo Jones, and set on rising ground in a 900-acre deer park in the triangle between Harting Hill and Compton Hill, Lady Hamilton was brought as a servant girl by a naval officer, to live in more amenable conditions than she had experienced in London; in this mansion, too, Sarah Wells, mother of H. G. Wells, was engaged as a housekeeper.

Sarah's father was an innkeeper at Midhurst, and she was 28 when, in 1850, she first entered the service of Lady Fetherstonhaugh. Joseph Wells was then employed as a gardener on the estate. Though Sarah said that at first she found Joseph ' peculiar ', this does not seem to have prevented her from walking with him on the downs. Their happy walks together were brought to a sudden end, however, when, in 1853, Sarah was forced to leave Uppark to tend her dying parents, and Joseph was given notice shortly afterwards. Despite the adverse circumstances they were married within a fortnight of the death of the second of Sarah's parents.

The two then went to live at Bromley, and it was here that their third son, Herbert George, was born in 1866. But life was not easy at Bromley. Joseph kept a shop, but his heart was in cricket at which he excelled, and he found himself better able to make money as a player-coach than by selling merchandise. Modest though his earnings were, Sarah might just have managed to keep the home going had not Joseph unhappily fallen in the backyard while pruning a grape vine, and so rendered himself lame for life.

With Joseph's cricketing days ended, the outlook appeared so bleak that, in 1880, Sarah Wells had no alternative but to split the family and return to Uppark, where for thirteen years she went faithfully about her work in black silk dress and cap and apron. Young Herbert George, now fourteen, was sent to Windsor to work as a draper's assistant, but, finding this distasteful, was allowed to join his mother at Uppark, where he spent the winter of 1880-81, dividing his time between playing with the servants, delving into old books, fiddling about with a telescope, and·producing a paper which he styled *The Uppark Alarmist.* Though it was not long before he was found employment as a chemist's assistant at Midhurst, this winter provided material for the rising author, who, disguising the place as ' on the Kentish Downs ', later introduced Uppark into his *Tono-Bungay* as ' Bladesover '.

XI

One of the best points from which to look down upon the village is Harting Hill. From here the views to north and east are superb. The Harting Downs, Telegraph Hill—one of the hill-top semaphore stations used for signalling messages from Portsmouth Dockyard to the Admiralty before the days of telephones—Philliswood Down, and, beyond, the five tumuli south of Treyford, known as the ' Devil's Jumps ', are knitted together to form a perfect set-piece of the land where Weald meets Down.

XII

South Harting is the scene of a gay Whit-Monday ceremony when one of the last surviving old-time Friendly Societies, the ' Red, White and Blue Club,' stages a traditional ' feast ' that may well be centuries old.

It is a day that starts early, and grows gayer and more festive with every hour. Almost at cock-crow the villagers may be seen decorating the *White Hart* with beech boughs, after which they proceed to the square to set up and adorn with red, white and blue streamers, the largest bough of all.

Soon after nine o'clock the members make their way to the *White Hart* to pay their subscriptions, an event which in itself calls for many a rollicking Sussex song. As soon as the subscriptions have been paid, and all have had their bite of lunch, some stalwart, who styles himself ' the mayor ', stands on the steps of the old inn and calls the roll. As he shouts each name, so the members fall into procession for their march to the church—first the standard-bearers, then the band, and behind them the rank and file, all wearing rosettes of the club colours and carrying sticks of pealed hazel, the latter as a symbol, some say, of the staves the pilgrims once carried on their downland treks to Canterbury.

Not a man or woman who has not been allotted some other task is excused attending this service to hear the vicar preach his traditional sermon at the cost of £1—a fee which, also by tradition, he must afterwards return to the club's funds! Any one who should display negligence in this respect is tracked down by the stewards and compelled to pay a fine of a shilling.

The ' feast ' takes place after the service, and it is amusing to see the villagers bustling to and fro with their bowls, dishes and hand trucks from the bakers' oven in the square, where they have been preparing and cooking the food, to the *White Hart*, where it is now to be eaten. Though present conditions have put a check on the amount of food to be served, in normal times these South Harting menus are memorable. Six yards of suet pudding, three 15 lb. gammons, 40 lb. of veal, 40 lb. of salt beef, 14 lb. of top side, a couple of legs of pork, one-and-a-half bushels of potatoes, and six dozen cabbages would not normally be considered untoward, and with this as much as 72 gallons of English ale might be served.

For how long South Harting has boasted a ' mayor and corporation ' is not quite certain, but the ' insignia ' is carefully preserved in a casket in the *White Hart*—a fine silken robe adorned with bottle corks. The duties of this august body are also preserved, and they make amusing reading. The ' town crier ', for instance, is required to ' shout the odds ' on the eve of all big races, while the ' treasurer ' is to ' stand drinks all round at his own proper charge and expense '. As for the ' mayor ', he is expected not only to check the levels of the ponds, and see to it that the parishioners cut the grass of the tennis courts and bowling greens, but, worse still, to ' question all strangers and visitors '!

CHAPTER FIVE: *Along the Western Rother*

FLOWING more or less parallel with the downs—zigzag-ging so sympathetic a course that often it loops northwards in harmony with their characteristic ' spurs '—the River Rother divides the hill country we have just explored from the un-dulating farmlands of the western weald next to Surrey.

If we head northwards from South Harting to Rogate and follow this diminutive river to just beyond Fittleworth, where the Rother joins the Arun, we not only see Sussex in one of her most soothing moods but we also behold a delightful panorama of the downs themselves as they roll along in their wooded beauty.

Rogate itself, pleasantly situated with its Early English church close by the cross-roads and its sadly ruined fortress on the river bank, was once the home of a Premonstratensian abbey, and, in the days of Edward II, when Ralph de Camoys obtained a charter from the king, was the scene of an important fair. To-day, however, it is but a place of memories, the only traces of Dureford Abbey, founded in 1169, being the frag-ments of a few arches that have been incorporated into a farm-house, and a small section of the old moat.

From Rogate the way leads us past the little church of Terwick to Trotton, whose beautiful bridge of five arches, spanning the Rother, was built at great cost in 1400 by Thomas, Lord Camoys, hero of Agincourt, after, it is said, one of his returning men-at-arms was drowned in making the then peri-

lous crossing here. Lord Camoys also rebuilt the church, and
he and his wife, Elizabeth, are buried in a magnificent tomb
in the aisle-less chancel.

The widow of Hotspur, Elizabeth has gained rather more
lasting fame than her second husband, as Shakespeare's
' Gentle Kate ' in the *Taming of the Shrew* :

> . . . Kate, the prettiest Kate in Christendom;
> Kate of Kate-Hall, my super-dainty Kate,
> For dainties are all cates : and therefore, Kate
> Take this of me, Kate of my consolation;
> Hearing thy mildness prais'd in every town,
> Thy virtues spoke of, and thy beauty sounded,
> Yet not so deeply as to thee belongs,
> Myself am moved to woo thee for my wife.

An exquisite brass, some nine feet long, shows ' Gentle
Kate ', whose praises Petruchio sang so extravagantly, dressed
in finely decorated kirtle and mantle beside her husband, who
wears his Order of the Garter.

Trotton Church contains a number of unusual features,
including a brass to Margaret Camoys, which was fashioned in
1310 by a French engraver and is generally regarded as the
second oldest in England to be set up in memory of a woman;
a reredos painting of the Last Supper; and a remarkable collection of medieval wall paintings, which were brought to
light as recently as 1904 after being covered with plaster for
several centuries.

Here, in the centre of the west wall, the figure of Our Lord
is seen sitting in judgement beneath a canopy of clouds, while
below Him Moses holds open the Tables of the Law. To the
right of Moses the Seven Deadly Sins are portrayed in the
naked form of a giant encompassed by Pride, Sloth, Avarice,
Gluttony, Anger, Envy and Lust; to his left a series of medallion paintings, arranged round a central figure, depict the
Seven Acts of Mercy.

Another interesting feature—though of no æsthetic merit—

is a memorial tablet to the dramatist Thomas Otway, who was born in the vicarage in 1652 when his father was curate here.

Though little remembered to-day, Thomas Otway was numbered among the leading dramatists of his time, surpassing his contemporary Dryden and even, in the opinion of Sir Walter Scott, excelling Shakespeare for the passion of some of his love scenes. Educated at Winchester and Oxford, he first tried his hand at acting, but, since he suffered such stage fright that he invariably forgot his lines, he soon decided to take to writing instead. The production of *Don Carlos*, when he was still only 23, brought Otway his first real success, prompting the Earl of Rochester to write unkindly that:

> Don Carlos his pockets so amply had filled,
> That his mange was quite cured, and his lice were all killed.

In fact, Otway made extremely little out of any of his plays. Behind these and other such utterances were a bitterness and intrigue that were to affect the whole future of the young dramatist. The beautiful Elizabeth Barry had played the leading part in Otway's plays, and with her he had fallen deeply in love. For a time she responded to his approaches, and passionate love letters passed between the two. Yet it was the Earl of Rochester who had first brought Mrs. Barry out, and the Earl was extremely jealous. Deciding that his ' favours ' were likely to prove of the more lasting value to her, Mrs. Barry eventually made her feelings quite obvious to Otway, who forthwith obtained a commission in the army, and went to the Netherlands to forget.

Within a year, however, the regiment was disbanded and officers and troops alike were left to find their own way home at their own expense. Ragged and almost penniless, Otway returned to London, where he was subjected to further libellous attacks by the Earl of Rochester. But the interval had been sufficient to allow him to recover his will to write, and in the years 1680 to 1682 he produced a number of plays of which his most famous were his tragedy, *The Orphan*, and his masterpiece of tragic passion, *Venice Preserved*.

Mrs. Barry, like Sarah Siddons, continued to act in his plays, but, though they obtained more than a fair measure of success, they brought him in but little money, and in the next three years of spasmodic and indifferent writing his spirit broke completely. His unhappy affair with Mrs. Barry had cut too deep, and poverty and misfortune brought him to an early grave at the age of thirty-three in sudden and unusual circumstances. It is said that starvation drove him from his humble lodgings in Tower Hill to beg for bread. On discovering his identity, a passing stranger gave him a guinea with which he at once rushed to the baker's shop. But his hunger was too acute. For one who had not tasted food for several days he attempted to devour the loaf too quickly and with the first mouthful choked himself.

III

At Trotton the Rother makes one of those northward loops to Chithurst—whose church is lined with the coffin lids of the monks from the long-vanished priory here—before turning southwards again for the pretty village of Iping, which also boasts an ancient bridge of five arches.

Nestling at the foot of Hammer Wood, where the iron founders worked in the days of the Spanish Armada, Iping is peopled almost entirely by the descendants of those men and women of Sussex who watched for the coming of Napoleon—a village wherein old ways, old thoughts, old beliefs, seem only to strengthen with the ages, and one in which the traditional songs of the countryside may still be heard.

Since the days of King Harold, Iping has boasted a mill by the water-side. Once they ground their flour here; later they employed the power of the Rother for making paper; now accumulators are made in the mill. Yet the beauty of its setting remains undisturbed.

Every village along this stretch of river once boasted its mill, just as to-day each retains its medieval bridge. At Stedham, eastwards beyond two further loops, whose 900-year-old churchyard yew has a girth of some twenty-eight feet, the power of the river once turned the giant water-wheels of no less than three mills, while Woolbeding, but a mile or two on, also possessed at least one.

It was to this hamlet, in a beautiful verdant valley, that Thomas Otway's father came as vicar when his curacy at Trotton was ended, and here the future dramatist disgraced himself by scribbling on the church registers. The vicarage where he played as a boy, like the church, approached along a walk of clipped yew trees, where his father ministered, still stands. But the glory of Woolbeding lies in the stone-built Elizabethan house whose well-planned gardens, containing one of the finest tulip trees in the country, abut on to the churchyard.

In this house, which was remodelled in Stuart or Queen Anne times and contains some interesting period furniture, miniatures and paintings, Charles James Fox was often entertained by Lord Robert Spencer, third son of Charles, second Duke of Marlborough. A close friend of the great Whig leader, Lord Spencer accompanied him to Paris for his interview with Napoleon during the Peace of Amiens, and in an alcove is a bust of Fox by Nollekens. A number of other prominent statesmen—Fitzpatrick, Hare, Grey and Disraeli—have found hospitality at Woolbeding in their time, while Charlotte Smith is also said to have written some of her books here.

IV

Charles James Fox may well have been acquainted with this district before he paid his first visit to Lord Spencer. For it

was as Member for the neighbouring market town of Midhurst
that he first entered Parliament in 1768 at the tender age of
nineteen, thereby entirely disregarding the Law of the Land
by doing so while he was still a minor.

The circumstances of his entry into politics were somewhat
unusual. His father, Lord Holland, and his uncle, Lord
Ilchester, father of Lord Stavordale, were worried because their
respective sons were showing a tendency to indulge in too care-
free living, and were anxious to find them some congenial
occupation. If only the problem of their age could be over-
come, Parliament was their choice.

Midhurst was then a ' burgage ' borough, privileged since
the early fourteenth century to elect two Members. But the
Midhurst elections of the eighteenth century were very different
from those of our own time. A ' burgage ' comprised simply
a measure of farmland in the centre of which a stone was set
up to denote the site and the ownership. Altogether there were
120 such tenements in Midhurst, and these were invariably
owned by one man who let them out to the country folk on
condition that at election time they cast their votes in accord-
ance with his instructions. Since the secret ballot was then
unknown, no tenant was likely to be foolish enough to anta-
gonize his landlord by disregarding his wishes.

Such a system, though amounting to dictatorship, solved the
problems of the two peers, who, as the elections of 1768 drew
near, made known their feelings to Lord Montagu of near-by
Cowdray Castle, who then owned all the Midhurst burgages.
The latter agreed to nominate the two cousins. And so it was
that the great opponent of Pitt, and one of the most dynamic
figures ever to sit on the Opposition Bench and later become
Prime Minister, embarked upon his long parliamentary career.

Though Midhurst lost its burgage rights with the Reform
Act of 1832, and has since declined in importance from a
borough to a parish, one of the old burgage stones can still be
seen in a wall in Knockhundred Row.

v

Set, as its name would suggest, in the heart of richly wooded country and heather-clad moors—much of it favourable hunting country—Midhurst is one of the most beautiful towns in Sussex. With its long main street—wide, spacious and airy—and its little side roads of medieval and Tudor houses, some with half-timbered or tile-hung overhanging upper storeys, it has an atmosphere of solid comfort tempered with sober prosperity. Here, every style of architecture down to the late Georgian and Regency are seen in perfect harmony. In the main street is the sixteenth-century *Angel Hotel*, where the Pilgrim Fathers are said to have paused on their way to embark in the *Mayflower*, and the grammar school, founded in 1672 by the quilt-maker, Gilbert Hannam, where the geologist, Sir Charles Lyell, was educated, and where H. G. Wells spent a year as a student teacher. Richard Cobden was also a pupil at Midhurst, but not at the grammar school.

Knockhundred Row leads off the southern end of this high street, climbing abruptly to Church Hill. Here, almost immediately opposite a finely proportioned row of seventeenth-century houses, is the chemist's shop to which H. G. Wells was sent from Uppark to work as an assistant. In his *Tono-Bungay* —in which he refers to Midhurst as ' Wimblehurst '—Wells describes how he used to dust the coloured medicine bottles and roll pills here, and how once he was unfortunate enough to break a dozen soda siphons during a friendly brawl with an errand boy. This was not the only occasion on which young Wells got into trouble: whenever the bearded barber, a few doors along, came out into the street to canvas customers he would dart out after him and proceed to sketch him.

Wells remained only a year as a chemist's assistant. When he discovered that it would be necessary for him to learn Latin if he was to qualify and set up on his own account, he decided to try his hand at teaching instead, and so, after an interval,

moved down to the grammar school. He left his mark, however. The cough mixture which he dispensed, like the pills
which he rolled, is still sold in this little chemist's shop, just as
the bottles of coloured water remain.

The oldest part of Midhurst lies beyond Church Hill—in
West Street and Wool Lane, to the west of Market Square,
where the old stocks and pillory are kept. Nearly every
building in this corner is either half-timbered or tile-hung, and
many possess the added interest of a contemporary inscription.
One shop in West Street, for instance, displays the initials and
date 'I.M.S. 1660', while one of the upper rooms of a cottage
in Wool Lane is adorned with the coat of arms of the Earl of
Southampton—who was mainly responsible for the building of
Cowdray—together with a number of such symbols as the tiger,
bull, eagle's head, sable and Tudor rose. These shops and
cottages contrast attractively with the fifteenth-century hostelry,
The Spread Eagle, a magnificent example of medieval craftsmanship, which is said to be the last inn in England to retain
a 'varlet' in Cromwellian uniform and contains among other
features a secret passage along which smugglers used to pass
on their way to the roof loft when hiding from the Excise Men.

VI

This corner forms part of the 114 acres known as the Liberty
of St. John of Jerusalem, which, from the reign of Edward II,
was vested in the Knights Hospitallers, who held jurisdiction
over the district.

Since the Dissolution of the Monasteries the liberty has been
incorporated in the manor of Cowdray, and until the last war,
when unfortunately the custom was allowed to lapse, an annual
Court Leet was held to appoint its constable. From time to
time the constable and his attendants would make a perambula-
tion of the liberty when all who 'obstructed the highway' were
amerced on the spot. Frivolous charges were often levelled

against the tradesmen. A greengrocer who allowed a box of apples to protrude too far on to the pavement; a furniture dealer who elected to cut out linoleum in the path of the passers-by; or a bicycle trader who carelessly left a tyre so that others could trip over it; all were liable to be fined anything from a shilling to two shillings.

Until the last holder of the office died a little while ago, Midhurst also boasted its own town crier who, at all public functions, paraded the streets at the head of the parish council, dressed in his traditional uniform and carrying his eighteenth-century silver mace. Every Shrove Tuesday, too, the pancake bell would be rung to remind the housewives—as was most necessary in the days when clocks were unknown and few could read—that it was time to fry the pancakes.

Unhappily only one of the town's many quaint old customs has survived the war. Each evening, sharp at eight o'clock, the curfew may still be heard in memory of a man who, lost in the dense forests of the Weald several centuries ago, was able to find his way home again by the sound of Midhurst's bells.

VII

The imposing ruins of Cowdray are situated to the north-west of the town, and may be approached across the water meadows almost opposite the grammar school. Started in the early years of the sixteenth century by Sir David Owen, completed about 1530 by the Earl of Southampton, and preserved as a ruin by Sir Aston Webb, on the instructions of the first Viscount Cowdray, shortly before the outbreak of the first world war, Cowdray numbered among the finest mansions of its time. Though to-day only a skeleton, sufficient is left of the banqueting hall, with its six-storeyed oriel window and vaulted entrance porch, the state bedroom, the kitchen with turreted tower, and the chapel with its four traceried windows, to give an impression of its past magnificence and of the high-feasting that took place within its walls, when, on the death of the Earl of Southampton, Cowdray passed to his half-brother, Sir Anthony Browne, Chief Standard Bearer to Queen Elizabeth.

Here, in 1591, having shown similar hospitality to Edward VI many years previously, Sir Anthony entertained the Queen for several days in lavish style, when, according to a contemporary document, homage was paid to Elizabeth at every corner of the park by men and women of every calling in the district, and fantastic tableaux were staged. In the mansion itself enormous quantities of food, including 3 oxen and 140 geese for breakfast, were prepared, the dinners of many courses being served on a table 144 feet long. Musicians and singers were at hand to satisfy the popular craze for madrigals and to play for the court dances and the masque. And when the queen chose to hunt, and proceeded to her bower in the park, the nymph who handed her her bow and arrows sang sweet songs while the deer were being driven to within easy range.

A year after this great pageant Sir Anthony Browne, now the first Lord Montagu, died, leaving behind him a curse on Cowdray to which its ruined state is attributed to-day. Though, unfortunately, no authentic records of the origin of the curse exist, it seems that at the time that Sir Anthony—who was awarded Battle Abbey at the Dissolution—inherited Cowdray, he incurred the wrath of some monks by interrupting them at their prayers and proceeding to make high revel. (One account goes so far as to say that he even slew the priest at Cowdray's High Altar, but I am assured that this is as much without foundation as the suggestion that the event took place at Battle Abbey.) As the last of the monks retired, he turned and uttered the words: 'The house of the despoiler shall perish by fire and water.'

Though Sir Anthony himself was spared the ordeal of seeing the prophecy come true, misfortune was to attend his descendants in great measure in later years. In September 1793, while

the eighth Viscount Montagu was abroad, a group of workmen, who were preparing the mansion in readiness for his
forthcoming marriage, stupidly set fire to some rubbish in the
north gallery. Since a high wind was blowing at the time, and
fire-fighting arrangements were far from adequate, the great
mansion was almost entirely gutted before the flames could be
brought under control. A week later the viscount himself was
drowned while attempting to shoot the Laufenburg rapids in
too frail a boat.

From the eighth Lord Montagu the estate passed to a cousin,
who died almost immediately. His sister then inherited the
property, and went to live with her husband and two sons in
the keeper's lodge. But the curse was not fully spent; hardly
had they moved into their new home than both sons were
drowned off Bognor. And further misfortunes have followed
the family since then.

Impressive monuments to these two sons and to the first
Lord Montagu may be seen in near-by Easebourne Church,
whose vicarage was originally the refectory of Easebourne
Priory.

VIII

Easebourne stands at the western entrance to Cowdray Park,
and the main road to Petworth, seven miles distant, takes us
through the heart of the lovely old deer park to Halfway Bridge
where a tributary of the Rother flows down from the Weald.
Two charming little villages lie to either side of this bridge—
to the south Selham, into whose small and partially Saxon
church a freshly cut sheaf is carried from the cornfields during
the Harvest Festival Service; to the north Lodsworth, cluster-
ing around its green in the midst of wooded hills and apple
orchards, with its old manor-house—now a farm-house—which
Cromwell occupied during a visit to Sussex. For several
centuries the inhabitants of Lodsworth enjoyed a number of

unusual privileges, including the exemption from owing suit
or service to any Hundred Court.

Though a little away from the river, the scenery along this
road, with the woods to the north and the downs to the south,
never wearies. A main road, it is nevertheless surprisingly
peaceful, with Tillington, scene of a Turner painting, the only
village between Halfway Bridge and the old market town of
Petworth.

IX

A royal manor in the days of Edward the Confessor and once
the property of Earl Roger de Montgomerie, Petworth is one of
the oldest and most unusual of Sussex towns. Little more than
a village, its character can scarcely have changed noticeably
since the eighteenth century when many of the homes of the
more prosperous citizens were re-fronted, and the cottages of
the humble folk built. Though Donkey Row is now North
Terrace, Lombard Street is still cobbled and is, like Middle
Street, essentially Tudor in character, while Hungers Lane—
thought to be one of the oldest streets in England—still has an
' atmosphere ' about it, reminiscent of the time when the
smugglers used to pass through here on their pack-horses to
their secret cave in Blackdown Hill. A place of innumerable
nooks and crannies and narrow ways, the streets of Petworth,
like those of Midhurst, are rich in houses of every architectural
style, including such fine buildings as the Jacobean almshouses,
Somerset Hospital, and Thompson's Hospital; the antique
dealer's shop in East Street, with its plaster ceiling and its
archway carvings of the Tudor Rose and the Percy Half Moon;
and the town houses of such families as the Dawtreys—who
can trace an unbroken link of eight centuries with Petworth—
the Mitfords and the Peacheys, all of whom, like the Percys
and Seymours of Petworth House, are remembered in the
church.

Standing on a northern eminence of the downs, with its main street encircling the old market hall, it is its lay-out, perhaps even more than its individual buildings, that makes Petworth so unusual, and, at the same time, so confusing. There is an old saying that once, many years ago, a heavily laden timber wagon, endeavouring to pass through the town, got caught in this street, and has not yet succeeded in extricating itself from this natural maze. During the last war tanks and other army vehicles were purposely sent through Petworth as a test for their drivers.

The confusion is accentuated to a certain extent by the great wall of Petworth House, which extends for something like thirteen miles and virtually encloses the north and west sides of the town.

x

Ancestral seat of the Percys, the Seymours and the Wyndhams this great baronial estate is now the home of their descendant, the third Lord Leconfield, who recently presented it to the National Trust. Its story goes back to the days of Henry I when the king bequeathed the manor to his second wife, Adeliza, and she, in turn, gave it to her brother, Joceline de Louvain, who is believed to have been a descendant of Charlemagne. Since then the estate has been inherited in unbroken descent by three interrelated families.

Joceline married Agnes, heiress of the Northumbrian family of Perci, and at the same time assumed the latter's name. For more than two hundred years the family then bore the title of Baron of Petworth, until, in 1377, Richard II created Henry de Perci Earl of Northumberland. This first earl held the position of Marshal of England, and was the father of Harry Hotspur whom Shakespeare immortalized in *Henry IV*. The sword which Harry Hotspur carried to his death at the Battle of Shrewsbury still hangs in Petworth House, and it may well be that 'Gentle Kate' first met her husband at this Sussex home of the Percys.

After ten further earls had carried the title down to 1670, Petworth passed to Lady Elizabeth Percy—the 'Percy Heiress'—who was married no less than three times before she reached the age of eighteen, her third husband being Charles Seymour, sixth Duke of Somerset. From the Seymours the estate passed two generations later to the Wyndhams, who enjoyed the title of Earls of Egremont. The third earl left Petworth to his adopted son, George Wyndham. Since, however, the latter was not the legal heir, he was unable to inherit the title, and so was created first Baron Leconfield, the name being chosen, presumably, in recognition of the fact that the third Earl of Northumberland—who was killed in the Wars of the Roses while fighting the Lancastrian cause—had been born at Leconfield in Yorkshire.

It was the sixth Duke of Somerset—who lived in such arrogant splendour that he earned for himself the name of the 'proud Duke'—who rebuilt Petworth House in the closing years of the seventeenth century, leaving only a section of the original manor-house and the thirteenth-century Perci Chapel untouched.

Stone-built at one end of a beautiful, well-wooded, undulating park, and notable for its massive west front of over 320 feet, in which are no less than sixty-three windows without a single classical order, Petworth appears to be in keeping with the reputation of its restorer—proud. But its pride lies more in its size and surroundings than in its architecture, which is of the plainest and most severe. As with Goodwood, it is the setting that makes Petworth. Completely encircled by a long wall, the deer park of 2,000 acres with its green sward leading down from the house to the brook, its rolling hills, well-wooded Pheasant Copse—in which are the descendants of the roe deer that were here when the park was first enclosed 600 years ago—and its Stag Park, which the third Earl of

Egremont reclaimed as farmland, provides a perfect set-piece for a house which, in more cramped surroundings, might well seem over opulent.

Like Goodwood, its interior is infinitely more pleasing than its exterior, the most remarkable features being the Jacobean-style Grand Staircase, whose walls and ceilings, depicting the myth of Prometheus and Pandora and the ' Percy Heiress ' in a triumphal car surrounded by her daughters, were painted by Laguerra; the North Gallery, the Marble Hall, the White and Gold Room, the Beauty Room, and the Carved Room whose panels of grapes, flowers, winged Cupids, birds, scrolls and musical instruments are, mostly, the exquisite craftsmanship of Grinling Gibbons, and number, in fact, among his best works.

In these rooms may be seen not only fine carpets, tapestries and pieces of period furniture, but also one of the most valuable private collections of paintings in the world. The collection was started by the third Earl of Egremont, Petworth's greatest benefactor, who spent more than £1,250,000 on the town and who, for his part in starting this collection and in promoting the Sussex Agricultural Society, then the first society of the kind in England, has earned lasting fame as ' the friend of art and agriculture '.

Some of the works were executed on the spot. Romney, as we have seen, used to journey over from Eartham to portray various members of the family, while Turner paid several visits to paint the river and parkland scenes, and was provided on each occasion with his own studio.

Foreign and English artists of all ages, from Hogarth to Rubens, from Rembrandt to Teniers, are represented in this valuable collection, which includes portraits by Van Dyck, Velasquez, Titian, Holbein, Franz Hals, Murillo, Lely, Kneller, Reynolds, Gainsborough, Lawrence and Romney, and landscapes by Turner, Hobbema and Cuyp. In the Carved Room is Holbein's painting of Henry VIII and Van Dyck's of

Charles I and Henrietta Maria. In another room is Holbein's
even more famous portrait of Edward VI at the age of ten,
while Van Dyck has also left us likenesses of the ninth Earl
of Northumberland and two of his daughters, one of whom,
the Countess of Carlisle, was one of the beauties at the court
of Charles I.

There is Titian's ' Cardinal Medici ', Hogarth's ' Peg
Woffington ', and Claude Lorraine's world-renowned ' Jacob
and Laban '; Corregio's ' The Virgin and Child ' and two
pictures of the Holy Family attributed to Andrea del Sarto . . .
But these are only a few of the more outstanding in a vast
collection.

XI

Another interesting point about Petworth House is that
certain of the interior marble work has been fashioned of local
materials. Many villages to the north of the town—notably
Kirdford and Plaistow—together with one or two places in
East Sussex like Streat and Ditchling—boasted marble quarries,
and in the old days this stone was used alike in the flagging
of farm-house kitchen floors and the interior decoration of
mansions and churches. No matter where it was quarried in
Sussex it was always known as Petworth marble. Chichester
Cathedral and a great many of the Sussex churches contain
pillars of Petworth marble, which, indeed, is also to be found
in such widely separated ecclesiastical buildings as Westminster
Abbey, York Minster and Salisbury Cathedral. This blue-
grey stone, mottled with green and yellow, which, when
polished, revealed the marks of the shells contained in its sub-
stance, lay between seams of clay, and varied from a few inches
to a foot or more in thickness.

Considerable skill was required of the craftsmen who worked
the quarries, for, with careful handling, it was possible to
excavate pieces of enormous size, as can be seen in the fact that

the archbishop's chair in Canterbury Cathedral was carved out of a single piece.

A number of interesting old trades were centred around Petworth in those days. In the Weald to the north, as we shall see later, the French craftsmen taught the English the art of making glass, while the charcoal burners were busy from morning until night providing the fuel for the iron founders. Of Petworth clay bricks were fashioned and exported to the West Indies, while in the woods the coopers—after whom so many families in Petworth are named—cut hoops for both beer and gunpowder barrels.

In the town itself there were cloth-makers and hatters, soap-boilers and cloggers to add to the list of normal village tradesmen; indeed, they numbered so many that the church bell used to be tolled at 5 a.m. to arouse the workers.

XII

In the face of such activity it is not surprising to find that the 'Pleasure Fair', held annually in the Market Square on November 20, dates back nearly seven hundred years.

Control of this fair is vested in Petworth's 'Tenant of the Tolls', who enjoys a number of centuries-old rights. From a hawker who sells fish in the streets, for instance, he may demand a toll of one penny, while from a costermonger who sells vegetables from a barrow on a Saturday morning he may exact double dues. Virtually the town's unofficial mayor, the 'Tenant's' powers are even more far-reaching on the common. The present holder of the office, a baker by trade, told me that no activity is allowed to take place here without his consent, and he recalled many a fight which he had engaged in with the gipsies who used to attempt to pitch camp on Petworth's cherished grasslands.

Slow to discard their old rights and privileges, Petworth folk also remain steadfast in many of their ancient beliefs. Since

Tudor times the ' Virgin Mary Spring ', at the foot of the
Sheep Down hills on the Fittleworth road, has been renowned
for curing sore eyes, and many a Petworth woman still likes
to bathe her eyes regularly with its ' magical ' waters, or at
least keep a bottle of them by her in case of need. In this, however, she is not alone: some of her friends in neighbouring
Fittleworth feel likewise.

XIII

Fittleworth once shared another custom with Petworth and
a few other neighbouring villages. At the time of the Spanish
Armada when invasion threatened and inland communications
were poor, plans were laid whereby certain of the village blacksmiths were to be the first to be advised of impending danger.
They were then to load their hollow anvils with gunpowder
and ignite them by the simple process of touching a cord,
previously impregnated with saltpetre, with a piece of red-hot
metal, and leaving it to smoulder its way into the powder. It
was reckoned that with a favourable wind the resultant explo-
sion would carry anything up to ten miles, and thereby give the
alarm to the more outlying hamlets.

When Philip of Spain, like Napoleon and Hitler after him,
found invasion less simple than he had anticipated, the blacksmiths, not to be outdone, elected to ' fire their anvils ' to
celebrate the return of peace instead. The old blacksmith at
Petworth used to tell me graphic stories of how he fired his at
the end of the Boer War and then set a light to an effigy of
Kruger, which he first trundled round the town in a wheelbarrow. Petworth's smithy has been closed for some years
now, but in Fittleworth's little, long, low forge in the trees
on the rising hill the return of peace is still remembered in this
time-honoured style.

But it is hard to think of war in this strangely peaceful
village. For many decades now artists have journeyed hither

to paint the scene, and their pictures line the walls of the old *Swan Inn*, where they stayed; an inn long famous for its wrought-iron sign that extends across the road in a way that seems to speak hospitality. With its upland commons and fir woods, its cottages and smithy, its Early English church on the hill-top, and, in the valley, the Rother flowing past the ancient mill on the last stage of its journey to join the Arun, Fittleworth is, indeed, a picture.

CHAPTER SIX: *The Arun Basin and Lower Arun*

I

STILL notable for its various woodland crafts, the Western Weald, in the basin of the Arun and its tributary, the Rother, was once numbered among the busiest corners of Sussex. Here, the glass-blowers set up their furnaces in the Middle Ages, and the charcoal burners prepared the 'billets' for their fuel. Before the last of the glass-blowers had departed the iron-founders arrived to give still further work to the charcoal burners; while others were equally busy felling—or 'throwing'—the giant oaks for the ship-builders and wheel-wrights.

Though the iron-workers were never so numerous as those of the Eastern Weald—who were older established—there were furnaces at Imbhams, West End, Ebernoe, Roundwick, Bark-fold, Pallingham, Frith and Shillinglee (seat of Earl Winterton, present 'Father of the House of Commons'). There were forges, too, at Burningfold, Barkfold, Mitchellpark and Chithurst, and a bloomery—another kind of forge in which the iron was made into rough ingots—at Lurgashall.

The rich woodlands, sluggish streams, and the clay, brought these craftsmen to the Weald, and many links with the iron-founders still exist in such field names as Furnace Field and Boremill Copse near Blackdown; Floodgate Field, Old Pond Mead, Hammer Patches and Colliers' Field near Kirdford; Minepit Close near Fernhurst, and Pond Tail and Pondhead Lag near Wisborough Green; Kiln Field and Minepit Field near North Chapel; and so on. Likewise, the glass-blowers are remembered on the Surrey border in Glasshouse Copse and Glasshouse Field.

But for these names it would be difficult to realize that this quiet, and still well-wooded Western Weald was once a miniature Black Country. The iron-founders and glass-blowers have been gone for so long that only the barest traces of their existence remain, while the men who ' threw ' the oaks have been superseded by craftsmen whose basic material lies in the underwood—by hurdle-makers, fencers and walking-stick makers, and by woodmen who cut thatching spars and bean sticks.

These once important centres of industry to-day boast only a farm-house, while many of the Wealden villages and hamlets are as remote in their ways and outlook as in their geographical position.

II

An entertaining instance of this remoteness is to be found in the little hamlet of Ebernoe, to the north of Petworth, of which Lord Leconfield is the lord of the manor. Two or three miles from the nearest main road, along which a bus passes but twice a day, Ebernoe is a place whose delightful inhabitants are inclined to scorn ' progress '. I have met several to whom the telephone is a quite unnecessary evil, and the wireless simply a means of disturbing the quiet. Even if electricity was available, oil lamps would still be their choice, while main water, they would argue, has not yet been proved any purer than that which they draw from their own wells! Indeed, they are so averse from moving with the times that they even refuse to alter their clocks for summer—because, as a native once explained to me, ' the old sun be the only thing what gives us the time, and so we goes by him here '.

Isolated geographically, with its school, church and cottages hidden behind a thicket, Ebernoe is independent spiritually and (in normal times when there are no controls), to a great extent, materially. Like the Saxon villages, which appointed their ' headmen ' to organize the life of the community,

Ebernoe has its ' king ', whose duty it is to make the hamlet as self-supporting as present conditions will allow.

Each man has his measure of land—which may comprise anything up to twenty acres—and enjoys his ancient common rights, and, under the guidance of their ' King ', they keep their cattle and grow their crops in the way they consider most beneficial to all. In many a cottage garden a goat or even a cow will be seen tethered in the orchard among the poultry houses and bee-hives, while most villagers like to keep their pig, which they still salt, cure and smoke in their out-houses. They brew their own beer and cider too, and, with age-old recipes handed down to them by their ancestors, make potent wines of cowslip, parsnip, rhubarb or elderberry, and the finest of all the country liqueurs, sloe-gin.

At work and at play Ebernoe remains in essence feudal. Even in their summer Horn Fair these country folk maintain a link with the medieval Boon Day feasts when, at the end of the day's work on the demesne, a sheep would be brought on to the field, and the harvesters gathered anxiously around to see whether it stopped to graze, knowing that if it did they had the right to roast it for their evening roast, but that if it escaped they must be content with less tasty fare.

A sheep still (normally) figures in Ebernoe's Horn Fair. On the little green by the roadside, the carcass is set to roast at 8 a.m., and, while the local cricket team do battle with bat and ball against some neighbouring village, the older folk take it in turns to baste the meat. Sharp at 1.30 p.m. the game is interrupted, and the feast begins. But before the first mouthful has been carved the horns are removed, and these are awarded at the end of the day to the batsman who makes the highest score for the winning side. The fair does not end with the drawing of stumps; like the gay gatherings of ' Merrie England ', the day is rounded off with dancing on the green, and ends only when the figures of the revellers are seen as silhouettes in the fast-fading light.

III

To the east of Ebernoe the main road from Petworth to Guildford takes us through the village of North Chapel. Pleasantly situated on a hill, enjoying downland views, North Chapel is memorable as being both the birthplace and burial place of Noah Mann, the local innkeeper and cobbler who, before he died at the tender age of thirty-three, became one of the stalwarts of the eighteenth-century Hambledon Cricket Club.

A hard-hitting left-hander, who once caused something of a sensation by scoring ten off a single stroke, Noah played with all the great cricketing dukes and earls of his time. He thought nothing of riding the twenty-seven miles from North Chapel to Hampshire's windswept Windmill Down to take part in the evening practice games, and then covering the distance back again. A popular character and a gifted horseman, his arrival at Hambledon was usually heralded with some mirth, for as soon as the familiar figure was seen in the distance the players would throw their handkerchiefs on to the ground; whereupon Noah whipped his horse to a gallop and attempted to pick up each without spilling or checking speed.

Though Noah Mann has been dead for more than one hundred and fifty years now, the Wealden country across which he used to hack remains almost wholly unspoilt. The timbered cloisters, roofed with Horsham stone, of Lurga-shall's partly Saxon church, have grown, if anything, a trifle more mellow, while the woods to the south of Fernhurst, by which he must surely have ridden, are only a little less dense.

IV

In two of these woods—Verdley Wood and Furnace Wood —may be seen the remains of the old iron mills, and in the latter are the remnants of a sluice gate and culvert and one or two slag heaps.

The departure of the iron-workers has not caused the woods to be deserted. In the many chestnut copses around Fernhurst, men and boys now ply a trade that is almost entirely peculiar to Sussex and her neighbouring counties—the making of cleft chestnut fencing, so much in demand for enclosing country gardens and large estates alike.

This south-eastern corner of England is the only place where chestnuts grow in sufficient profusion for the making of such fences, and probably there are no more than 500 men employed in the entire industry. As a plantation is of no further use for eight years after felling, as much as £30,000 may be expended in a single season on buying suitable acres of chestnut, and the craftsmen are obliged to move from copse to copse.

Since much of the work is undertaken in winter their first thought, on arrival at a new copse, or 'frith', is to set up temporary worksheds, comprising a framework of chestnut poles overhung with a canvas awning, with but a single wall of twigs and branches to afford protection against the prevailing wind.

It takes at least two years to master the mere elements of this trade, a craftsman once told me, and each pale in a fence represents work extending over twelve months. In the autumn the trees are felled about a foot from the ground, and after that the poles are trimmed. Carefully balancing each pole on a special block, the woodman removes all small offshoots with his handbill, and then passes it on to another man, who, with the aid of a marked table, saws it to the required length, which may vary from two to six feet according to the height of the fence to be made.

After the bark has been 'rinded' the poles are smoothed, trimmed afresh, and stacked in the open to season. In five months' time cleaving, a most complicated operation upon which the quality of the ultimate fence largely depends, begins.

Though the growth and grain of the wood do not always allow, it is the aim of every craftsman to cleave stout, straight-limbed poles such as will yield pales of not less than two inches on the face and one-and-a-half inches to each arris, and it is an object-lesson to see with what care he wields his adze with just that correct twist of the wrist to enable him to keep as straight a course as possible while at the same time avoiding knots. The first two or three pales are comparatively simple to cleave, but a normal pole may yield as many as twenty-five pales, and each is more difficult to cut than the one before.

The cleaving finished, the craftsman takes up his fag-hook and proceeds to point each pale. Then the pile is loaded into a ' notch ', and wired together by means of a ' grip '. A notch load represents one bundle, which, in turn, is reckoned to contain sufficient pales for an average length of fencing.

All that remains now is for the pales to be wired together, and this is done with the aid of a weird, hand-operated contraption consisting of four revolving spools of wire connected to a drum which is worked by a man at a bench a few yards away.

v

Fernhurst, a charming valley village, is in the heart of the most varied corner of this western Weald. All around the scenery is glorious. To the south the woods and commons drop gently down to the valley of the Rother; to the north they climb their way more abruptly into Surrey. To the west is Linch, wild and with fine commanding views; to the north-west the Marley Heights and Common comprising something like 150 acres of steep woodland and high common, with the ruins of Shulbrede Priory (now a private house), which Sir Ralph de Arderne founded in 1240, standing near the by-road to Linchmere. But perhaps the most sensationally beautiful—and certainly the most interesting for their associations, first with the iron-workers and then with Tennyson—are the Blackdown commons of wild wood and heather to the north-east that rise so abruptly to 918 feet to form the highest point in the county.

Amidst the trees of Aldworth, on the eastern slopes of Black-down, Alfred, Lord Tennyson, built the great white house, with its two stately terraces, that was to prove his last home. He laid the foundation stone in 1868 on Shakespeare's reputed birthday (April 23), and here, for twenty-four years, he lived the simple life of a country gentleman, walking, riding and entertaining the highest in the land, yet never too proud to pass a friendly word with the more humble folk about him. Sussex took kindly to Tennyson, and he to Sussex, and it was doubtless on looking down across the Weald to the South Downs beyond from the heights of Blackdown that he saw

> Green Sussex fading into blue
> With one grey glimpse of sea.

Perhaps this was his last vision of England before he died in 1892 in the house of his own creation, and it is pleasing to think that this corner of Sussex he loved so well—Blackdown, Quell-wood Common and Boarden Door Bottom, together with the lane along which the Poet Laureate strolled so often that it now bears his name—is safe in the hands of the National Trust, and so will remain for ever as he knew it.

VI

From Tennyson's Aldworth a quiet lane takes us past Jay's Copse and Gospel Green, back across the main Petworth-Guildford road, and then up country by Shillinglee Park to Pickhurst. Although it is believed that glass may have been made in Sussex in the time of the Romans, Pickhurst is the site of the first glass factory in England of which there is any authentic record. According to a deed of 1226, the glass-maker, Laurence Vitrarius, who appears to have come over from Normandy, was granted some twenty acres here, and it is known that by 1240 he was making both white and coloured glass for ' King Henry III's Abbey of Westminster '.

Laurence Vitrarius was followed by his son, William le Verir, and thereafter these rich woodlands of the Sussex-Surrey border—in which there was such a ready supply of timber for the charcoal burners—served as the cradle of the English glass-making industry, until, in the late sixteenth century, Jean Carré moved to London, and, by employing the Italian, Jacob Verzelini (who later succeeded him), introduced the Venetian tradition at the expense of the French.

One after the other—the Aleymaynes, Holmeres and Schur-teres; the Peytoes, Bongars and Jean Carré (who arrived in 1567), to mention but a few of the more important—these French craftsmen settled in Sussex to make not only window glass but also ' urynalls, bottles, bowles, cuppis to drink, and such lyke '. The domestic articles they bartered at the fairs or hawked around the countryside, but the window glass they transported to London and sold by the ' shev ' or ' ponder '.

They set up their glass-houses as near as possible to the top of a hill so as to make the fullest use of any natural current of air. They employed sand from the local sandpits, and obtained their potash by burning green bracken and then leaving the ashes to evaporate in pans of water. Though they had to rely entirely on such materials as were available, and though their furnaces and kilns were, naturally, somewhat crude, nevertheless, fundamentally, they employed much the same methods as the craftsmen of our own time. Moreover, many of the terms in use in the trade to-day—' rigaree ', ' cullet ', ' puntee ' and so on come from them. Their pieces may have been rough and too often opaque, yet it was they who *first* taught the art to the English.

In fact, it was made a condition that for every two foreigners who settled in Sussex or Surrey at least one Englishman must be shown the secrets. There must certainly have been plenty of instructors, for in Tudor times, when religious persecution was torturing the Continent, they arrived in such numbers that Pierre Bongar, who owned a glass-house at Wisborough Green, found it necessary to seek permission to hold special French services in the local church for the benefit of his Huguenot colony. What is more, no less than twenty-seven of the sites of their glass-houses have been discovered. Doubtless many more lie buried beneath the tangled underwood of the Weald, for even when a site is located on a map it is usually hard to find, the only clue to the exact whereabouts being a few fragments of broken glass.

VII

Like the woods around Fernhurst, those near the old glass-making centre of Pickhurst, to the south of Chiddingfold, have given rise to another essentially local industry. For more than a hundred years now the Lintott family have been making walking sticks of all kinds, from canes for service men to crummocks for Scotsmen, from lambing sticks for shepherds to riding whips, and, of course, the simple country walking stick. In addition to serving an enormous home market, it is estimated that they export something like 300,000 sticks each year to such countries as America and the Dominions and Colonies.

Sticks are cut from planks, or drawn from the hedgerow, in many parts, but the Lintott family, in common with another firm at Witley, just across the Surrey border, claim to be the only people to cultivate them scientifically. Some of their sticks they make in two sections with handles fashioned of holly; some as a single piece whose crook handles they bend while damp round a metal ring. Their speciality, however, is a stick with a straight handle at right angles to the main limb, made as a single unit without any twisting or bending.

To bring about such a seemingly impossible growth, ash

saplings are planted in well-prepared beds, and left for two years, at the end of which time they are uprooted and cut short. By then each will contain a number of buds, all but one of which, together with the root, are nipped off; whereupon the stem is laid flat in the trench with the single bud pointing upwards. After a further three years this bud will have grown to the length of a normal stick, so that what was originally the stem becomes the handle, while the new shoot forms the main stick.

Considerable skill and knowledge are necessary to ensure that the bud grows in the way required and that no other buds burst from below ground, while care must be taken to see that a May frost does not ruin the plantation. If there is any doubt about the weather at that time of year the grower will always light his smudge fires.

As soon as the sticks are uprooted they are taken into the workshops and placed in beds of oven-heated sand to render them more pliable. When the craftsman is satisfied that they are no longer liable to split he straightens the sticks by pulling them, one by one, through his ' horse '—a heavy wooden plank containing niches on either side and set at an angle like an easel. After straightening, they are set in cold sand, and finally trimmed of their nodules.

VIII

By contrast with the hills and woods around Fernhurst and Blackdown, the eastern half of the Arun basin is flat. Soothing country of twisting lanes and chequered fields, harbouring many lovely old farm-houses and barns, it contains only four villages of any consequence—the two old marble centres of Plaistow (pronounced Plastow) and Kirdford; Loxwood and Wisborough Green. Each is of interest in one way or another. At Wisborough Green, of course, is the church in which Bongar held his French services for the Huguenot refugees, while Kirdford, long renowned as a centre for the growing of Cox's Orange Pippin apples, can show two links with the glass-blowers in the remains of a furnace at Slifehurst Farm, and a church window which is believed to have been made in the district.

At Plaistow is a farm-house that served as a summer residence of the Archbishops of Canterbury; Loxwood, on the other hand, claims distinction as the birthplace of a strange religious sect whose creed has spread as far afield as America.

Founded in about 1850 by a London cobbler, John Sirgood, they are known as the ' Cokelers '—a name given to them by the local inhabitants, because at their first meeting they drank cups of cocoa which, then a scarce commodity, had to be brought down from the capital. Their aim is to help each other according to the teachings of the Bible, and these ethics they follow in their business as much as in their private lives. In a number of villages they run a communal store whose business is organized by a secretary and four trustees. Every member of the sect is allowed to hold shares and, in fact, a large number put their whole savings into these shops which at the same time are provisioned by Cokeler farmers. Probably it is no exaggeration to say that the seeds of the now powerful Co-operative movement were sown by these Sussex folk. The Cokelers own Loxwood's communal store, and here they may be seen bustling about in Victorian costume, showing to all a courtesy that is in keeping with their attire. They have their own chapels in various parts of West Sussex; and their many kindnesses to those in distress (whether members or not) prove them to be so sincere that, despite some of their beliefs, they are beloved even by their critics.

IX

The road from Loxwood to Wisborough Green follows the course of the Arun, and from here the river flows through lush

Winchelsea, The New Inn

Georgian and Tudor Architecture, Midhurst

meadows to be joined by the Rother just beyond Stopham's medieval stone bridge.

An enchanting corner with its church and cottages clustered along two sides of one of the smallest greens I have yet seen, Stopham itself is hidden away up a quiet lane on the hill-top. Built soon after the Conquest and boasting a yew tree that can be hardly less old, Stopham Church possesses one of the most interesting collections of brasses in the country, nearly all of which are to the de Stopham Barttelots. The de Stophams came over with William the Conqueror, were awarded the manor now bearing their name, and were united with the Barttelot family in the early fourteenth century when their heiress, Joan de Stopham, married Richard Barttelot. As a result of this union, the present youthful holder of the baronetcy, Sir Brian de Stopham Barttelot—whose ancestral home, Elizabethan in style but restored beyond recognition as such, stands not far from the bridge—can claim the distinction of having inherited his position as lord of the manor in an unbroken link from his de Stopham ancestor of Norman times.

Various members of the de Stopham family are remembered in the north window of the nave, but the oldest brass is to John Barttelot, who died in 1428, having been elected M.P. for the Sussex Cinque Ports in 1392. A lawyer by profession, and treasurer of the ' Hospital of Arundel ', he is seen wearing a fur-lined legal long coat with full sleeves and waist belt buckled, together with hose and long, pointed shoes that are fastened across the instep. There is also a brass to his son, who, having fought at Agincourt, is appropriately portrayed in full armour, though, unfortunately, he has been given a nineteenth-century head, complete with bristling moustache.

There are seventeen brasses altogether, and an unusual point about them is that many of the boys and girls represented at the feet of their medieval or Tudor parents are dressed in Jacobean costume. Moreover, it will be noticed that whereas one coat of

arms lying by itself shows left-hand gauntlets pointing upwards, the arms of all the other Barttelots have the glove
turned downwards.

The reason for this strange discrepancy is that a certain confusion was caused when Squire Richard Barttelot died in 1614
and his son, the first Squire Walter, anxious to erect a splendid
tomb to his parents, applied to the College of Heralds for a
copy of the family's correct arms and quarterings. Hitherto
the Barttelots had adopted the upward pointing gauntlet as
seen in the Bayeaux Tapestry. As, however, the original grant
could not be traced, and as the Gounters (the ancestors of those
who figured in the escape of Charles II) had only recently been
given a coat showing three silver right-handed gauntlets pointing upwards on a sable shield, the Garter King at Arms refused
to ratify the old coat, but, instead, produced a richly blazoned
document with gloves pointing downwards and a crest figur-
ing a swan.

On receipt of this Squire Walter commissioned a brazier to
fashion the finest brass to be seen in Stopham Church to-day.
At the same time he ordered that all the other shields be
changed accordingly.

This was done so thoroughly that, whether by design or
accident, the costumes of the figures were likewise altered.
The brazier, however, engraved one shield too few, which
explains why one is seen with the family's original coat of arms.

x

At Stopham the Arun takes a sudden sweep eastwards for
Pulborough, a mile or so away, before turning south again for
Arundel, Littlehampton and the sea. A straggling village of
rather doubtful charm, Pulborough's real claim to beauty lies
in its splendid views of downs, meadow and river, and in its
eastern mound on which are ranged the church, attractively
approached through a lych-gate at the top of a flight of grass-

lined steps; *The Chequers*, in whose grounds are the remains of a monastery chapel; a Tudor cottage that was once the resort of smugglers; and, near by, the timbered farm-house, known as Old Place, into whose fabric the remains of the Henry IV mansion of the Apsleys is incorporated.

Notable to-day for its bird life, and for its coarse fishing, Pulborough served as a Roman strong-point. From the western mound by the station the Romans guarded the ford of the river at this vulnerable section of Stane Street, while excavations of a century or so ago showed that they built a causeway across those low-lying meadows to the south, which are still liable to serious winter flooding.

A number of discoveries have been made in this district from time to time, including the remains of a Roman villa at Wiggonholt and a Roman ' fosse ' near the church at Coldwaltham. Bignor itself is only about five miles away, while Hardham, the next place south from Pulborough along the modern causeway, was, as we have seen, one of Stane Street's posting-houses, and contains in the masonry of its tiny eleventh-century Church of St. Botolph a certain amount of brick and tiles salvaged from the old Roman buildings.

Hardham is in the same parish as Stopham, and its church is as famous for its collection of murals as is Stopham's for its brasses.

Executed soon after 1100, it has been suggested that these wall paintings, which were concealed for many generations, may be the oldest complete series in England, and an unusual feature is that they appear to have been coated with varnish, which, at the time of their uncovering in 1866, gave them an enamelled effect not unlike that of an oil-painting. Beneath this glaze the colours were found to be so thick and tough that Mr. P. M. Johnston, who prepared an interesting paper on the subject for the Sussex Archæological Society, formed the opinion that the technique adopted by the artists was a combination of pure tempera and oil-painting, the finer details being picked out in oils after the ground colours and broad masses had been laid on in distemper, and the whole then coated with varnish.

To obtain their colours it is thought that the artists may have used burnt earth, ochre, lime and soot, and, for certain of the greens, verdigris scraped from copper that had previously been buried in a manure heap.

Though, unfortunately, damp has caused some of the walls to crumble and many of the rich reds, greens, pinks and yellows to fade, considerable portions of these essentially Byzantine paintings survive in various states of preservation on the walls of both nave and chancel. Their interest, however, lies in their age and curious method of execution rather than in their beauty. They might even be described as crude, yet the meaning of some of the subjects is quite apparent—the Nativity; the Flight of the Holy Family into Egypt; the visit of the Shepherds and the Magi; the Massacre of the Innocents; Joseph's dream; the Fall; Adam and Eve after the Fall; the Tortures of the Damned; St. George routing the Saracens at the Battle of Antioch; and St. George being broken on the wheel.

South of Hardham the Arun cuts a way through the verdant Amberley Wild Brooks—whose meadows are grazed by farmers at an annual rental according to their head of cattle—to the twin villages of Bury and Amberley, which face each other across the river—Bury, with the home of John Galsworthy at the foot of its long steep hill and its church by the ferry, on the west bank; Amberley on the east.

Beloved of artists for its attractive lanes of old cottages, its partially ruined castle (once the seat of the Bishops of Chichester) standing above the meadows, and its church at the end of the main street, Amberley has been described by writers of all ages as one of the most charming villages in Sussex. And its character is only enhanced by the beauty of its setting in one of the downland valleys.

The Sussex rivers may lack the beauty of the Wye and the grandeur of the Thames, yet to boat down the Arun from Amberley on a summer's day is an experience that none should miss. Other pleasure boats may come and go, but never in such numbers as to cause more than a slight checking swirl, or disturb the anglers who are dotted about the banks. The whole winding course of perhaps six miles is sublimely peaceful and takes us past only the smallest of hamlets: Houghton, with its 800-year-old *George and Dragon* ale-house, where Charles II paused for a tankard of ale on his memorable flight, after narrowly avoiding being captured in the woods at Arundel, and whither, in later times, the smugglers took their casks by means of a secret underground tunnel leading from the river; North Stoke, and then South Stoke, the chancel arch of whose church is composed of hard chalk mounted on marble pillars; and finally, if we follow a backwater, the enchanting little village of Burpham, where the remains of the camp which Athelstane fortified as a strong-point from which to guard the river may still be seen.

Between Houghton Bridge and Burpham the river and its backwaters contain few buildings. Then, suddenly, we get our first vision of Arundel Castle, standing proudly on the hill-top; the perfect 'journey's end'.

XI

Home of the Ancient Britons (who named the river the Tarrant) and later used by the Romans as a station when they built their coast road from Chichester to Pevensey; once the property of Alfred the Great, who is thought to have built the original castle, and later of King Harold; then awarded by the Conqueror to Roger de Montgomerie, who extended it and made it the impregnable capital of one of the county's six rapes, Arundel is still the perfect feudal town—a place steeped in tradition and boasting among its many documentary treasures

the muniments granted by Henry VIII and the confirmatory
charters of Queen Elizabeth and Charles II.

Though its castle was largely rebuilt in Victorian times, its
setting still savours strongly of baronial might. Arundel's steep
hill, rising as the main street from the ruined Maison Dieu—a
fourteenth-century hospital for twenty poor men—on the west
bank of the river, to the castle's southern gateway and the
Victorian Gothic Roman Catholic Church of St. Philip Neri
round the bend beyond, still maintains its slightly continental
flavour. Many of the town's side roads are lined with Tudor
cottages and Georgian houses of considerable charm, yet they
are completely overshadowed by the castle.

Three times this castle has been besieged—first by Henry I,
who captured it from the Montgomeries and left it to his queen,
Adeliza; then by Stephen, who sent his troops to arrest Henry's
daughter, Matilda, his rival claimant to the throne, who sought
Adeliza's hospitality here; and, finally, by the Roundhead Sir
William Waller, who mounted his guns on the tower of St.
Nicholas's church and battered it into submission in some
eighteen days. By the time the Roundheads—who afterwards
set up their headquarters here—had departed, the building had
suffered badly, and time and neglect caused the walls to
crumble still more. So that to-day all that is left of the original
building are the ten-feet thick walls of the keep which Alfred
the Great built and Earl Roger strengthened; the inner gateway, built in 1070 by Roger de Montgomerie, with, above, the
room in which the Empress Matilda renounced her claim to
the throne; the thirteen-century Barbican Towers of flint and
orange sandstone, in which the marks made by the cannon balls
can still be seen; the Well Tower of the same period; the Bevis
Tower, named after the giant warder, who ate one ox and
drank two hogsheads of beer each week, and rode about the
estate on his horse Hirondelle (from which the name of
Arundel is derived) carrying his sword Mongley; and the tilt-
yard where the knights held their jousting tournaments. Even

the Fitzalan chapel, in which are many monuments to the dukes and earls who have held Arundel through the centuries, is a careful Victorian restoration.

Yet, even though Arundel Castle has been largely rebuilt, the work of restoration has been carried out so sympathetically, and the setting is so perfect, that the old saying, ' there are many beautiful places in the world, but there is only one Arundel ' is well justified. Standing in its beautiful deer park of 1,200 acres, whose trees are the haunt of myriads of birds and whose chalk-bottomed Swanbourne Lake (mentioned in the *Domesday Book*) harbours a serpent, they say, the castle is magnificent from all angles. And when the sun is in the south-east it literally sparkles. Turner, Prout, Constable and Vicat Cole all painted the Arundel scene in their time, and modern artists still follow in their footsteps.

Impressive for its own sake, an added dignity is brought to the building in the knowledge that Arundel Castle is the seat of the Premier Duke and Earl Marshal of England, and that for nine centuries each owner has inherited the title of Earl of Arundel, from Roger de Montgomerie, who was the first of that style, to the present Duke of Norfolk, who is the thirty-seventh. For more than seven hundred years, too, it has been held by but two families.

When Henry I's widowed queen married a second time, her husband, William d'Albini, became the fourth Earl of Arundel, and from him the castle was handed down in direct succession until 1243, when it passed to the eighth earl's cousin, John Fitzalan, who was lord of the manor of North Stoke, farther up the river. When, more than three centuries later, the twenty-second earl died in 1580 without male issue it descended to his daughter, Mary Fitzalan, whose portrait is to be seen in the castle among the many other family paintings. Mary married Thomas Howard, fourth Duke of Norfolk, Earl of Surrey and Earl Marshal of England—who, unhappily, was later beheaded by Elizabeth for favouring the cause of

Mary, Queen of Scots—and by her wedding brought the castle into the family who are its possessors to-day.

XII

In a town that has stood guardian over the southern shores for so many centuries, and has witnessed the activities of smugglers, sheep stealers and cattle rustlers, it is only to be expected that the inhabitants themselves may still cling a little to the defensive in some of their time-honoured customs.

Thus, on the Monday evening nearest to February's full moon, farmers, nurserymen, brewers, inn-keepers, builders, and lawyers from miles around Arundel still forgather at *The Norfolk*, an old coaching-house in the shade of the castle's southern walls, to hold their annual dinner and discuss plans for bringing criminals to book.

It is thirty years since they caught their last thief, yet they still read their minutes and make their reports, and when the dinner is ended they will post their handbills round the town offering to those who help in their capture such tempting rewards as £20 for a murderer and £5 for a robber, down to ten shillings for a trespasser in search of game.

Styling themselves the Society for Prosecuting Felons, Thieves and Other Miscreants, they are the last survivors of the volunteer parish police forces such as once operated in country districts throughout England before the days of Sir Robert Peel. They have met every year since 1769, and, having existed so long, they have no intention of breaking their habit just because another police force is now stationed in the town!

CHAPTER SEVEN: *The Western Coastal Belt to Brighton*

ARUNDEL is just seaward of the Downs, and from here the river has but five miles to flow before entering the sea at Littlehampton Harbour. To the west of this final stretch is the flat country next Chichester and the Hundred of Manhood.

Rather more wooded than the Manhood, this district contains a number of interesting villages and hamlets. Ford and Yapton, for instance, both boast small and unusually pleasing churches with traces of Saxon stone work; while the approach by the farm to Eastergate's church, with the ducks, geese and pigs wandering at will in the path of the worshippers by a lovely old half-timbered granary, might almost have been designed to serve as a timely reminder of the traditional relationship between Church and Land.

Eastergate leads into Westergate, whose inn sign of the *Labour in Vain* depicts a white woman scrubbing a black baby. A rather improbable story tells how the inn gained its name because of an unfortunate incident connected with a former landlord and his wife. The two went to the tropics, but after a while, it seems, the wife was called back to England, where, within a short time of her return, she was unlucky enough to give birth to a black baby. Fearing the anger of her husband, she set to work, day after day, trying to scrub the baby white. . . . But her labour, in the true sense of the word, proved in vain.

Two other quite pleasant villages in this area are North Bersted and South Bersted, the latter boasting an Early English church with curious frescoes, in whose graveyard are some remarkably fine holly trees and a yew that may well be eight centuries old.

To-day South Bersted is virtually a suburb of Bognor Regis, the most westerly of the Sussex coastal resorts; 150 years ago, however, the position was just the reverse. When Sir Richard Hotham saw Bognor for the first time in 1785 and determined to make it fashionable, it was a hamlet of South Bersted; a sandy fishing cove with just a few cottages, an ale-house, and a chapel of ease, erected for the benefit of the fishermen and farmhands whose jobs did not allow them to go as far afield as the parent church at South Bersted, where Hotham is now buried. Its character and atmosphere were then so different that the wide stretch of firm, dark sands—which must certainly rank among the finest in England—where prawns, shrimps and lobsters are still landed in great numbers, is probably the only feature to survive unimpaired from the Bognor of yesterday.

Sir Richard Hotham, who in 1780 was elected M.P. for Southwark, was a successful hatter who succeeded in amassing a large fortune of which he devoted no less than £60,000 to the development of Bognor. After buying up all the cottages and farmlands in the hamlet he boastfully renamed the place Hothampton, and proceeded to build a number of large houses, chief of which were Bognor Lodge, Bersted Lodge and the Dome. At the same time he enlarged the ale-house into a well-equipped hostelry, boasting extensive stabling accommodation, and laid out the Crescent, Spencer Terrace, Hothampton Place, East Row, the Steyne, and Rock Buildings.

Sir Richard, however, proved to be less suited to town planning than to selling hats, and is sometimes unkindly remembered as the ' Mad Hatter '. Though Bognor grew, the ' quality ' failed to arrive in sufficient numbers to justify his extravagant expenditure, and when he died in 1790—having fought and lost a law suit in the venture—he left only £8,000. Indeed, Bognor Regis was never to become the fashion centre that the hatter anticipated. Princess Charlotte, daughter of

George III, and later the young Princess Victoria (afterwards Queen Victoria) both came to stay at Bognor Lodge at different times. But their visits did no more than provide a temporary prestige, which was rekindled in our own time when, for five months in 1929, George V passed his convalescence at Craig-weil House (since demolished) and in gratitude for the courtesy shown him, granted the town the right to use the royal affix. The patronage by royalty has merely helped to increase the population of what has become a rather characterless seaside town.

II

Something of the rural charm which Hotham destroyed in his attempt to develop Bognor still lingers in the cluster of thatched cottages in the neighbouring village of Felpham.

In one of these cottages William Blake lived from 1800 until 1803 while executing a number of book engravings for William Hayley, who, grieving deeply over the death of his son, had left Eartham and now lived the life of a squire in the large house by the church, in whose graveyard he was later to be buried.

Born in 1757, the son of a hosier, William Blake worked as engraver, painter and poet, and, though he remained poor throughout his life, he achieved recognition in connection with each art after his death. Apprenticed to the engraver, James Basire, he gained fame as a painter for his *Canterbury Pilgrims*, *Jacob's Dream*, and *The Last Judgment*, and for his twenty-one illustrations to the *Book of Job*, a work which he undertook at the age of seventy. As a poet he has been called ' the greatest mystic of the Western World ', and is widely known for his *Jerusalem*, the adopted ' hymn ' of the Women's Institute, whose words were set to music many decades later by Sir Hubert Parry, who lived and died at Rustington, but ten miles along the coast from Blake's Felpham.

Throughout his life Blake was influenced by a vivid faith in

the unseen. Some of his visions were fantastic, and disturbing
to those about him, as, for instance, when he told the country
folk at Felpham how he had witnessed the funeral of a fairy
and described how he saw a number of creatures that were no
bigger than grasshoppers laying out a body on a rose leaf for
its pall and heard them singing as they performed the last sad
rites.

His strange faith not only characterized his works in a way
that failed to capture the imagination of most of his contem-
poraries, but his resultant eccentricities brought him few
friends. William Hayley was one of the few to befriend him,
and though Hayley was rich where Blake was poor, the latter
valued this friendship which brought him to Sussex.

Not even the angry scene with the soldiers stationed at the
near-by *Fox Inn*, which led to Blake's trial and acquittal at
Chichester on a charge of seditious libel, prevented these three
years from proving the happiest of his life. To Blake, Felpham
was ' Heaven ' where, as he wrote in one of his poems :

> The Ladder of Angels descends through the air,
> On the turret its spiral does softly descend,
> Through the village then winds, at my cot it does end.

A number of famous people visited Felpham around the
turn of the eighteenth and nineteenth centuries. On a wall of
the old *Fox Inn*, which unhappily was burnt out recently, the
debauched George Morland was once obliged to paint one of
his lovely country scenes in order to pay for his drinks; while
in 1819, the year before Hayley died, the little village was to
welcome no less a figure than the First Gentleman (George IV),
who came to see his old tutor, Dean Cyril Jackson, as the latter
lay on his deathbed in the manor-house here.

III

The seven miles of coast between Bognor Regis and Little

hampton have suffered particularly badly from coast erosion. Even in the last century whole villages have disappeared under the sea. Indeed, Middleton, next to Felpham, lost its original church so recently that some of the older folk can still recall the time when a number of bodies were washed ashore from the old graveyard. As soon as the tide receded again a football match was staged on the sands when one of the skulls was made to do service as the ball! The old man who recounted this incident to me some years ago expressed the widely shared opinion that the loss of the village was a just retribution for the amount of smuggling that used to take place along this shore. Every man in Middleton, he told me, was involved, and he could remember his father being paid fourpence a time for carrying kegs of rum across several miles of fields to various secret inland hide-outs.

The waves have, in fact, caused such havoc that the recently restored thirteenth-century chapel of Bailiff's Court at Atherington, together with the modern mansion that has grown up in the medieval style around it, are the only buildings of any note now standing between Middleton and Littlehampton. As it is, this chapel is all that is left of an imposing grange that was once inhabited by monks from the Abbey of Seez in Normandy, to whom Roger de Montgomerie granted the manor of Atherington. The sea has reduced many buildings to ruin and engulfed vast acres.

Atherington is in the parish of Climping, whose manor Montgomerie likewise awarded to the nuns of Almanesches. Climping's Early English cruciform church—whose tower and elaborately carved west doorway are so splendid that they have given rise to a Sussex catch-phrase, ' Climping for perfection ' —happily stands at a safe distance from the sea, protected to the south by the Ryebank Rife. From here a toll bridge takes us across the Arun into Littlehampton, the ancient port of Arundel.

IV

It was at Littlehampton that the Empress Matilda landed in 1139 when she came to seize the throne of England. She made her way to Arundel Castle by the river, and along this river the prisoners captured at Crécy by Richard Fitzalan were taken for internment in this same Sussex stronghold. At one time this stretch of the Arun was an important waterway capable of taking brigs up to 200 tons burthen, while the harbour itself was numbered among the most important for many miles along the coast. Merchant vessels entered week after week with their various cargoes, and the old Sussex song, *The Littlehampton Collier Lads*, is still sung in memory of the days when, in the slack months of winter, the farmhands augmented the crews of the local colliers that fetched the coals from Newcastle:

> People say we're a noisy lot
> When we come home from sea.
> We call for liquor freely,
> And cheerily are we;
> But when our money all is spent,
> To sea we go again.
> We are the lads to rough it through
> We never do complain.

Just as to-day many of the sailing-boats and pleasure craft that now berth in this harbour are built by Littlehampton's waterside, so in the past the cargo boats were constructed by the local shipwrights.

To-day, however, Littlehampton is more famous as a seaside resort than as a harbour. Yet passengers crossed from here to France many years before Newhaven came into prominence, and had it not been for local opposition to necessary developments that would have spoilt the surrounding countryside and destroyed the simple charm of the town itself, this seaboard at the mouth of the Arun would have been the chosen cross-Channel port.

Among those attracted by this quaint river port were Constable, who came to paint the windmill; Byron, who delighted to swim in the Arun; Samuel Taylor Coleridge, who wanted a rest; and Henry Francis Cary, the translator of Dante, who found it refreshing to walk along the sands reading *Homer* in Greek to his son. Coleridge happened to pass Cary on one of these occasions, and was so surprised to hear Greek words being spoken that he introduced himself, with the result that the two struck up a friendship.

Alas, beauty has not been preserved. Though much of the surrounding countryside, like the distinctive common which the Duke of Norfolk gave to the town, is still at least soothing, and though the harbour itself retains its slightly continental tone, the old windmill and cottages have gone, and a hideous pleasure fair now mars their site. Littlehampton has grown, and, in doing so, has developed streets of no conceivable architectural merit.

Unfortunately Littlehampton is not alone in this respect. Though *Sussex by the Sea* is now the county's best-known song, the coast-line is no longer in any way comparable with the inland beauty of Sussex. The sea—so near to London—now brings holiday-makers in their thousands, while the sunny climate has turned this belt into a convalescent home for those in failing health. Thus the whole coast from Littlehampton to Brighton and beyond is a tale of development which becomes steadily more depressing the more easterly one travels. Villages that 100 years ago were no more than quiet fishing hamlets are now riddled with bungalows of the worst type, while once pleasing little towns have grown beyond recognition.

Even so, the coast is infinitely more interesting than many writers would have us suppose, and the development between Littlehampton and Worthing is, in the main, less dense and less noxious than between Worthing and Brighton.

v

Within easy distance of Littlehampton there are at least five villages that have not yet completely surrendered their past to the present.

At Poling they still make pottery by hand out of local clay, and fashion their carts and wagon wheels in the wheel-wrights' shop down the lane leading to the radar station.

Rustington—Sir Hubery Parry's ' dear Rusty ', and one-time home of the artist, Albert de Belleroche—is still rich in old buildings. Many of these are reputed to have their ghosts, ranging from the dachshund dog which makes its home in Pound Cottage to the lady in black who haunts the vicarage, or the one in grey who, in company with a gallant cavalier, periodically visits the near-by manor-house of West Preston. And those that have no ghosts have memories of smuggling days and tell of secret passages leading from the seashore.

Lyminster—once the home of a nunnery and now noted for its water-cress beds—also has its legend which is centred around its ' Knucker Hole '. At the edge of this ' bottomless ' pond —into which one may dive down to the antipodes—St. George, they say, won a glorious victory over a dragon that once menaced the district!

Two other villages of charm are East Preston and Ang-mering. Clustered round a central green from which all its roads radiate in a most delightful manner, Angmering must on no account be confused with its namesake on the coast, which is anything but attractive.

A certain traditional rivalry exists between the inhabitants of East Preston and Angmering. It is said that when Ang-mering's church was restored a certain amount of gipsy labour was employed, and that an unwelcome strain was thereby introduced. In view of this the East Preston folk used to regard the women of Angmering as sluttish, and so were loath to see their sons marry them. Naturally, the men of Angmer-

Regency Architecture, Hove

Royal Pavilion, Brighton

West Pier, Brighton

ing strongly resented this attitude, with the result that free fights between the respective villagers were at one time common.

The remains of a Roman villa have been unearthed at Angmering in recent years, while Highdown Hill near by was the site of a late Bronze Age camp and Saxon cemetery. Many interesting bronze implements have been discovered in the pits and graves here, and these are now housed in Worthing Museum.

VI

These five villages are on the eastern side of the final stretch of the River Arun, and the whole of this area, extending as far along the coast as Worthing and Lancing, is the seat of a world-famous glass-house industry where the finest quality grapes, tomatoes, peaches, cucumbers and sundry other produce are grown.

This industry owes its origin indirectly to the Great Exhibition of 1851. When the Prince Consort ordered that his ' beautiful glass-houses ' be taken down from Hyde Park and re-erected at Sydenham as the Crystal Palace, a certain Worthing doctor obtained a small quantity of the glass and built a green-house in which he proceeded to grow grapes for his patients.

Seeing how well the doctor's vines flourished, a schoolmaster, George Beer, of the same town, designed a much larger and more elaborate green-house, where he tried his hand, with equally satisfactory results, at growing tomatoes, or ' love apples ' as they were then called.

Doctor and schoolmaster alike did their utmost to keep their activities secret, but their strange glass buildings aroused such curiosity that their efforts were in vain, and in a short time others were starting upon a similar venture. As the news spread beyond Worthing, so apprentices from the Lea Valley in Hertfordshire, and even from as far afield as France, Holland and Belgium, came to Sussex to learn this new ' mystery '.

In those days the all-important manures were made of offals and blood from the slaughter-house which were mixed with live sprats from the beach and left to rot to a point where nobody could stand the smell any longer.

To-day, everything is highly scientific. Growers spend as much as £200 an acre on the sterilization and fertilization of their soil, and, by means of furnaces and water-pipes, can keep their glass-houses at a desired temperature. The art, however, lies not merely in stoking up the furnaces when the weather is cold and damping them down when it is hot. On the contrary, the grower must keep pace with climatic conditions and the season of the year, and regulate his fires in sympathy with the normal strength of the sun.

Though the glass-house industries of the Lea Valley and of the Continent are now more extensive than those of Sussex, Worthing produce is still regarded as being of the finest quality. Moreover, Worthing is still the ' capital ' of the Sussex growers, and in the season special fruit trains leave this seaside town several times a week loaded with many tons of produce for sale at Covent Garden and other markets in various parts of England.

VII

Like her sister, Princess Charlotte, at Bognor Regis, Princess Amelia was one of the first to make Worthing popular when she was sent there by her father, George III, to allay her love affair with one of his equerries. A number of buildings of her time are dotted about the town. In Liverpool Terrace, for instance, there is a delightful Regency sequence, and in Marine Parade many graceful bow-fronted houses of the same period. Sash windows, and ' dog's teeth ' along the eaves, still reveal the Georgian origin of many of the shops in Warwick Street and elsewhere, while in Anne Street is the theatre (now a grocery warehouse) where Sarah Siddons is believed to have acted.

Essentially a modern town, most of Worthing's old corners are to be found in the ancient villages that have gradually been incorporated into the borough in the process of expansion.

Originally, Worthing came into the parish of Broadwater, and though this position has long been reversed, the splendid cruciform church of Broadwater, with its fine twelfth-century central tower and its long and stately chancel with Early English buttresses, still stands. Two of our best-known naturalists, W. H. Hudson and Richard Jefferies, who died at Goring (also included in the borough), are buried in the near-by cemetery.

Worthing has been associated with quite a few writers. It was here that Oscar Wilde wrote *The Importance of Being Ernest*, and William Henley *Hawthorn and Lavender*, while in the Salvington district is the little thatched cottage that was the home of John Selden, lawyer, antiquarian, writer, linguist and Member of Parliament, whose *History of Tithes* caused so great a sensation that he was compelled to recant it.

Born in 1584, John Selden was the son of a small farmer who supplemented his land earning by offering his services as a fiddler at the various county fairs. His mother hailed from Russington in Kent—not, as is locally believed, from Rustington in Sussex.

At the age of ten young John was sent to the Chichester Free School where he took so readily to Latin that he surprised his parents by composing a distich in that tongue which is still to be seen, carved over the lintel of his birthplace:

> Welcome honest man to me:
> I may not be closed, walk in and take a seat.
> Thief, I am not to be made unfastened for thee;
> And therefore I bid thee to quickly retreat.

Happily for Selden, his poor parents did all they could to

encourage the boy in his reading, and after only four years at Chichester, sent him to Oxford and thence to London to study law.

As a conveyancer and chamber counsel, he soon found himself in demand on account of his profound antiquarian knowledge of estates, and so was quick to earn a high income. Not content with that, he chose to steer a more dubious passage as defender of the liberty of the people, an objective that was to govern his entire life. Making an intensive study of the history and origin of the various laws of the land, he devoted his energies, both in Parliament and by his pen, to defending those liberties which he considered were being abused.

In 1621, three years after the publication of his book on tithes, he was imprisoned for recommending Parliament to repudiate King James's doctrine that all the privileges then enjoyed had originally been royal grants. Seven years later, when M.P. for Lancaster, he was instrumental in drawing up the ' Petition of Right ', and within a few months found himself, as a result, in prison once more. As Member for Oxford University in the Long Parliament, he showed his complete fairness by championing the cause of the bishops when their right to sit in the House of Lords was usurped, and he was one of the most fervent opponents of the execution of Charles I, even though, hitherto, he had so frequently opposed the king that the latter had once demanded Selden's arrest.

Though Selden enjoyed high office in Parliament before he finally retired from public life in disgust at the execution of the king, he is remembered best for the sincerity of his convictions, and for standing steadfast by them in an age when Parliament was darkened by intrigue, and the seeds of dictatorship were being sown.

VIII

Tarring is the most interesting of the villages now included in the Borough of Worthing. Once the property of King

Athelstan, who gave it to the Church of Canterbury in 941, it is steeped in tradition and still possesses a number of age-old buildings, notably some half-timbered fifteenth-century cottages, with roofs of Horsham stone, in the High Street, and the remnants of what is believed to have served as one of Thomas à Becket's palaces.

There are many fig trees in the gardens hereabouts, and it is said that these have sprung from a tree—whose gnarled trunk may still be seen—which Becket brought from Italy and planted here in 1162 during one of his visits to this palace. Figs prosper in this warm, sunny climate, and the fig-gardens have attracted many migrant birds. In 1835 a local clergyman noted that the rare beccafico—a bird of the warbler family, unknown in any other part of England, but still considered a delicacy in Italy—used to arrive at Tarring each year as the figs were ripening. Often these birds would alight on the fishermen's boats in an exhausted condition, but after regaling themselves on the figs they became 'lumps of fat' and flew away again.

Tarring has had many adventures, and, in consequence, boasts one or two charters granting its people unusual privileges. More than five hundred years ago, when French pirates made a practice of plundering the village as soon as the menfolk set off for the markets of Steyning and Chichester, Henry VI granted the inhabitants the right to hold a fair of their own, and, though this has been allowed to lapse, one or two of the older folk can still remember the excitement when the sheep hurdles used to be set up in the narrow main street.

Later, Elizabeth exempted them from serving on juries because of the way they rallied to her call at the time of the Spanish Armada. The church, it is believed, was then used as a look-out tower, and, in recognition of this the white ensign is still flown from its staff on all national occasions, though, as the last rector himself pointed out, it is doubtful whether, in fact, Tarring really has the right to do so!

Smuggling numbered among these adventures, and in the graveyard of this church—as in many other Sussex churchyards —there are a number of oblong hollow tombs in which the smugglers used to hide their contraband.

The first plough ever to break the soil of Victoria was forged in Tarring's smithy when the Henty family set sail from this village for Australia to help her found her sheep industry after the agricultural depression had set in following the Battle of Waterloo, and Thomas Henty felt that there were no prospects at home for his eleven children.

A successful sheep-breeder who owned many acres at Tarring, and was fortunate enough to obtain the fine flocks of merinos which the King of Spain had given to George III, the story of Thomas Henty's emigration with his family—the many journeys across the seas with their stock and equipment; their adventures in trying to tame the aborigines and their years of hardship and disappointment before at last they found success—is part of the story of the colonization of Australia and the development of one of her major industries.

IX

East of Worthing the country deteriorates badly. A by-pass now separates the Saxon church of Sompting—once the home of the Knights Templars and the Knights Hospitallers and unique in possessing the only ' Rhenish helm ' tower beyond the banks of the Rhine—from the village itself, where is a farm that is mentioned in the *Domesday Book* and the house where Trelawny, friend of Shelley, once lived. While Lancing College, one of a group of Sussex schools which Canon Nathaniel Woodard founded in the last century, now looks down from its hill-top position on to the buildings and hangars of the Brighton, Hove and Worthing municipal airport of Shoreham.

Shoreham is fortunate in possessing two churches of great

age and beauty that once prompted Swinburne to write a song about the place. While the flint-built cruciform church of Old Shoreham, with its central tower and its partly Saxon nave, stands on the eastern bank of the River Adur by the picturesque old timber toll-bridge from Lancing, the twelfth-century church of New Shoreham is set in the very heart of the town, and, for its round and octagonal piers, triforium arches, rounded windows with dog-tooth mouldings, flying buttresses, and its stately proportions throughout, is considered one of the finest parish churches in Sussex.

Though Shoreham still has several other interesting old buildings, such as the museum, known as *The Marlipins*—originally the toll-house where the harbour dues were collected for the de Braose family, who were lords of the manor and may well have built both the churches—this ancient sea-board too has shown a complete lack of sympathy for its past in its modern development. Such old buildings as are left are now largely eclipsed by jerry buildings of the very worst type, though, happily, the disgraceful beachland dwellings, known as ' Bungalow Town ', which comprised among other hideous erections a number of converted railway carriages, were blown up in the last war for defence reasons.

Apart from the churches, Shoreham's chief interest lies in its harbour, the mouth of which has shifted more than once during the centuries. Here, tradition has it, Aella landed with fresh supplies from Germany, and drove the inhabitants into the dense forest that once covered the Weald. As early as the Norman Conquest it became the seaport for the Rape of Bramber, while in the reign of Edward III Shoreham supplied no less than twenty-six ships for the navy, and acquired considerable commercial status as a landing-place for large cargoes of wine and Caen stone from the Continent.

One of Shoreham's proudest boasts is that it has witnessed the entrance of one king and the exit of another. It was here that King John landed with his army to succeed to the throne of England upon the death of Richard I; from this same southern water-way that Charles II eventually set sail in the stillness of that early morn of October 1651 to find refuge in France at the end of that hazardous flight which took him through the greater part of Southern England.

The loyal Colonel Gounter, whom Charles met with Lord Wilmot when he sheltered in the old rectory at Racton, had at last succeeded, where others had failed, in finding some one who, taking it all round, was felt could be trusted to ferry the king across the English Channel. Colonel Gounter was well acquainted with a merchant named Francis Mansel, who lived at Chichester, and, being of French extraction, had considerable trade connections with France. To him he pretended (though later he confided the truth) that he had two friends who were in trouble as a result of a duel, and begged that he might be put in touch with some one discreet enough to undertake a secret mission. Accordingly, Mansel introduced the colonel to Nicholas Tattersall, the owner of the trading brig, *Surprise*, who agreed to undertake the mission for the sum of sixty pounds.

Since Tattersall was not the type to inspire complete confidence, Mansel kept in close contact with him while Colonel Gounter went to tell the king and Lord Wilmot of the plans he had made. A few days later Tattersall and ' Mr. Jackson ', in company with Colonel Gounter, Wilmot and Mansel, supped at *The George*, an inn at the bottom of West Street in Brighton. Though the inn was quiet, the meeting was not without its anxious moments. Almost at once the landlord, Anthony Smith, recognized the king; but he was a Royalist, and soon put the company at their ease. Then Tattersall himself revealed that he, too, had seen beneath the disguise, and made this a good excuse for trying to obtain better terms. Happily, though, Tattersall proved to be no more than an opportunist, and, after protesting, quite incorrectly, that the wind was in the wrong direction, and doing all he could to emphasize the obligation which everybody owed to him, eventually agreed to take the king across to France that very night, and soon left to get ready to sail. Thus, at two o'clock next morning, the party set off on their horses for Shoreham where the king and Lord Wilmot, after bidding farewell to Mansel and the faithful colonel, took up their position beneath the cabin of *Surprise*, and so set sail for France, while Colonel Gounter, fearful that the wind might drive them ashore, galloped his horse along the coast-line until he was satisfied that all was well.

x

In Charles's time the way from Brighton to Shoreham was open country, save only for a few cottages, where now it forms one long built-up area, denser than anything we have yet seen, although Southwick contains an attractive green and a number of interesting old buildings including the restored church of St. Michael and All Angels, which was given to the Knights Templars in the thirteenth century by Earl Simon. Brighton, too, was not Brighton in those days, but the little sea-swept village of Brighthelmstone which the Normans had valued at an annual rental of some four thousand herrings, and Defoe considered to be worth no more than £8,000 even in his day— a village with a stream running down its single street whose inhabitants were nearly all fishing folk.

It is doubtful whether any two places owe so much to but two men as do Brighton and its sister town of Hove. It was Dr. Richard Russell who first put Brighthelmstone on the map as a seaside resort; the Prince Regent who caused it to grow into one of the most fashionable towns in England.

Dr. Russell was a man of modest birth who ran away with the daughter of a Sussex squire, and took up medicine for no better reason than that his father-in-law stipulated that he must do so. He bought a practice in Lewes, where, partly through the influence of his father-in-law, who was squire of Malling, he was successful in building up a considerable clientèle among the more well-to-do. Many of his patients were children suffering from glandular and tonsular troubles and from various skin diseases.

In the early years of the 1750's Dr. Russell—whose portrait hangs in the town's art gallery—paid a visit to Brighton where he was surprised to find that the children suffered none of these maladies, but that, on the contrary, they appeared to be quite unusually healthy. This the doctor attributed to the sea water, and proceeded to write a book upon the advantages to be gained from bathing at Brighton. Later, he discovered that St. Ann's Well contained mineral waters such as could be drunk according to the fashion at Bath and elsewhere, and immediately publicized that as well.

Since only the bravest took to the water in those days, his book about the sea caused so great a stir that the doctor found it opportune to move from Lewes and build himself a house on the Steine where he was soon being consulted by people from all over the world.

XI

As ' Sea-water Russell ' thereby increased in wealth so Brighton grew. So that when, in 1784, the Prince Regent bought his ' respectable farm-house ' here, Brighton was already a place of quite definite renown.

Yet its fame was as nothing by comparison with that which it was to enjoy under the latter's patronage. Whenever the Regent came down from London fashionable London followed along the Brighton Road behind him. Probably no other town in England welcomed quite so many famous people as did the ' Queen of Watering Places ' in the months of those late eighteenth and early nineteenth century summers. As year by year for the next quarter of a century ' Prinny ' spent more and more of the country's money in developing his farm-house into the Royal Pavilion, so, all around, beautiful squares were laid out and magnificent sequences of houses erected to accommodate those who followed him down in steadily increasing numbers.

It is said that no one of consequence failed to visit Brighton at least once. Every one from the Duke of Queensbury ('Old Q'), whose perfect manners were always liable to be relieved by a spasm of swearing, to rakes like Sir John Lade, who gathered round the Prince and led him into foolish escapades; from Dr. Johnson, who froze so many into silence by his ready wit, to Fanny Burney, who, by contrast, kept many a company entertained by her keen sense of humour; from Wellington, who, at the dinner table of the Pavilion, sat patiently listening to the quite fantastic tales of the Prince's personal achievements in the military field, to Byron, who penned his disapproval of the heir to the throne's extravagant expenditure; every one, it seems, came to Brighton at some time or another.

The Prince came ostensibly to bathe, and he, like the others, would venture into the sea in company with the 'dippers' whose first duty was to see that no one drowned. There were two dippers of special renown—'Smoaker' and Martha Gunn. The 'First Gentleman' patronized the former, and a story is told how, when once the Prince ventured out too far, 'Smoaker' swam out and dragged him ashore by the ear, muttering that he was not going to be blamed for allowing the Prince of Wales to drown.

But there were other things that caused the Prince to come so frequently. A year or two after his first visit he met Mrs. Fitzherbert, who had been widowed twice before she was twenty-six. After their morganatic marriage Mrs. Fitzherbert had bought a house in the Steine, and here the Prince was able to make the most of her company, away from affairs of state and the interference of his father, the king, with whom he could never agree.

It was a gay and festive scene that greeted the Prince and the ' fashionables ', and the ' First Gentleman ' enjoyed it to the full. There were the races at Brighton and Lewes—which he never missed if he could help it—riding on the downs, cricket on the ' Level ' (one of the first cricket grounds in England and now an open space) and bathing in the sea. There were the waters of St. Anne's Well and the German Spa to be taken, and all day long the bepowdered lords and ladies would promenade both the Steine and the front, while the dog and goat carts, ' flies ', curricles and such like drove through the streets with those less energetic. The public dinners, balls and gambling parties, arranged by such Masters of Ceremonies as Mr. Wade, or, in later times, Colonel Eld, can have been only a little less elaborate than the sumptuous feasts that took place in the Royal Pavilion itself. And for those who preferred a more sedate evening, Sarah Siddons was often to be seen at the theatre.

XII

Though Brighton has developed year by year since then, and, like all seaside resorts, now has its full share of ugly buildings, happily the town maintains much of its Regency tone. In Brighton alone there are no less than thirty-seven streets and squares of this period whose proportions are so perfect that if a single house in any one sequence was to be demolished the whole effect would be ruined. In Hove there are a further seven such streets, while in both towns there are many others of great merit. Many of these terraces, with their curved façades, their bow windows, their iron verandas, and various classical orders, can vie with the best in Bath, and it is gratifying to know that, largely through the efforts of the novelist D. L. Murray, who lives in Brighton, a Regency Society has been formed to safeguard them against the hands of the despoilers.

If only for its beautiful architecture and its rich associations, Brighton is still the gay 'Queen of Watering Places' whose streets are yet haunted by the ghosts of the 'grave and gay'. The home of Dr. Russell has gone, but the Royal Pavilion—a strange building of Eastern influence whose many domes and cupolas prompted the Rev. Sidney Smith, Canon of St. Paul's, to remark that the dome of St. Paul's must have come down to Brighton and pupped—together with the Dome, which once served as its stables but which has been converted into one of the finest concert halls in the South, remain.

Mrs. Fitzherbert's house in Old Steine still stands close by Gideon Mantell's, while the homes of many other famous people may yet be found in the various streets of Brighton and Hove—of Harrison Ainsworth, who based his *Ovingdean Grange* upon the Tudor mansion in the near-by village of Ovingdean; of George Canning, Charles Dickens and Sir Roland Hill; of Richard Jefferies who wrote *The Life of the Fields* here, and Herbert Spencer; of 'Phiz' (Hablot Knight Browne) and John Leech; of Winston Churchill, who attended the Misses Thompsons' Preparatory School in Brunswick Road, Hove, to mention but a few.

The George, where Charles II supped that last night in England, has vanished, but the grave of Nicholas Tattersall, who took him across the sea to safety, may be seen in the churchyard of St. Nicholas along with the graves of many of the beaux and belles who followed the Regent to Brighton, and of Martha Gunn and the immortal Phoebe Hessell, who served in the army to be with her lover, was twice wounded in battle, and later ran a street stall in Brighton, where she died at the age of 106.

The Chain Pier, a favourite promenade for William IV, which was built on the suspension principle in 1813, was destroyed by a gale in 1893, but Volk's railway, the first electric railway in England, still runs, while the Aquarium, which was opened in 1872, is said to contain the finest collection of fish in the world, just as Booth's Bird Museum houses an almost equally remarkable variety of stuffed birds.

Brighton has grown, but it has not forgotten even the oldest features of its past. In the 'lanes' and 'twittens'—a series of narrow alleyways of medieval and Tudor buildings in the very heart of the town—we may still find traces of the original Brighthelmstone, while on the beach there is a colony of fishermen who retain their rights to dry their nets on the esplanade.

Though conditions have changed for them, the fishermen have not yet forgotten their Good Friday habit of skipping, nor become less superstitious about taking buns to sea. They can still talk, too, of the days when the 'smacksmen' (crews of the fishing smacks) turned out in blue jerseys and brown trousers with gold ear-rings dangling from their ears, and the skippers of the luggers, or 'Hogge-Boats', wore top hats to give them just that extra distinction; when they hung their nets in the Steine to dry and were involved in endless legal tussles with those who would deny them their ancient rights and privileges. They can talk of the Press Gang and of coastal defence; of the packet boats crossing to Dieppe, and of pleasure cruises in the old *Skylark*, skippered by the redoubtable Captain Collins. . . .

Even their old mackerel prayer is not forgotten:

> Watch! Barrell! Watch!
> Mackerel for to catch.
> White may they be like blossom on a tree.
> God sends thousands; one, two, three.
> Some by the heads, some by their tails.
> God sends thousands and never fails.

Brighton has grown, but remains as interesting and, in parts, as architecturally perfect as ever.

XIII

Two of the famous people who came to Brighton in the

town's most fashionable age—the Duke of Wellington and
Cardinal Manning—must have been acquainted with the district from boyhood, for they, with Bulwer Lytton, learnt some
of their earliest lessons from the vicar of near-by Rottingdean,
Dr. Redman Hooker, who, like so many country parsons of his
time, ran a school in his vicarage. While in the charge of
Dr. Hooker, the Duke of Wellington—then young Arthur
Wellesley—often worshipped at St. Nicholas Church, Brighton,
and in later years this church was restored as a memorial to
him by Hooker's grandson, the Rev. Wagner.

Rottingdean itself has been associated with quite a number
of people of note. Burne-Jones lived in a house that is still
standing, and designed some of the windows of the church in
whose graveyard his ashes are now buried. Lady Baldwin, too,
lived here for a time, while the village was also the home of
Kipling before he moved to Burwash.

Rottingdean, with its pond and green, its wealth of old
houses and the windmill towering over it from the downs
behind, is but a few miles eastward from Brighton, and,
though development has taken place on the coast itself, the
village has been left surprisingly unspoilt. In one respect it
can claim greater distinction than Brighton—it was the first
place in Sussex to have electric light!

CHAPTER EIGHT: *The Middle Downs*

I

BY contrast with the coastal belt, the middle stretch of the South Downs, which runs roughly parallel with the shore, is so unspoilt that we can traverse the hills from Ditchling Beacon, to the north of Brighton beyond Stanmer Park, right back to the Arun without being more than occasionally conscious of the mass development that has taken place to the south.

Everything possible is being done to ensure that the natural beauty of these downs continues unimpaired. While both the East and West Sussex County Councils possess and exercise powers to control the amount and character of building that may take place here, the Society of Sussex Downsmen—a voluntary body, comprising something like a thousand lovers of the South Downs—maintain a constant watch against any threats of spoliation, whatever their nature. In addition to carrying out regular patrols on horseback, cycle and foot to see that holiday-makers do not uproot the wild flowers and saplings, and that motorists do not offend the law prohibiting the driving of cars more than fifteen yards on to the turf, they maintain their own trust, and, as far as their funds permit, buy up any buildings or land that may be in danger.

Standing out against the skyline, barren and sharply defined, with their many prehistoric sites to remind us that once it was the hills and not the coast that drew the populations, these Middle Downs are generally considered more characteristic of

134

the county than those at the western end. Though far less
wooded than the downs we have already explored, they are as
rich in such wild flowers as the rare round-headed rampion
(known locally as ' the pride of Sussex '), the orchis, scabious,
horshoe vetch and bird's-foot trefoil (' shoes and stockings '),
the lady's bedstraw and harebell, viper's bugloss, clematis and,
of course, the wild thyme.

Many rare butterflies flit from flower to flower, while the
goldfinch, yellowhammer, grasshopper warbler and stonechat
may all be seen upon these hills. The succulent wheatear too—
so long a delicacy at Sussex banquets—still pays its annual visit,
while the nightingale sings so constantly that it used to be said
that once a year all the nightingales in Christendom were taken
to Heathfield Fair in a sack and then sent to the downs to
make sure of maintaining their numbers.

To think of these downs is to think instinctively of sheep.
Since the dawn of civilization men have grazed their sheep here
in such numbers that they have become part of the hills. While
the nibbling sheep give the turf its velvet, springy tread, the
grass and wild flowers, in turn, help to make the Southdown
breed among the most noted in the world, and the mutton so
remarkably tasty.

Three or four decades ago the downs were thick with sheep,
and their bleating and the distant tinkling of their bells,
together with the barking of the dogs that watched over them
as they nibbled the herbage, or clustered around a dewpond to
drink, made pleasant and familiar music.

The shepherds wore high leather gaiters, slate-coloured
smock frocks—beautifully smocked by their nimble-needled
womenfolk—and ' chummy ' hats, not unlike those worn by
the old-time parsons. When the weather appeared threatening
they usually carried a large umbrella on their backs, and always
they had their crook, which, very often, had been handed down
to them by their forefathers as a family heirloom. At lambing
time, when they lived in a hut by the lambing-pen and often

acted as both midwife and foster-mother, they would carry, as well, a candle lantern of horn.

As shearing time approached the sheep were washed in special sheep-washes. These 'washes' were formed by damming a brook, and some of them are still used for the annual 'dippings'.

Sheep-shearing with its arduous work, lightened by a plentiful supply of ale and merry-making, was the highlight of the year. 'Gangs' of from ten to twenty shearers worked under the 'Captain', who contracted with the farmers to shear at so much a score. Before work began an initial meeting, known as 'White Ram Night', was held at some convenient inn when each member subscribed a shilling. At this meeting shears were invariably offered for sale, and the whole programme of work was decided upon.

The 'Captain's' right-hand man was the 'Lieutenant', and these two wore gold and silver bands, respectively, round their hats. There were also the 'tar boy' whose chief duty was to daub tar on an unlucky cut as a protection against the dreaded sheep pest—'the fly'—and it is from him that the old saying 'to spoil a ship for a ha'porth of tar' is derived, the Sussex folk referring to sheep always as 'ship'.

At the end of each strenuous day of shearing there would be a supper and sing-song, at which one of the most popular songs was *Rosebuds in June*. When the shearing was ended the 'gang' foregathered once more at the inn to hold their 'Black Ram Night' when the 'Captain' made a final share-out and any money owing for shears was paid.

Alas, the number of flocks has lessened sadly as the result of two world wars, and times and conditions are causing few young men to follow the calling of a shepherd. Even so, we may still occasionally happen upon a shepherd of the old stock folding his sheep at eventide with the aid of his faithful Old English Bob-tail dog. He no longer wears his characteristic smock and ' chummy ', but he has not forsaken his crook, and often he will be found to be remarkably superstitious.

Like his predecessors he may still be averse to accepting money on a Sunday, and he may well continue to hope that when he dies he will be buried with a lock of wool on his chest in the expectation that on the Day of Reckoning this will be taken as a symbol of his calling and his reason for not having attended church as regularly as might have been desired!

II

Often as we wander along these downs the sheep will be our only companions, and we shall be constantly reminded of them in other ways.

On the heights of Ditchling Beacon, for instance, may be seen one of the old dewponds for which these Sussex hills, like those of Wiltshire, are famous. These shallow ponds—some of which are thought to be two or three centuries old—never run dry in even the most severe of droughts, and so are a boon to farmers who otherwise might experience the greatest difficulty in watering their upland sheep and cattle.

A certain mystery is often made concerning the method of constructing these dewponds, and in a number of respects they are the object of much controversy. In fact, a craftsman once explained to me that a hollow of great circumference is dug to a depth of perhaps five or six feet. The surface is then trodden firm and lined with straw, which, in turn, is covered with a thick layer of well-puddled clay. The art, it seems, is to see that each layer is constant and in taking precautions to ensure that the clay does not crack as soon as it begins to harden.

The straw acts as an insulator against the heat of the earth below. Thus, the clay provides an isolated cold spot, which chills the night air above it, causing it to condense.

III

Rising to a height of 813 feet, Ditchling Beacon is the third highest down, and once formed a link in the great chain of bonfires that used to be lit as a warning when invasion threatened, or, when the dangers had passed, as a means of celebrating victory.

Now quiet and deserted save for the walkers and picnickers and the downland birds and animals, the Beacon was an important site in earliest times. The Romans had a camp here, and before them the Ancient Britons built their earthworks upon these hills. Fragments of these can still be seen, while the village of Ditchling, which lies on the Wealden side of the downs, can even now be approached along ' the Nye ', one of those sunken trackways used by the Ancient Britons and many others, including the smugglers, who wished to pass over the hill-top without being silhouetted against the skyline.

It is said that Alfred the Great once owned Ditchling, and that his palace stood on the rising ground opposite the village's Early English flint-built church. An imposing half-timbered and gabled Tudor manor-house, with outside stairway and chimneys typical of the period, now stands on this site. Once a ranger's home, it was given to Anne of Cleves by Henry VIII, who, after their divorce, also awarded his former queen the manors of Preston, near Brighton (where there is a lovely Georgian manor-house), and Southover, near Lewes.

At Ditchling Anne of Cleves led the life of a much-beloved lady of the manor—kindly to all and attentive to the poor—and in her house we can still see the room in which she slept, the drawing-room with Tudor arched fireplace where she used to sit and read on winter evenings, and the little upstair room which she set aside as her private chapel. A small altar with candles now stands in this chapel in her memory.

IV

Long celebrated for the fine quality of its gooseberries—one of the highlights of the year being the local flower show when, as has been the practice since 1822, a copper kettle is awarded to the winner of the ' gooseberry class '—Ditchling is remarkable in that whereas some atrocious building has been allowed to take place here in recent decades, it has managed to retain sufficient charm to attract such artists and craftsmen as Sir Frank Brangwyn and Eric Gill, both of whom made their home here at one time. Even to-day it boasts quite a colony of both artists and craftsmen.

With its rich assortment of Tudor chimney stacks and wavy roofs, its sixteenth-century manor and its 200-year-old ' peg-and-post ' windmill, Ditchling is undoubtedly a delightful village whose beauty is enhanced by its splendid panorama of the downs, which, from this vantage-point, can be seen stretching in a long majestic line from Black Cap, near Lewes, in the east, to Duncton Hill in the west.

To the north of the village are bleak, windswept commons to give added variety. Here, in 1734, a pedlar, Jacob Harris, was hanged on a gibbet for battering three people to death at a local inn. When last I visited the common the fenced remains of the gibbet—known locally as ' Jacob's Post '—were still there, and it used to be customary for people to carry away pieces as a cure for ague, just as once they came here to drink the waters of the local spring to rid themselves of rheumatism. For some time after Harris was hanged barren women used to journey from miles around to touch the pedlar's body in the belief, then widely held, that to hold the hand of a hanged man would increase fertility.

V

Ditchling Common commands extensive views of both

Weald and Downs with the Sussex forests melting away into the Surrey hills. Immediately to the north is Burgess Hill, where there is a colony of ecclesiastical wood-carvers and an interesting hand pottery, and to the north-west, Hurstpierpoint, home of another of the public schools founded by Canon Woodard, with, near by, Albourne Green where Bishop Juxon, whom we met at Chichester, lived in the old palace, and during the civil wars escaped being captured by the Roundheads by posing as a bricklayer. To the south-west are Clayton's twin windmills, ' Jack and Jill ', beckoning us back to the downs.

Beyond Clayton—in whose church are a number of interesting wall-paintings—the main Brighton-London road cuts through the downs at Pyecombe, where for many generations some of the most famous of the shepherd's crooks were forged. The Sussex shepherds are still most particular about the shape of their crooks, some favouring one style and others another, with the result that the village blacksmiths have always taken a special pride in their making. Indeed, some of the old-time craftsmen used to fashion them to such perfection that they could play tunes on a set of six, and I have heard that, while their principal aims were good shape and balance, some used to judge them by their music.

Smoke still issues from Pyecombe's forge, but this corner is now anything but peaceful. Yet at Saddlescombe, but a mile or two on, we are again in as quiet country as any.

Saddlescombe, too, has a smithy, and here may be seen the equipment used some forty or fifty years ago for shoeing oxen when those sturdy black beasts were still employed for ploughing these Sussex slopes. Fashions change but slowly in this downland hamlet. One of the last places to forsake the ox, it still relies upon a donkey to turn the water-wheel.

VI

The Devil's Dyke is in the neighbourhood of Saddlescombe.

A prehistoric site of some two thousand years ago, in which a number of interesting relics have been found, tradition has it that this deep cleft in the chalk was cut by the devil for the purpose of letting in the sea and thereby flooding the country-side. The devil, it appears, was annoyed by the great number of churches in this part of Sussex and obtained permission (from whom it is not stated) to inundate them, provided that he was able to complete his task between sunset and sunrise. He had got so far when an old woman in a near-by cottage, having much washing on hand, arose betimes. Seeing her light shining from behind a red curtain, and mistaking this for the rising sun, the devil threw down his shovel and took to his heels with such gusto that his footprints still remain!

The extensive views from the top of the Dyke make this one of the best known of the Sussex beauty-spots, which, however, might well have disappeared by now but for the magnanimity of a Brighton alderman, Sir Herbert Carden. When the site was threatened by speculative builders and amusement pur-veyors some years ago, Sir Herbert bought the Dyke, and resold it on extremely advantageous terms to the Brighton Corporation, who, hitherto, had proved all too slow in realiz-ing the dangers.

Due north of the Devil's Dyke is Poynings, whose church is attractively set by a winding lane at the foot of the downs. From here a quiet by-road takes us through the lonely hamlets of Fulking, whose *Shepherd and Dog* inn nestles on the hill-side—a place much beloved by Ruskin, who often came here to admire the sunsets, and who, in fact, first gave the hamlet water—and Edburton, whose ' Little Grey Church '—contain-ing altar rails believed to have been the gift of the seventeenth-century Archbishop Laud—Michael Fairless introduced into *The Roadmender*.

All along this route, almost as far westwards as Upper Beed-ing, the downs are seen at their most barren, and, in parts—as,

for instance, at Truleigh Hill, above Edburton—are so close
as to be almost overpowering.

I

At Upper Beeding we recross the River Adur into Bramber,
leaving the two tiny churches of Botolphs and Coombes—the
former partially Saxon and the latter partially Norman—but
two or three miles down the Adur Flats by the western bank.

To-day Bramber is no more than a one-street village of old
cottages. Only the square south tower and a few fragments of
the six-feet thick walls of the Norman castle remain to remind
us of its past importance as the capital of one of the county's
six rapes when the Adur was a busy commercial waterway into
the Weald that had to be strongly defended at all costs.

After the Conquest, Bramber (mentioned in the *Domesday
Book* as Brembre) was given by William the Conqueror to one
of his followers, William de Braose, who built his moated,
motte-and-bailey castle on the site of a Saxon fortification. In
those days the now shrunken Adur passed by the foot of this
castle mound, and traces of the old landing-stage used by the
barons were recently discovered close to the Norman church,
which, like the castle itself, was badly despoiled in the Civil
Wars.

For two centuries the de Braose family—who, as we have
seen, received the harbour dues at Shoreham—were among the
most powerful in Sussex, until, in the thirteenth century,
William de Braose unfortunately quarrelled with King John
and, in consequence, was forced to flee to Ireland. Whereupon
the castle was seized by the Crown, and William's wife and
children, having been held as hostages, were put in gaol where,
it is said, they were starved to death after William had neglected to pay the ransom demanded for their safety.

After a short time, however, Bramber was restored to the de Braoses from whom it passed, first to the Mowbrays and then to the Howards. John Howard, the first of that name to inherit the manor, was created Duke of Norfolk and Earl Marshal of England by Richard III, and was killed in 1485 while fighting the latter's cause at the Battle of Bosworth Field. The Howards continued to occupy Bramber until the seventeenth century, when, as we have seen, they came into possession of Arundel Castle, and thus enjoyed the distinction of becoming lords of two rapes.

In the Civil Wars Bramber Castle was defended for the Roundheads by James Temple, who later sat as one of Charles I's judges, and though sadly ruined, remained the property of the Dukes of Norfolk until 1915 when the present duke sold the castle and its twelve-acre hill; twenty years later it was acquired by the National Trust.

II

Bramber possesses three features, each of which, in its way, may well be unique. While the church is believed to be the only one in England to contain its chancel in its tower, the twelfth-century black-and-white house, known as St. Mary's, is regarded as the oldest example of medieval domestic architecture in Sussex and the second oldest in the country.

Once the property of the Knights Templars, it is chiefly noted for its superb woodwork which includes two inlaid doors, believed to have been made from galleon timbers, and a considerable amount of panelling, some of which is adorned with Elizabethan paintings. It is approached through some splendid gates, which, likewise, afford one of the finest examples of Sussex wrought-iron work. This is saying a great deal, for the pieces made by these old-time craftsmen were adjudged so highly that their work is to be found as far afield as Spain.

The third unusual feature is a museum of taxidermy, formed

last century by Walter Potter. Here, among many other tableaux, rats are seen playing dominoes and guinea pigs cricket, and the whole story of the *Death of Cock Robin* is depicted in stuffed animals, from the birds of the air that ' fell a-sighing and a-sobbing ' to that lone fly that proved to be the only witness to the tragedy.

III

In the time of the de Braoses and the Mowbrays Bramber sent its own Member to Parliament, but from 1467 until the passing of the Reform Act of 1832, when it was classified as a ' Rotten Borough ', the village was linked with its neighbour, Steyning, as a Parliamentary Division.

One of Bramber's most famous Members was William Wilberforce, and an amusing story is told how once, on passing through the village and inquiring its name, he replied: " Bramber? Why, that's the place I am Member for! "

IV

Originally the inland port for Bramber and a Saxon market centre, Steyning was once a royal town of considerable consequence. There is a pleasing tradition that it was founded about 750 by St. Cuthman, a shepherd boy of the West Country who had already proved himself to have divine power over his sheep.

When his father died St. Cuthman fell on hard times, and was obliged to trundle his invalid mother round the country-side in a wheelbarrow in search of food. In the course of his wanderings he travelled far through many counties until at last the wheel of his barrow crumbled at the point by the Sussex Downs where Steyning now stands, and he found himself un-able to proceed farther. Taking this to be a portent, he made a rough shelter of branches for his mother, and proceeded to fell trees with the aid of improvised tools, and build a wooden church. This long and arduous labour of love was almost frustrated as the building was nearing completion when one of the great trunks began to bend under the stress. At this point, the old tale goes, a stranger appeared and chided him for his lack of faith. Whereupon St. Cuthman replied that nothing was impossible for those who feared God, and, bidding the stranger stretch forth his hand to help him, set the pillar straight again. As the church was thus completed St. Cuthman heard the voice of the stranger again: ' I am Jesus to whom thou buildest this house ', and turned to find that the figure had disappeared.

Here, in this church, St. Cuthman proceeded to convert the people to Christianity, and when he died his body, which was later translated to Winchester Cathedral, was buried in this building. Thus Steyning became a noted pilgrimage centre.

In due course a second church arose, and here King Ethelwulf was laid to rest in 857. Then Ethelwulf's son, Alfred the Great, built a palace at Steyning. And so the little town steadily grew in importance until, by the time of Edward the Confessor, it even boasted a mint.

Anxious that William the Conqueror should succeed him to the throne of England, the Confessor awarded Steyning to the Abbey of Fécamp in Normandy, together with the manor of Brede, a parish at the far corner of East Sussex, which then included Hastings. At the same time he gave Bosham to the Norman bishop, Osbern, who was kinsman both to himself and to William, and who later became Bishop of Exeter. It is said that he made these generous gifts in order to provide William with three possible ways of entry into England. So the Battle of Hastings might equally well have been the Battle of Steyning. Indeed, though Steyning was to be spared the horrors of war, the fact that King Harold, on succeeding Edward the Confessor, confiscated this manor was one of the excuses put forward by William the Conqueror for eventually invading this island.

After the Conquest William restored Steyning to the Abbey
of Fécamp, whose monks then proceeded to build the present
church, which, though heavily restored during the last century,
still contains a beautiful arcaded nave, clerestory and chancel
arch of the later Norman period, and which, fittingly, is
dedicated to Steyning's founder, St. Cuthman.

v

When the sea began to recede in the fourteenth century
and the River Adur gradually changed its course, Steyning
dwindled in importance to such an extent that an eighteenth-
century writer was moved to describe it as ' a mean con-
temptible place with hardly a building fit to put a horse in '.
Certainly no one could be so damning to-day. An old-world
market town with a tannery where for generations some of the
finest parchment has been made from the skins of the downland sheep, Steyning is unquestionably one of the most enchanting towns in Sussex—a busy little place, hardly more than
a village, whose atmosphere bespeaks country life and farm
folk.

Set on the crest of a hill with just a few by-ways branching
off the one long main street, Steyning boasts, like Midhurst, a
wealth of medieval, Tudor and Georgian homes, with the prim
eighteenth-century houses round the diminutive Chantry Green
—where, in 1555, one John Launder was burnt at the stake—
contrasting delightfully with the gabled, partly tile-hung
Grammar School farther down the street. Founded in 1614
by William Holland, who gave £100 towards the cost of
equipping the fleet that defeated the Spanish Armada, this
school has sprung up around the fifteenth-century Brotherhood
Hall of the old Steyning Guild, and provides a remarkable hotch-potch of styles, all of which, however, blend
perfectly.

Among Steyning's many charming old buildings the most

notable are the old Prison House and Workhouse, Saxon Cottage, Mint House, the old tithe barn, and Market House, where, in 1655, George Fox addressed a meeting of his Society of Friends. Before they acquired their own meeting-house here the Quakers used to hold regular gatherings in this hall, and when William Penn, who lived but five miles away at Warminghurst, set sail to found the state of Pennsylvania, a number of Steyning folk went with him.

The people of Steyning are keenly alive to the charm of their town, and, under the presidency of the artist, Bertram Nichols, who makes his home here, have their own preservation society, one of whose principal objects is to see that all development is carried out sympathetically.

VI

Steyning is in the heart of some of the most perfect of the downland country, and if we follow the road to Washington we soon come to Wiston Lake, with the famous clump of beech trees, known as Chanctonbury Ring, crowning the hills beyond at 815 feet. The site of an ancient camp, a number of coins, including some that were minted at Steyning, were unearthed at Chanctonbury during the last century, and are now in the British Museum.

Like Ditchling Beacon, Chanctonbury also has a dewpond. But it is for its trees that this hill-top is now best known. They stand out as so fine a landmark for so many miles in all directions that they have helped many to find their way, while to those who live within their view they are a part of home. They were planted in 1760 by Charles Goring, whose Elizabethan ancestral home on the slopes of Wiston is still in the possession of his descendants. Charles Goring planted the trees while still a boy, and in this house there is a portrait by Lawrence showing him holding a twig.

In Sussex it is a general belief that the Ring is haunted, and few care to walk round this clump of trees after dark lest they bump into the ghost of the Saxon with flowing white beard who was killed at the Battle of Hastings and now seeks his buried treasure, they say. Such is the romance of trees and downs and ancient camps that though the ' ghost ' is but an imaginative figure in R. D. Blackmore's *Alice Lorraine*, he is now accepted by many as a reality.

VII

At Washington, a Saxon settlement with fine commanding views of the Weald to the Hog's Back and the North Downs, we join the Worthing-Horsham road, and from here we can explore both the southern and the northern slopes of the remaining sector of these Middle Downs. If first we turn southwards towards Worthing we soon come to Findon in whose little smithy—which has been in the same family since the days of George III—a number of Derby and Grand National winners were shod when horses used to be trained on the downs at near-by Michelgrove.

Findon is the scene of an important sheep fair—the Great Fair—which is held every year on September 14, and of a Lamb Fair, held each July.

Originally the flock masters used to sell their sheep by private treaty, and the fairground at the foothills of the downs was specially chosen so that they could drift their sheep to the fair. For the last fifty or sixty years, however, they have been sold by auction, and the sheep are now, mostly, brought in by lorry. In the first place, too, the fair was confined to Southdowns where now almost every breed is represented. Buyers come from as far afield as the Eastern counties, Warwickshire, Gloucestershire and Wales, and it is amusing to hear the farmers bidding and chattering in their various native tongues. At the Great Fair as many as 10,000 to 17,000 ewes and lambs and about 250 rams may come under the hammer according to the season, while the number of lambs sold at the smaller July Fair fluctuates from 1,000 to 2,500.

VIII

These southern slopes on either side of the Adur are unusually rich in ancient sites. The most notable are the remains of a Roman peasant village, with the remnants of furnaces and a granary for the drying and storing of corn, on Thunderbarrow Hill, just to the east of the river above Shoreham; and, to the west, an Iron Age hill fort at Cissbury, by Findon, together with a series of Neolithic flint mines both here and at Myrtle Grove and Harrow Hill.

Both as a hill fort and for its flint mines, Cissbury is one of the most interesting sites of its kind in the country, and in the museum at Worthing may be seen a wide variety of local discoveries, dating from the Neolithic Age to Saxon times, including pottery, oyster shells, bones and skulls, flint implements, and beach pebbles which the inhabitants used to store as ammunition for their slings.

Though never so strongly defended as some of the Wessex forts like Maiden Castle, E. Cecil Curwen and R. F. Ross Williamson, who in 1930 prepared a paper on the subject for the Worthing Archæological Society, tell us that this camp, which is situated on a hill 603 feet high, enclosed approximately 60 acres. Roughly pear-shaped, it measures about half a mile at its longest point and about a quarter of a mile at its widest. It contained entrance gates to south and east, and its defences comprised two ramparts that were separated from each other by a ditch.

It is thought that the camp was first constructed between 400 and 250 B.C. and that it continued to be fortified until 50 B.C. when it became the centre of a small farming community. Much of the site then fell to the plough, but in Roman times it appears to have been refortified, probably by the Celtic inhabitants, as a strongpoint where they could shelter from the Saxon pirates who then made periodic raids along this part of Southern England.

The large group of flint mine shafts at the western end of Cissbury provide the most interesting feature to-day. These flint mines—which, before their excavation in 1875, were taken variously to be the sites of huts, water-holes or cattle pens—are far older than the camp itself, and it is incredible to think that those Neolithic folk who so scientifically excavated their flint by means of these galleries we see to-day had to use the antlers of reindeer for their picks and the shoulder-blades of oxen for their shovels.

Of the flint they excavated they fashioned tools of many kinds. Besides the arrow-heads with which they hunted their beasts, they made sickles for reaping corn, keen-edged knives for sundry purposes, and saws with 27 teeth to the inch. They made scrapers for the tanners, axes for the woodmen, drills, chisels and gouges for the carpenters.

As I show in my *English Country Crafts*, they formed a tool-producing centre that served the needs of farmers and crafts-men of all kinds, and they ground their implements sharp by means of other stones, afterwards polishing them by friction. Their methods were as varied and enterprising as were the tools they fashioned numerous, and if we examine some of these flint implements in Worthing Museum to-day we can readily appreciate that they and others like them must have been the models upon which most of the modern metal tools have gradually evolved.

IX

From earliest times almost down to the present day the flint of these downs has been of commercial importance to Sussex. For centuries after the mines of Cissbury and elsewhere had been filled in the flint was used alike for making roads and building churches and houses. There are people who can still remember watching the old roadside ' stone-crackers ' at work, and it is said that the reason why so many of the cottagers are even yet averse to opening their windows too wide on even the hottest day is that they have not forgotten the fearful white dust raised in the summer by the iron tyres of the various horse-drawn vehicles.

But it is in the homes themselves—especially in the architecture of the towns and villages within easy reach of the downs—that the flint has left its greatest mark. Homes of brick and flint, or of flint alone, are a common and most pleasing feature of downland Sussex. Sometimes the flint will be seen in its natural state. Sometimes it will have been ' knapped ' to a uniform size, but in either case it is laid in ' courses '. For the very reason that they are built of local materials, they tone perfectly with their surroundings, while age has given many of the homes an added warmth and mellowness.

x

From Findon we can descend Long Furlong to the woods of the twin villages of Clapham and Patching where, in the old days, they used to seek the truffle, an edible-fungus still considered a delicacy. The truffles are found just below the surface, usually near the roots of the beech trees, and used to be hunted with the aid of keen-nosed ' truffle-dogs '—not unlike poodles in appearance—which were rewarded for their efforts by being given pieces of bread smeared with the fungus. This breed of dog is said to have been introduced into England by a Spaniard who took two such animals to Wiltshire in about 1670, and was fortunate in earning a considerable amount of money by his truffle-hunting.

The truffles found in these Sussex woods were sold in the London markets, while the women of Sussex devised many tempting recipes for cooking this delicacy.

Truffle-hunting has died out, but in the lovely primrose
and bluebell woods craftsmen may still be found making
hurdles and sheep-feeding cages for the downland shepherds
as well as cutting spars for the thatchers, tent pegs and bean
sticks. One of these families, whose work often takes them
within sight of the little woodland church where their ancestors
are buried—a church which, besides being unusual in its setting, also contains a number of brasses and other monuments—
have been plying their trade in these same woods since the
days of Charles II, and there is something delightfully peaceful in watching these men of tradition working so near to
Nature.

Hazel is the wood favoured by the hurdle-makers. The
stouter branches they cut short, trim and point to serve as their
main stakes; the finest they merely trim; the medium they both
trim and split, using a fromard for the latter, and the bole of
a not too stout tree as their splitting post.

Where they are making hurdles they set their uprights into
a curved block of wood containing ten holes, and then weave
their medium strands backwards and forwards, finishing off
at the top with a few rows of the finest stems. But in the case
of a cage they drop their uprights into a ' wheel ' with twelve
holes.

Though considerable skill is required to twist back the hazel
rod at each end of a hurdle without allowing it either to break
or splinter, the making of a cage is more complicated. Here
two of the finer rods—known as ' ethers '—are plaited alternately in and out of the stakes to a few inches above the wheel,
after which the split rods are threaded through to about a third
of the height. A space is then left so that the sheep can poke
their heads through and help themselves to the hay. Above
this space work continues as before. When the last row has
been woven and the rods have been beaten down and the
uppermost one nailed, the ends of the stakes are trimmed off
to avoid possible injury to the sheep.

It is an interesting fact that both hurdles and feeding cages are an evolution of one of the earliest forms of house-building, that known as ' wattle-and-daub '. Though the feeding cages of Sussex—which are almost entirely peculiar to the county—are made in one piece, they show a distinct resemblance to the huts of Glastonbury's famous primitive Lake Village, which are circular with hurdles set between upright timbers and daubed with clay. Incidentally, it is from this form of building that yet another popular expression of speech—that relating to ' mud-slinging '—is derived, the man responsible for the daubing being known as the ' mud-slinger '.

In addition to the hazels and beeches, Patching and Clapham boast a remarkable number of walnut trees. These were planted at the time of the Napoleonic scares in order to provide timber for the musket stocks, which were usually made of walnut.

Another pleasing feature of Patching is its pond, and at near-by Hammerpot is a disused decoy pond which used to supply the wild duck for the kitchen of Arundel Castle. Close by this pond is a row of cottages which, as New Place, was the home of Sir Edward Palmer, whose three sons, born on successive Sundays, were all knighted by Henry VIII.

XI

By contrast with these southern slopes, there are only three points of real interest in the last few miles of the northern side. After branching westwards off the Horsham road from Washington we come in turn to Sullington Warren, a wild expanse of heather and pine now in the hands of the National Trust, with the little church and farmstead (the latter boasting one of the largest tithe barns in England) nestling side by side up a quiet lane in the shadow of Kithurst Hill; Storrington, a village possessing a number of lovely old houses, and a centre for beagling; and, a mile or so on towards Pulborough, the restored, but still imposing, Elizabethan mansion of Parham House, formerly the seat of the Ashby de la Zouches but now the home of the Hon. Clive Pearson.

Set in a deer park of 350 acres, Parham was once the property of the Manor of Westminster to whose abbey regular supplies of venison were sent from this corner of Sussex. Queen Elizabeth once dined at Parham, and in the park is an oak tree under which she is said to have sat. Though this tree is known as Betsy's Oak, in fact it is more likely called after a man named Bates, an archer at Agincourt and a member of the retinue of the Earls of Arundel. For this lovely sandy park, in which the bracken and the tall, slender fir trees thrive so well, was an important residence long before the present mansion was built, and boasts a small fourteenth-century church with a leaden font bearing the arms of Andrew Peverell, who was Knight of the Shire as far back as 1351.

Though the deer still roam in Parham, it is for its heronry that the park is most famous. These birds are the descendants of a number of herons which the steward of Lord Leicester brought from Wales to Penshurst in Kent in the time of James I. After some two hundred years the herons migrated to Michelgrove where they remained until about 1829 when the Duke of Norfolk bought the mansion there and destroyed it, at the same time felling a number of trees in order to provide the materials for the building of Shoreham's toll-bridge. From Michelgrove, but a few miles across the hills, the herons transferred their affections to Parham where their descendants constitute one of the now all too few such bird colonies in England.

XII

A minor spur of the downs branches north-westwards from Storrington, encompassing a series of further delightful little villages—Thakeham (where country dancing once more forms part of the May Day celebrations), an enchanting hamlet with the church tucked away round the bend at the bottom of the hill, the close neighbour of a row of medieval half-timbered cottages and a beautiful Georgian house; West Chiltington, whose fifteenth-century church contains one of the largest lepers' squints in England, and still displays the old stocks and whipping-post beside its churchyard wall; and William Penn's village of Warminghurst—whose deer park and thirteenth-century chapel were once the property of the Abbey of Fécamp—where Edward Shelley (one of the poet's Tudor ancestors), a bearded courtier in a fur-lined cloak, who was a master of the household of three successive sovereigns, Henry VIII, Edward VI and Queen Mary, is pictured with his wife and nine children in a brass. The Shelleys are also remembered in some of the brasses in Clapham's church.

Though all too little is known of Penn's life at Warminghurst, it is certain that he once owned an extensive property in this village, and that it was in his house here—one or two of whose walls are now incorporated in a farm-house—that, with the aid of his friend, Algernon Sidney, he prepared the first draft of his Constitution of Pennsylvania shortly before he sailed for America.

For exactly how long William Penn made Warminghurst his home is in dispute, but at least it can be said that this corner of Sussex was one of the breeding-grounds of the Quaker movement. Moreover, a number of American writers have noted the similarity between their tongue and the Sussex dialect and have been surprised to find that autumn is referred to as ' the fall ' by the country folk hereabouts—which seems to indicate that many of Penn's early settlers hailed from these parts.

The movement is still particularly strong around here. At the ' Blue Idol '—a fine half-timbered meeting-house, which the Quakers built near the Coolham-Billinghurst road, a little to the north of Warminghurst, in the latter half of the seven-teenth century—the Friends still meet as regularly as when they used to foregather here under the inspiring leadership of Penn himself.

But at Coolham we have left the downs, and are on the fringe of the Forest Ridge.

CHAPTER NINE: *The Wealden Forests*

I. WEST OF THE BRIGHTON ROAD

I

THE Coolham-Billinghurst road forms part of a long high-way stretching from beyond Haywards Heath in the east to Petworth in the west, and cutting off the South Downs and the plain immediately to their north from the Wealden Forests.

These forests—St. Leonard's, Holmbush, Peasepottage, Til-gate, Worth, Balcombe and Ashdown—form the last link with the great Forest of Anderida which once extended for 120 miles across the north of Sussex as a great natural barrier separating her from Surrey and Kent.

Though the forests have dwindled considerably in both size and density, the area they encompass to-day as woods or moor-land is still considerable. No longer the ' impenetrable barrier ' of medieval and Tudor times, the famous Brighton Road, as well as several other lesser highways, now brings travellers from London to the coast across these woods. Indeed, one of the best ways of exploring the forests is to take the stretch of this road from Crawley in the north to Bolney in the south as our base, and work first a western arc round St. Leonard's, Holmbush and Peasepottage, and then an eastern one round Tilgate, Worth, Balcombe and Ashdown.

II

Bolney, our starting-point for the western circuit, is on the southern slope of the Forest Ridge, close by a windy common, and, like Ditchling for its gooseberries, is renowned for its cherry orchards, and for its church bells which Samuel Beech-ing gave to the village after one of his beasts had taken a first prize at Smithfield, it is said.

Henry Huth, the nineteenth-century book collector, is buried in Bolney's churchyard. A man of German extraction, Huth was remarkably gifted at languages, capable, while still a boy, of speaking many Eastern tongues. To encourage his learning his father sent him all over the world, and it was during these early travels that he started his invaluable hobby. He specialized in collecting old works, including many long-forgotten ballads and tracts which he printed and bound him-self. After his death, Huth's son continued the work, and the importance of the enterprise can be gauged by the fact that when, in 1910, the latter sold the entire collection, with the exception of some fifty volumes which he presented to the British Museum, it realized £300,000.

The way westwards from Bolney takes us past Oakendean, another cricketing stronghold of the late eighteenth century, to Cowfold, a peaceful village near a tributary of the Adur, asso-ciated rather dubiously with the poet, John Gay.

In the church here is the largest and finest brass in Sussex, erected to the memory of Thomas Nelond, Prior of Lewes, who died in 1433 and was buried here at his own request. Nearly ten feet in length and close on five feet high, it is so magnificent a piece of craftsmanship that antiquaries journey from miles to take rubbings of it. The prior is seen in the habit of a Cluniac monk, his hands clasped in prayer. Above him, under a canopied arch, are the Virgin and Child, while to his right is St. Thomas à Becket, and to his left, St. Pancras, the patron of the Lewes Priory. The latter holds a palm branch in his right hand and a book in his left and tramples proudly upon a warrior whose sword is drawn.

Towards the end of the last century a further monastic influ-ence was established at Cowfold when, upon the expulsion of the religious orders from France, a number of Carthusians from that country established a monastery at Parkminster, a mile or so to the south of the village, to St. Hugh of Lincoln. They consecrated their buildings in 1883, and the tall white spire—nearly two hundred feet high—is now one of the more notable of the Sussex landmarks.

III

Two rather charming little villages—Shermanbury, where Michael Fairless wrote the *Roadmender*, and Henfield, once a seat of the Bishops of Chichester, who held the area known as Streatham Manor while the Prior of Lewes held Wantley Manor—lie to the south of Cowfold.

The church and rebuilt Elizabethan manor-house at Shermanbury occupy what appears to be the site of a Saxon burgh, or fort of a shireman or sheriff, and it seems probable that it is from this that the village gets its name. Now no more than an agricultural hamlet, its importance as such is accentuated in an unusual way by having the names of the various farms in the parish painted on the pews of the church. Each pew represents one farm and denotes the size of the holding; thus where one bears the name ' Green Trees ' another has ' Little Taylors ' painted on it. And so on.

Though its two inns, *The George* and *The White Hart*, were noted houses of call in the days when George IV was making Brighton fashionable, Henfield, with its lovely views of the downs from Wolstonbury to Chanctonbury, its single street of old houses, and its common and marshes, is, to-day, not so very much busier than Shermanbury, and is noted for its bird life and rare plants. A local naturalist of Victorian times, William Borrer, recorded well over 6,500 different plants in his garden here, and more than once reported seeing the rare golden oriole on a thorn bush on the common.

Birds of the tame variety have also left their mark at Henfield. From the eaves of a thatched cottage near the church hang a series of wrought-iron cats, each holding a bird in one of its paws. It is said that this cottage—known locally as the ' cat house '—was once inhabited by a canary fancier, who was a smith by trade. When one day the vicar's cat seized and killed one of the smith's prize canaries, he fashioned these metal images and hung them in this obtrusive position in protest, hoping that the vicar might feel a certain pang of conscience each time he passed by the cottage on his way from the vicarage to the church! More likely the images were suspended in order to frighten away birds from nesting in the thatch.

In this church is a monument to Henry Bishop, who, during his term as Postmaster General in the first three years of the Restoration, introduced the idea of post-marks. Henfield has another minor claim to distinction as the birthplace of Dr. Thomas Stapleton, a prebendary of Chichester Cathedral, who, deprived of his office upon the accession of Queen Elizabeth, became a professor at the Catholic colleges of Douai and Louvain, and gained fame for his prose translations of Bede and for his Latin biography of Sir Thomas More.

IV

From Shermanbury we can get back to the Forest Ridge by following a delightful cross-country route that takes us over Partridge Green and the deer park of West Grinstead—where Pope wrote *The Rape of the Lock* under an oak tree during a visit to his friend, John Caryll—to Knepp Castle and Kneppmill Pond, a picturesque lake of 100 acres, said to be the largest sheet of water in Southern England.

There are two Knepp Castles—an ancient and a modern. The first was one of the strongholds of the de Braose family and a favourite hunting-seat of King John, but was so seriously damaged in the Civil Wars that all that is now left is a mere fragment of the keep, which stands, surrounded by the outline of its original moat, on a knoll by the Worthing-Horsham road. The second was built by Sir Charles Merrik Burrell, son of Sir William Burrell, an eighteenth-century antiquary, who devoted a number of years of his life to gathering material for an exhaustive book on Sussex, but was prevented by paralysis from writing it, and so, instead, left his precious folios to the British Museum. Alas, this building, too, is now largely ruined, having been ravaged in 1904 by a fire which also destroyed many treasures, including a number of Holbein paintings and a valuable library.

Knepp is in the parish of Shipley, and both here and at West Grinstead are monuments to the Burrells, whose descendants still live in these parts.

v

The whole of this area between the South Downs and the Forest Ridge is rich farmland, and many of the farms round Shipley, Coolham (where we rejoin the Haywards Heath-Petworth road) and Billingshurst bear such appropriate names as 'Slaughterbridge', 'Purveyor's', 'Sauceland', 'Barnhouse', and 'Sproutes'.

The pretty, though busy, main road village of Billingshurst straddles the Roman Stane Street, and faces the old glass centre of Wisborough Green across the River Arun. One of the oldest of the Sussex villages, its church, which is attractively situated on a mound, contains a certain amount of Roman brickwork, which helps to strengthen the local belief that Billingshurst is called after the Roman engineer, Belinus, who planned this important highway through the woods.

As the last part of its name would suggest, Billingshurst has always been associated with woods, and if we follow Stane Street up to Roman Wood, on the Surrey border, and the near-by delightful hill village of Rudgwick, where nearly every house is old, we pass through the heart of much beautiful parkland—a country of halls, granges and small manors, enclosed in miniature well-treed estates.

Some of these houses—like many of the old manors and farm-houses throughout the county—are roofed with the lovely mellow greyish-brown 'Horsham stone' already mentioned. This stone, which is not altogether unlike that of the Cotswolds, used to be excavated from the quarries around Slinfold, and is of such weight that extra heavy roof timbers were needed, and the builders were obliged to adopt a special technique.

Slinfold—a village on the Horsham side of Stane Street—was the home of the medieval ancestors of the poet, William Cowper, to some of whom there are tablets in the church.

Another poet is linked with these parts. It was at Field Place —a low, rambling house, partly Tudor and partly Stuart, in the midst of trees, a little more than a mile to the south of Warnham—that Percy Bysshe Shelley was born on August 4, 1792. His ancestors too had lived in Sussex for many generations, and here he spent the first ten years of his childhood, weaving his imaginative tales of the snake in his parents' garden, of the 'great tortoise' that haunted the deep of Warnham's lily-carpeted pond, in which he used to sail his boats, and of the 'dragon' in St. Leonard's Forest.

Yet, though a tablet in the house tells us that this was the 'shrine of the dawning speech and thought' of the poet, it is a mistake to associate Shelley too closely with Sussex. After leaving home at the age of ten to go to school at Isleworth, whence he passed to Eton and Oxford, his connections with the county were few, and his visits very occasional and usually of the saddest. His father, always a tyrant, appears to have made no attempt to understand the boy's curious temperament. He was, not unnaturally, angered when Shelley was sent down from Oxford for preaching in favour of atheism; and he was hardly less disgusted at his association with Miss Hitchener, a Hurstpierpoint school teacher who printed and distributed his illegal broad-sheets on Ireland—copies of which he himself floated in bottles to mariners at sea—among the Sussex farmers. He strongly disapproved, too, of his son's unfortunate marriage, while still in his teens, to Harriet Westbrook, the daughter of a coffee-house keeper, from whom, however, he separated after only four months in favour of Mary Godwin, his second wife, with whom he lived for some time before their marriage. Shelley's father carried his disgust so far, however, that the poet found himself barred from his boyhood home at an early age.

Once, when his mother wished to see him, it is said, Shelley was obliged to disguise his identity by dressing in the scarlet uniform of a soldier; while even when his grandfather, Sir Bysshe Shelley, died in 1815, and the poet journeyed to Field Place to discuss the estate, of which he was one of the principal beneficiaries, he was refused admittance.

Against such a background of bitterness it is not surprising that Shelley was never inspired to write eulogies concerning his native county. In fact, apart from the house and the pond, there is little with which we can associate him. Even his memorial tablet in Horsham Church, three miles away, where many of his forefathers are buried, is humble enough, considering that it commemorates one of the most famous of the county's literary sons.

VI

One of the oldest towns in Sussex, Horsham was privileged as far back as 1295 to send two Members to Parliament and was granted a royal charter to hold fairs and markets even before that. There are a number of interesting theories as to how it obtained its name. While some say that the district was renowned in Saxon times for its horse meadows and that many of the horses used for local transport used to sink in the clay up to their hams, others recall that many of the horse-shoes for the army of Edward I were made in the local smithies out of the Wealden iron. Again, some give the town an even older origin by linking it with Horsa (of Hengist and Horsa fame), who is said to have fought a successful engagement in the neighbourhood.

Whatever the justification for these claims, the native still likes to maintain a link with the horse by pronouncing the name of the town ' Horse-um ' rather than accept the more modern, but now quite general ' Horsh-um '.

Horsham—for long the only sizeable town, other than Chichester, in ' wild west Sussex '—has been associated with a remarkable variety of things besides horses. In the Middle Ages it was one of the principal centres for the making of bolts for the cross-bows used by the English archers in France. The seat of the Sussex Assizes from 1307 until 1830, it was also the scene of many hangings and burnings at the stake, and it was here that, in 1735, the cruel torture of pressing to death was practised for the last time when a man convicted of murder and robbery tried to avoid sentence by following the then customary dodge of pretending at his trial to be dumb.

The last public hanging took place here as recently as 1844 when John Lawrence was sentenced for murder. Henry Burstow, who witnessed the event, has left a graphic description of the scene, which shows all too well the barbarous outlook of the people little more than one hundred years ago.

So that the maximum number of people could watch the proceeding the execution was timed for noon on Easter Saturday (April 6), the day selected that year for the Horsham Teg Fair. Among the 3,000 who thronged to see the sight was Lawrence's brother, who drunkenly boasted that he was a greater scoundrel than the condemned man. Though Mr. Kenrick, the curate, managed to persuade one or two of the schoolmasters to march their scholars to Denne Park out of the way, scores of children were present, some with their mothers, some unattended. Costermongers from Brighton and else-where sold gingerbreads and oranges, crying as they went: 'Oranges, beautiful oranges, they'll melt in your mouth like butter, run down your throat like a wheelbarrow; they are sugar outside, brandy in the middle, and the rind will make you good boot soles.' The beer shop enjoyed an excellent trade, while pedlars travelled around the town singing the eight verses and chorus of *The Last Dying Confession*, copies of which they then sold at a few pence each.

A year later, when Horsham Gaol was pulled down and Lawrence's body was exhumed, hundreds experienced a further 'thrill' in paying twopence a time to examine the corpse in the stables of *The Queen's Head*, where it was left pending reburial.

Horsham's associations are by no means all concerned with war or torture. One of the town's proudest memories is of its bell-ringers and singers whose fame spread afar during the last century, largely through the industry of the Burstow family and of the Rev. John Broadwood.

As early as 1843, when so many of the old songs and carols that had been handed down through the generations by word of mouth were already largely forgotten except by the older folk, the Rev. John Broadwood started to make a collection of traditional songs which was afterwards continued by his niece, Lucy Broadwood, and has since been augmented by Dr. Vaughan Williams, W. H. Gill and George Butterworth.

Many of the songs which he recorded were given to him by Henry Burstow, who was born at Horsham in 1826. Though Henry himself was a cobbler, his father ran a clay-pipe business in the town, and used to travel round the countryside in a pony-cart selling his wares. In that way he picked up the words and music of no less than 200 songs. Henry, as interested in the subject as his father, managed to augment these to 420, and in 1906 devoted 41 consecutive evenings to singing these songs to his wife in celebration of her 78th birthday.

A singer all his life, and a bell-ringer from the age of fifteen, Henry Burstow, then 80, crowned this achievement the following year by ringing a complete peal of 5,050 changes in Billingshurst Church in two hours and thirty-seven minutes.

These two families were instrumental in making Horsham one of the most musical towns in Sussex, and it is largely through them that so many of the traditional songs are still remembered. Moreover, bell-ringing, with its 'Stedman Caters', 'Grandsire Triples', 'Bob Royals', 'Union Triples' and many other changes, is still a practised art in a few Sussex villages round about.

Horsham was also renowned for its gingerbread, which, as mentioned, was on sale at Lawrence's execution. Nearly every fair throughout England once boasted its gingerbread stalls, yet few recipes were more tempting than those used by the women of Horsham.

Miss L. N. Candlin, writing recently in *The Sussex County Magazine*, recalls that three traditional gingerbreads were made at Horsham—'hard', which was rich and dark; 'toy', a daintier variety of a somewhat lighter colour; and 'Parliament', which was more after the nature of a thin biscuit.

The gingerbreads were made in moulds, and were often decorated in gilt with such emblems as cats and dogs, the fleur-de-lis, the Tudor rose, coats of arms, or even with the figures of such military heroes as Wellington. Every bakery in the town made them, and they were sold at each one of Horsham's five fairs. As a boy, Shelley himself was often brought 'a fairing' of gingerbread.

VII

Unhappily, Horsham has expanded greatly in the last few decades, and in doing so has lost much of its old-world charm. The heart of the town is still a maze of narrow streets and fascinating nooks and crannies, graced with many centuries-old buildings, while in the Carfax, where they baited the bull as recently as 1813, is the iron ring by which the wretched beast was tethered. Yet though the centre is still old, a considerable area is modern and busy. Horsham Park, a fine example of late seventeenth-century brickwork, remains, but the *Black Horse* is only a Victorian successor to the inn of the same name where the ' Pinks ', or Independent Tories, used to meet in the early years of the nineteenth century. A great many of Horsham's principal buildings, such as the Grammar School, founded in 1532, and the church of St. Mary, with its fine oak shingled spire, where the Shelleys are buried, were either rebuilt or heavily restored in that period.

Unquestionably the most charming corner is the Causeway, where rows of old gabled houses and pollarded trees lead us from the hustle and bustle of the shopping centre to the quiet of St. Mary's Church.

VIII

Two or three miles to the south-west of the town, on the way to Itchingfield—where, appropriately, is sited a factory for the making of insect powder!—is the public school, Christ's Hospital, better known as the ' Blue Coat School ' on account of the long, blue coats and yellow stockings worn by the boys.

Founded in London by Edward VI as a direct result of a sermon which Ridley preached to the boy king on the hardships caused by his father's (Henry VIII's) Dissolution of the Monasteries, Christ's Hospital has given many famous men to the world, including Charles Lamb, Samuel Taylor Coleridge and Leigh Hunt.

The school removed to Sussex in the early part of this century, and is now accommodated in buildings designed by Sir Aston Webb on an estate of some 1,200 acres.

Horsham provides the perfect western gateway to St. Leonard's Forest and its two northern offshoots, Holmbush and Peasepottage Forests. From here we can either wander into the woods on foot, or encircle them by road.

The main road to Crawley—which passes within a mile or two of Rusper, in whose church is a medallion to Lucy Broadwood, and Ifield, burial place of Mark Lemon, the famous editor of *Punch*, who died here in 1870—takes us along the northern edge of Holmbush and Peasepottage Forests, but an infinitely better view of these Sussex woods is gained by branching off this road at Roffey for Colgate and the village of Peasepottage. The scenery hereabouts is delightful, and at Colgate it is possible to mount the Beacon Tower and look down from 481 feet upon a sea of oaks, beeches and firs, ashes, birches and sweet chestnuts. From this high vantage-point we can see right across Sussex, into Kent, Surrey and Hampshire, according to whether we face east, north or west.

At the same time an even quieter by-way skirts the southern edge of St. Leonard's, passing close by the ruins of the Jacobean mansion of Slaugham—a hamlet where Tennyson once lived—to join the Brighton Road at Handcross.

To the north of this road are two of the hammerponds used by the old iron-masters. The overflow of these ponds provided the power by which the great drop hammers employed for breaking the ironstone were operated. Wherever there was a suitable stream within close proximity of a good deposit of iron the lord of the manor would cause it to be dammed, and it is reckoned that at one time there must have been between one hundred and forty and one hundred and fifty such ponds in Sussex.

Just as on the downs one instinctively thinks of sheep, so in these Wealden forests we remember not only the men who felled the oaks for the ship-builders and for the construction of such buildings as the Tower of London and Westminster Hall, but also the iron-workers and the charcoal burners who provided the fuel for smelting, and who, in doing so, used so much of the precious oak that Queen Elizabeth was petitioned to curb their activities lest there should be insufficient left for building the ships to fight the Armada.

Even before the days of the Romans, iron was worked in the Weald, and though the industry declined almost to insignificance upon their departure, Sussex became once more the ' Black Country ' of the South in Tudor times, and remained so until the late eighteenth and early nineteenth centuries when Northern coal finally ousted Southern charcoal. Though the best deposits lay in the low-lying country nearer Kent, a number of links with the old industry are still to be found in the forests in the form of hammerponds, minepits, remnants of furnaces, or, simply, in such place names as Hammer Hill, Crooked Cinder Lane, Furnace Farm and Little Mill Close around St. Leonard's, and Little Forgefields, Furnace Wood, Cinderbank and Minepit Wood in the Ashdown district.

The iron-workers had two distinct methods of manufacturing their iron. By the ' bloomery ' process they could produce wrought iron of a steely nature such as could be forged without further treatment into such light articles as tools and small weapons; on the other hand the material needed for heavier pieces they had to cast in blast furnaces, and then convert into wrought iron by means of forges.

The Sussex blast furnaces were really a primitive version of those used in the industrial areas to-day, but Ernest Straker shows in his *Wealden Iron* that the bloomery hearths of the Weald were of an altogether different character. Here a slightly concave circular platform, perhaps nine feet in diameter, was made of rough sandstone. Surrounding this a gravelled pavement was laid to provide standing room for the workmen and a platform for the bellows. Alternate layers of charcoal and ore were arranged on the hearth, and the heap was covered with a thick coating of clay. The bellows—arranged in pairs in order to ensure a constant draught—were worked either by hand or foot, and had to be operated for several hours at a time. Gradually ' the purer constituents of the ore, mainly silica, remained above the iron as slag, and were in part drawn off through openings for that purpose '.

Whereas the bloomeries were set up by small streams, the furnaces required far more water, and so were built by the rivers and hammerponds.

As with most crafts, the iron-workers had a vocabulary of their own, and it is only by studying this that one can really appreciate the significance of some of these place-names. For instance, while ' mine ' was the word given to the ore itself, a ' minepit '—of which there are several in St. Leonard's—denoted an open quarry. ' Dyk ', ' flash ', ' gil ', ' spillway ' and ' pen pond ' were all connected in some way with water, whereas ' shaw ' and ' stumlet ' had to do with woods. So, too, the charcoal was always known as ' cote ' and the slag as ' cinder '. And so on.

Many of the old hammerponds—some of which covered more than twenty acres—are dry now; the rest are carpeted with lilies, thereby providing a picturesque memorial to an age of Wealden prosperity that is past.

Wild flowers are a beautiful feature of St. Leonard's Forest, particularly the lily-of-the-valley around which a legend is woven. Once, the story runs, a monster or dragon, more than nine feet in length and shaped like an axle-tree, haunted the forest. At the sound of man or beast it would raise its neck ' with great arrogancy ' and cast its venom ' a full four rods '. To but breathe of the poison was sufficient to cause an agonizing death, and many stories used to be related concerning the finding of the swollen bodies of men and dogs who had been bold enough to try and bring the creature to its doom. Happily, St. Leonard—after whom the forest is named—was more fortunate than the rest, and after a valiant tussle succeeded in slaying the monster. But his victory was not without blood-shed, for it is said that the lilies-of-the-valley mark the spots where the blood of the courageous saint was spilt, and will grow nowhere else in these woods.

This lovely forest is a land of legend. The country folk round about—some of whom cling as faithfully as ever to the custom of sticking pins into the ash trees to cure their warts— still warn riders about Squire Paulett, the headless phantom who springs up behind and hugs people to death. So, too, they declare that the nightingale has never been heard in St. Leonard's since that day when a temperamental hermit, irritated by the songster, laid a curse upon the bird!

2. THE BRIGHTON ROAD

Crawley, the terminal point of the route round Holmbush and Peasepottage Forests, is the half-way house on the Brighton Road—half-way between London and Brighton, that is.

In the old coaching days the romantic *George Inn*, whose unusual gallows sign still spans the highway, could provide sufficient accommodation to allow for the change of as many as fifty coaches a day. In that great coaching era when the Regent was busy turning Brighton into one of the greatest seats of fashion, every one of note who journeyed down from London passed through Crawley, from the rakish Lord Barry-more, who once took a couple of horses up the staircase of Mrs. Fitzherbert's house in Brighton's Steine, to Prinny himself, an admirable coachman, most 'adept with the ribbons', who once covered the fifty-six miles from Carlton House (his London home) to Brighton in four-and-a-half hours.

From early morning until late evening *The George* was the scene of constant hustle and bustle, and, from the lips of the strange medley of travellers, its landlords must have heard some of the wisest and also some of the silliest and most depraved talk imaginable. One joke that never seemed to flag concerned the length of Crawley's High Street at one end of which is *The Sun Inn* and at the other *The Moon*. Why, some traveller would ask, must this street be the longest in England?

Whereupon, as someone shouted 'Because it reaches from the sun to the moon', the company would fall to laughing and send the ostler hurrying for another round of drinks.

Equipages of every kind stopped either at Crawley, Friar's Oak or Handcross for a change of horses, but the little town drew not only those who were journeying to and fro twixt London and Brighton. Near-by Crawley Down, a little to the east, was one of the secret rendez-vous for the illegal prize-fights of the Regency period. No fashionable 'buck' would ever miss such events as these if he could possibly help it. Not even the prince himself could resist breaking the laws when so famous a bruiser as Tom Cribb—who lived at Crawley—was billed to fight, and was often to be seen among the vast concourse of dandies and blackguards that used to intermingle on this famous down.

Most of the great bruisers entered the ring here at some time or another, and Conan Doyle draws an imaginative picture in *Rodney Stone* of the excitement in Crawley on the night before Jem Belcher was due to fight. Every window of *The George* was aglow, while the long procession of lighted vehicles that converged on the town from London resembled 'a writhing serpent with golden scales'.

Crawley has certainly witnessed many varied scenes; many changes of fashion too. Where the spanking horses and carriages were once admired for the smartness of their turn-out, and the daring of those coachmen who raced their way through Crawley, covering the distance from London to Brighton with incredible speed, once provided an important topic of conversation, to-day the highlight of the year is the procession of obsolete cars which cover the same distance in the annual 'Old Crocks Race'.

Alas, Crawley is shortly to witness further and more serious changes as one of the chosen sites for the development of a satellite town.

3. EAST OF THE BRIGHTON ROAD

I

The Brighton Road forms a dividing line between the forests we have just explored and those of Tilgate, Worth and Balcombe. Though all these lovely beech woods run into each other, the three forests immediately to the east of this highway are now mostly enclosed, and so assume more the character of private parks.

Taking the Brighton Road once more as our base, we can work our way right round not only Tilgate, Worth and Balcombe, but also round Ashdown Forest, which marks the eastern limit of the Ridge.

From Crawley we follow the road to Three Bridges, the first town in Sussex to boast a railway station, and now, as a result, anything but pretty.

Worth, the ' capital ' of the forest bearing its name, is a mile or so away and is of particular interest on account of its church whose Saxon cruciform ground plan is the most complete in England. Standing close to the forest, approached by a lych gate, which opens into an avenue of trees, it contains many Saxon features in its masonry, including a circular eastern apse of the tenth century, finely proportioned chancel and transept arches, a series of two-light windows, each divided by a heavy circular baluster, in the nave, together with such interesting external features as ' long-and-short ' quoins at the corners, a double plinth whose lower stage projects beyond the upper one, and a Saxon string course, connected to the base by pilasters, which can still be traced round the greater part of the building.

Though a certain amount of restoration has been carried out, Worth Church is not only the largest, but probably also one of the finest examples of Saxon work now left to us, and so is a pilgrimage centre for antiquaries.

There are an unusual number of fine houses in this vicinity —substantial brick-built yeomen's houses of the fifteenth and sixteenth centuries, some of them tile-hung, some half-timbered, many roofed with Horsham stone: all well cared for and affording an atmosphere of well-tempered prosperity.

In Paddockhurst Park, in the forest area to the south-east, is the priory, containing an interesting collection of stained-glass windows recording the history of music, used by the monks of Downside, while in Crabbet Park, to the north, is the home of one of the greatest of all the iron-masters, Leonard Gale, owner of Tinsloe Forge, who bought the property in 1698. Not far from here, at Rowfant, is the Tudor house where Frederick Locker-Lampson, the Victorian lyricist, confidant of three First Lords of the Admiralty, made his Rowfant Collection of books and manuscripts by famous writers and poets.

II

At Crabbet Park we are on the edge of Crawley Down, a district now as renowned for its marbles contests as it once was for its cock-fights and prize-fights. Every village round about boasts its team of marbles players, who foregather every Good Friday in the courtyard of *The Greyhound* to contest 'the championships' as their forebears have done for 300 years.

These contests arouse such widespread interest that the results are sent to the far corners of the Empire for the benefit of those Sussex folk overseas who used to compete here in earlier decades.

On 'Marbles Day' several hundred people from various parts of both Sussex and Surrey will journey to Tinsley Green to watch these stalwarts play the 'ring taw' version of this medieval game on a ' bed ' that is said to have been used in no less than eighteen reigns. The busmen of Crawley, competing against the farmhands of Copthorne for the silver challenge cup, use the same terms—' flip an alley ', ' flick a tolly ', ' die shot ', and so on—as did the marbles players of ' Merrie England '. To many gathered round the rink such words are strange, yet few can fail to find amusement in the backchat—especially in the badinage between the two rival teams of Copthorne, the ' Sharpshooters ' and the ' Spitfires '.

As skilful in their battle of wits as in flipping their marbles, one team has been known to credit its captain with being able to flip a marble clean through a small cylinder from a distance of ten feet. Another once claimed that one of its members could hit a fly in flight on the forehead with one marble and then finish it off by directing a second at its heart!

III

Tinsley Green and Copthorne are adjacent villages on the Surrey border, the latter close to the road leading into East Grinstead, where some of the finest stained-glass windows are designed and made for churches all over the world in the workshops of the stained-glass artist, Mr. Geoffrey Webb. When last I was at East Grinstead I was able to watch a memorial window to the last war being executed here.

It is an object-lesson in fine craftsmanship to see how these craftsmen at East Grinstead cut and piece together the various coloured glasses to their own designs to form such translucent windows of exquisite artistry. The artist has to make three separate drawings of his design. First he makes an accurate scale draft which he colours and shades to give the effect for which he is aiming. From this he draws his ' cartoon '—a life-size sketch revealing only the outlines—and finally comes the ' cut-line ', a plan showing the shapes and sizes to which the various pieces of glass are to be cut by the glazier.

Laying each piece of glass in turn upon this ' cut-line ' the glazier cuts along the ' lead lines ' with a wheel cutter. Then, when each piece is cut to size and shape, the artist carefully arranges them in position on his glass easel, holding them firm by means of liquid wax. He then places his easel in an upright position against the light so as to give the correct effect and, with the aid of his sketch and cartoon, sets to work painting in his outlines and shadows.

When the pattern is complete, it is dismantled and each piece of glass ' fired ' in order to fuse the monochromes, after which the glazier cuts his grooved leads and patiently ' builds up ' the window as though it were a jig-saw puzzle, soldering the leads at each of the joints.

The stained-glass artist must study not only the architecture of his church, but also the aspect, and the effect which the weather is likely to produce with the years. For it is the light that shines through that plays the all-important part; and that light must always appear to shine brightly.

IV

One of the most important towns on the London-Eastbourne road, East Grinstead is a place of two expressions in that, whereas it has grown into an extremely busy centre, ruined in parts by the incursion of unattractive modern buildings, it nevertheless still possesses a number of architectural treasures.

Some of the old houses in High Street, with their dormer windows, crooked lintels, roofs of Horsham stone or mellow tiles and their medieval timbering, show that East Grinstead must once have been among the most charming towns in Sussex. While in the restored church—where there is a tablet to Charles Abbot, Lord Colchester, Speaker of the House of Commons during Napoleonic times, who lived near by—are rare concave fluted and octagonal pillars of the late Perpendi-

cular style such as may be seen in the great Cotswold ' wool '
churches of Chipping Campden and Northleach, although this
rare feature is also to be found in another Sussex church, that
of Alfriston.

There are many other fine buildings, including the *Dorset
Arms*, an attractive old coaching inn, and Judge's Terrace, so
called because the Winter Assizes were once held here. But
the glory of East Grinstead is Sackville College, founded as an
almshouse in 1609 by the second Earl of Dorset, member of the
great Sackville family of Knole in Kent, after whom the college
is named. Stone-built round a quadrangle, and containing
large mullioned windows and four exquisite old doorways, the
northern one of which bears the Dorset coat of arms and is
crowned by a lantern, these almshouses are a splendid example
of Jacobean architecture. There are two principal rooms—the
Chapel with original carved oak door, aumbry and lock, and
the Hall, once reserved for members of the Dorset family but
now used by the warden.

Among those to fill the role of warden here was the Victorian
hymnologist, John Mason Neale, who wrote at least forty-six
hymns, including *Jerusalem the Golden*, *O Happy Band of
Pilgrims*, and *Art thou weary, art thou languid*. Dr. Neale,
who died here in 1866, held the post for some twenty years,
during which time he founded St. Margaret's Convent in Moat
Road, though, alas, he was never to see the buildings completed, his death occurring within a year of the laying of the
foundation stone. Dr. Neale was one of the leading figures in
the Oxford Movement, and, on the centenary of this movement
in 1935 a stained-glass window containing his portrait, together
with likenesses of Nathaniel Woodard, John Keble, Walter
Farquhar Hook and Hugh James Ross, was placed in the
church.

Every evening at eight o'clock the curfew is still rung at
Sackville College.

Another pleasing link with the past is to be seen in an iron milestone telling us that East Grinstead is but thirty miles from Bow Bells. This milestone was doubtless made locally, since this town—once a burgage borough like Midhurst—was an important iron centre. There was an iron mine here before the time of William the Conqueror, and in the churchyard there are no less than four iron gravestones. Besides that, the district round about is particularly rich in place names connected with the industry, two of the more uncommon being Cansiron and Shovelstrode.

v

The ruins of another Jacobean home are to be seen in Brambletye House at Forest Row, less than three miles to the south-east of East Grinstead. The scene of a novel by Horace Smith—a Regency and early Victorian author who also amassed a fortune on the Stock Exchange—this once impressive mansion was deserted as long ago as 1683 when its owner, Sir James Richards, fled to Spain after being warned on a hunting expedition in Ashdown Forest that he was suspected of treason. As the house has never been occupied since, the ruins are now fragmentary.

Forest Row is by the banks of the infant Medway, and from here we can follow the river to Hartfield, another centre of the old iron-masters, who, when cut off by the swamps and mires of winter, often used to ' put up ' at the *Dorset Arms* here.

Every Good Friday an interesting dole ceremony is performed at Hartfield when the poor of the village receive a bounty over the tomb of Nicholas Smith, who lived here more than three hundred years ago. A man of gentle birth, Smith decided to test the generosity of the various Sussex villages round about by disguising himself as a tramp and journeying from one to another begging for food. To his disgust, he found that wherever he went he was treated with scorn and contempt. At Hartfield, however, he was shown every kindness. This so pleased him that he made his home here, and when he died left a sum of money to be divided annually among the poor.

All this country once belonged to the Sackvilles, whose seat, before they moved to Knole, was at Withyham, the next village east of Hartfield. All that is left of the great mansion in Buckhurst Park, to the south of the village, which they inhabited as far back as the days of Henry II, is the Perpendicular gate tower. A comparatively modern mansion—owned by Earl de la Warr, one of their descendants—has taken its place. But in the church—rebuilt in 1666 after a fire had seriously damaged the original fabric—is the Dorset Chapel where many of the family are buried, and here may be seen many memorials to the Sackvilles, including a monument by Flaxman to the fourth duke, who died in the year of Waterloo, and another by Sir Francis Chantrey to Arabella, Duchess of Dorset.

Withyham — whose lovely timbered Tudor farm-house, known as ' Duckings ', drew the praise of Richard Jefferies— was also the home of John Waylett, an itinerant bell-founder of the early eighteenth century, who used to travel round the country repairing the cracked bells of the village churches, setting up his temporary forges in the graveyards after the style of the craftsmen of the Middle Ages.

Two enchanting little villages lie to the west of Withyham —Groombridge with its pretty triangular green set on a steep hill leading across the Kentish border to Tunbridge Wells, and Eridge Green, seat of the Abergavennys, whose monogram is displayed over the doorway of many of the cottages.

The Abergavennys are the descendants of the Nevill family, who came to England with William the Conqueror, and at Eridge Park is preserved *My Ladye Nevells Booke*, a collection of forty-two pieces for the virginal by William Bird, the ' father of English music '. Written in the script of John Baldwin, the famous scribe of Windsor, and beautifully bound in Morocco, it is generally acknowledged to be the finest Tudor manuscript extant.

Lady Nevell, we are told, was ' the scholar of Birde ', and it is thought that the great music master gave the volume to his pupil in 1591. One of the most interesting pieces included in the work is *Sellingers Rownde*, a variation of one of the most popular tunes of the time—*The Beginning of the World*—and still a favourite item at Sussex folk-dance parties.

Crowborough—an unpleasantly overgrown town whose famous beacon constitutes the fourth Sussex high-point—lies almost immediately south of Withyham, and affords as excellent an eastern gateway into Ashdown Forest—home of one of the first greyhound coursing cubs—as does Horsham a western one into St. Leonard's.

VI

Whereas, technically, St. Leonard's is a chase—having always been in private ownership—Ashdown, as the former hunting-ground of kings and princes, is a forest in the true sense of the word. Here many of the medieval kings used to hunt the stag, and even when Edward III granted the forest, together with Pevensey Castle, to his fourth son, John of Gaunt, Duke of Lancaster—the son of one king and the father of another but never to reign himself—Ashdown continued to come under forest law.

In character, too, this sanctuary of bird life is quite different from the forests to the west. With its wide stretches of moorland, its ponds, lakes and swamps, where the bog pimpernel, marsh orchids and many other wild flowers abound, its little streams, weirs and mill-races, its noble avenues of chestnuts, and its parks of pine and rhododendrons, its scenery is altogether more varied, while some of the views from the heights are magnificent.

If we stand on high ground near the centre of this forest we find ourselves surrounded by as impressive a patchwork of forest scenery as is possible to contemplate. One way we see vast stretches of moorland, glowing with heather, furze and bracken, and sheep grazing by the wayside; another we see dipping fields of corn or ploughland dropping from our feet like giant saucers. Here we notice great clumps of oak, silver birch and beech—so dense that from a distance it is impossible to see their trunks or branches through the foliage; there, by contrast, we find single lines of trees dividing one field from another.

Though by far the greater part of the forest is moorland, the whole country rolls in such lovely dips and folds that few can fail to be stirred by the scenery hereabouts, while the south-western panorama is one of the most impressive in the county. Here the South Downs may be seen in their distant blue standing out as a noble ridge along the horizon, the ridge dark and gaunt, almost menacing, when the sky is overcast, yet sparkling silver when the sun is out.

Unlike St. Leonard's, Ashdown has no dragon, but it was once a hide-out for smugglers, and as such is still said to be haunted by various of these law-breakers who met their fate around the Crowborough district. One of these, they say, may still be seen of a night riding round the district on horseback searching for his lost kegs with the aid of a lantern.

VII

From Crowborough we can make our way along the sparsely populated southern side of these moorlands past Poundgate, Duddleswell and Nutley, and then cut up country by Pipping-ford Park and the Isle of Thorns to Wych Cross, which, with its fifteen acres of National Trust woodland property, virtually marks the western limit of Ashdown.

Wych Cross is but two miles south of Forest Row and stands on the East Grinstead-Lewes road. Dotted about between this highway and the Brighton Road are a few further villages that merit a visit for one reason or another—Horsted Keynes, with its picturesque mill and thirteenth-century church; West Hoathly, noted alike for its commanding views, its strange rock formation, known as ' Big upon Little ', and for its medieval priest-house of stucco and half-timber which, like the house at Ditchling, Henry VIII awarded to Anne of Cleves; Balcombe, in whose forest the skeletons of wild animals of prehistoric times have been unearthed; and Ardingly, where is a third public school founded by Canon Woodard. Near Ardingly is the restored late Elizabethan mansion of Wakehurst Place. Once considered among the most perfect examples of the period in Sussex, Wakehurst Place was the seat of the Wakehurst and Culpeper families, to whom there are monuments and brasses in the church. In one of these brasses—which must surely rank among the most interesting in England—Nicholas Culpeper, who lived here 400 years ago, is seen with his wife and eighteen children, his eight daughters in their tight gowns of the period lined up on one side and his ten sons with their long flowing locks on the other.

But perhaps the prettiest villages in this area are Lindfield, with its wealth of lovely architecture of all periods and its long main street climbing the hill from the swan-favoured pond at the bottom to the church at the top; and Cuckfield (pronounced ' Cookfield '), another place of lovely old houses and hammerponds. One of these houses—the Elizabethan mansion in Cuckfield Park—is said to be the original of Harrison Ainsworth's *Rookwood*, the novel which gave the author his first success and made Dick Turpin famous for a ride which, in fact, he never undertook. Whether or not there is any justification for linking this house with Ainsworth seems doubtful, for though he must have known Cuckfield Park, he nevertheless sited this hall in Yorkshire. Shelley certainly knew the house, and Cuckfield is one of the few Sussex places mentioned by him.

Andrew Boorde, variously writer, physician, Carthusian monk and confidential missionary of Thomas Cromwell, who travelled extensively throughout the greater part of the world in pursuit of his many callings, was born at Cuckfield in 1490.

Bolney, the starting-point for our exploration of the Wealden forests, is less than three miles from Cuckfield.

CHAPTER TEN: Down the Ouse to Newhaven

A LITTLE to the north-west of Lindfield and Cuckfield, in St. Leonard's, the River Ouse finds its source. A network of small nameless streams flow into this river at various points from the southern slopes of Ashdown, Balcombe and Worth, so that together the Ouse and its tributaries provide the principal forest drainage.

From its source to its mouth it loops and curls and twists and turns for thirty miles or so. Though for much of the way it is little more than a stream itself—and, indeed, never acquires any great width until it has passed Lewes—and though, like most of the Sussex rivers, it lacks the beauty of so many of the water-courses of other counties, nevertheless it traverses remarkably varied, if not always particularly attractive country. From the forests, where is it often concealed by the foliage, it passes into wide open plain; then, after cutting a passage through the chalk downs, it flows leisurely across a further plain to enter the sea at Newhaven.

It is a lonely river, too, in that along all its thirty miles it skirts only one town of any size—Lewes, the county's capital. For the rest, villages and small hamlets afford the only centres of population within near reach of its banks. Yet to those who love Nature it would never seem lonely. Said to be one of the routes followed by the migrant birds, it teems with wild life. Many uncommon visitors, including the hoopoe, bittern, golden oriole and rough-legged buzzard are reported to have been seen here in the past, while one may often catch a glimpse of a playful otter, splashing in the water, or, on land, of a badger, or ' brock ', stoat, fox or squirrel.

II

After passing to the north-east of Lindfield and Haywards Heath—the latter a singularly unattractive place, said to take its name from a highwayman called Hayward who used to 'operate' on its vanished heath—the Ouse swoops round the south of Sheffield Park, former seat of the Earls of Sheffield, whose mansion has been replaced by a modern building.

This lovely park, with its four lakes and its avenues of trees, has a place in the annals of cricket. The Sheffields were among the foremost patrons of the game during the latter half of the last century. In 1891 the third earl captained the team that visited Australia, and for many years it was customary for the 'Aussies' to start their tours over here with a match in Sheffield Park.

The first Earl of Sheffield, John Baker Holroyd, who bought the property in 1769, was a close friend of the historian, Edward Gibbon, and was the editor of the latter's *Miscellaneous Works*. Gibbon stayed at Sheffield Park on several occasions, and when he died of dropsy in 1794—the disease having been brought on partly through his over-eating and lack of exercise—Lord Sheffield had his body brought from London and laid to rest (as a memorial stone shows) in the Sheffield mausoleum in the partly Norman church at near-by Fletching, in which parish the park is situated.

Within easy walking distance of Fletching—the camping ground of Simon de Montfort's army before the Battle of Lewes—is Piltdown Common. Here, in 1912, part of the skeleton of the earliest known inhabitant of our island was found by Charles Dawson, geologist, solicitor and steward of the manor of Barkham, close by the east bank of the river.

The story of the discovery of this prehistoric being, who is thought to have lived in this corner of Sussex at least 250,000, perhaps even 500,000 years ago, is admirably told, and its significance fully explained, in *The Earliest Englishman* by

Sir Arthur Smith Woodward, the well-known anthropologist, who, over a space of several years, joined with Dawson in digging among the gravel and ironstone deposits for missing portions of the skull and helped the latter in piecing it together.

Charles Dawson—to whom a memorial stone has been erected on Piltdown—had made an important collection of reptile fossil bones in the Wealden sandstone some years previously, and so already possessed considerable experience of local geology. One day, when on his way to attend the Court Baron at Barkham Manor, Sir Arthur tells us, he was surprised to find some unusual brown flints on the road. On inquiry he learnt that the gravel containing these flints had been dug on the spot and that, in fact, two labourers were engaged at that very moment down a side lane gathering some more of this material.

When a suitable opportunity occurred, Dawson hurried from the court to the scene of the digging. Realizing at once that this gravel was part of a shingle bank formed by a river many thousands of years ago, he asked the men to save anything ' unusual '.

Dawson kept a watchful eye on their operations, and, at last, on one of his visits, one of the men took from his waistcoat pocket a piece of what he believed to be a coconut. This ' coconut ', he volunteered, had been complete when he discovered it, but since it did not seem to him to be anything out of the ordinary and was cumbersome, he had smashed it with a spade and tossed aside the remaining fragments.

Thus, with one blow was destroyed a head that had survived the Ice Age and the storm and tempest of thousands of years. Indeed, it was several years before Dawson, aided by Sir Arthur and a French priest, had found all the missing fragments and was able to reconstruct the skull.

This skull is now in the Natural History Museum, South Kensington, and in the museum of the Sussex Archæological Society at Lewes is a cast of this head of what Sir Arthur was pleased to call 'The Dawn Man'—an ugly creature whose features must convince all who see it, as it has now convinced the anthropologists, that we are, in fact, descended from the ape!

III

Facing Barkham across the river is the old glove-making centre of Newick, a pleasant village with a green and pond, in whose churchyard Viscount Brentford—better known as Sir William Joynson-Hicks, or 'Jix'—whose son, at the time of writing (1949), is Conservative Member for Chichester, was laid to rest in 1932.

Newick leads us westwards to the wide open commons of Chailey, whose white smock windmill—considered by many to be the most perfect in the county—together with the old workhouse, are now the home of the well-known Heritage Craft School for cripples.

Chailey itself is a little to the south of the common on a tributary of the Ouse known as the Longford Stream. But here we are getting a little away from the main stream, and if we would explore the east bank as well as the west, we should return to Piltdown and then follow the river down to Isfield, home of the Shurleys, whose Tudor mansion on a slope to the north of the village, close by an old Roman road, is now no more than a farm-house.

The Shurleys were among the most highly respected of the county's gentry—related to a family of the same name who were lords of the manor at Wiston—and in the lonely church on the north bank of an eastern tributary of the Ouse, not very far from the old paper mill, may be seen some of their tombs. The finest of these is to Sir John Shurley, who died in 1631, and who was, we are told, 'of a magnanimous heart, of an exemplary industry, of a justice beyond exception . . . stout in good causes, yea, and good in all causes'.

Sir John married twice, and so is depicted in an elaborate canopied tomb, lying in his gilded armour between his two wives. Guarding the trio from above are a number of cherubs who are ranged on either side of the family coat of arms. At the base the nine children of his first marriage (there were none by his second)—two sons and seven daughters—all dressed in robes, kneel in prayer. Both sons and two of the daughters died young, one of them in extreme infancy, and are therefore carrying their skulls.

Beyond Isfield the country grows steadily less wooded, yet the way down to the next hamlet of Barcombe Mills, where the old Iron River flows almost parallel with the Ouse, is none the less soothing for its confluence of streams. From north, east and west they wind their way across the lonely meadows to join their parent, thereby affording a scene that is delightful for its pastoral simplicity, especially when viewed against the down-land background to the south—a scene that stirred Cowper to write:

> Here Ouse, slow winding through a level plain
> Of spacious meads, with cattle sprinkled o'er,
> Conducts the eye along his sinuous course
> Delighted.

A toll-bridge takes us across the river into Barcombe village, and from here we can join the main Lewes road by following a lane through Hamsey down to Offham. Here we are on the edge of the downs once more with Plumpton—once the property of Earl Godwin and now, like Lewes, famous for its race-course—the only village separating us from Ditchling Beacon, to the west.

Here, on the northern slopes, by Plumpton Place, may be seen a large ' V ' of trees which a number of local inhabitants planted in 1887 to commemorate the golden jubilee of Queen Victoria.

To-day no more than a small, but charming, brick and flint manor-house, standing on an island on one of three lakes,

Plumpton Place was originally a moated grange with a draw-bridge, and is popularly associated with Leonard Mascall.

An agriculturist of Henry VIII's time, Mascall wrote and translated many books on such country subjects as fishing, ' the Government of Cattell ', the grafting of fruit trees, and so on, and it is claimed—though without substantiation—that at Plumpton Place he introduced into England both the carp, which he set to breed in the moat, and the golden pippin apple, which he planted in the grounds.

Plumpton is also the reputed birthplace (some say he was a native of Rottingdean) and boyhood home of one of the most remarkable of all the downland shepherds—John Dudeney. In 1790, at the tender age of eight, young John set off for the hills to follow the calling of his forefathers. Though his pay comprised only the earnings from the wool and lambs of but one of his master's sheep, he was able to earn a little extra money by catching wheatears with the aid of traps which he set under the turf. These birds he sold to the gentry at about three shillings a dozen. Out of these humble earnings he managed to set aside a few shillings each year which he then spent at the various Lewes fairs on books.

At seventeen he was fortunate in obtaining a better post on the downs near Kingston, a few miles to the south of Plumpton, beyond the village of Falmer, where he earned the princely sum of £6 a year. Here, by his sheep walk on Newmarket Hill—a land rich in tumuli and sarsen stones (the latter known as ' grey wethers ' for their likeness to the sheep when seen from afar)—John Dudeney excavated a cave in the chalk to serve as a study and library, which he concealed with a large flint stone. Day after day he would retreat here to teach himself all those things which to-day he would have learnt at school —and much more besides. At last, after several years of study on Newmarket Hill—during which time he never once neglected his sheep—he realized his ambition by becoming a schoolmaster at Lewes, where, in 1852, he died an honoured citizen, co-founder with Mark Anthony Lower, one of the county's greatest antiquaries, of the local Mechanics Institute.

IV

Within the shade of Mount Harry, less than a mile from Plumpton, Simon de Montfort and the barons defeated Henry III and his followers at the Battle of Lewes on May 14, 1264, and so turned the tide of English political history. Though the hill does not take its name from the conquered king, as has so often been written, but from some heathen god, it is said that many of the pits in the turf hereabouts are the scars of that hard-fought struggle to regain the rights granted by Henry in the *Provisions of Oxford*.

When Simon de Montfort reached Fletching on his march from London, he sent the Bishops of London and Worcester as emissaries to Henry III and his royal army, who were then encamped at this spot, promising him that the barons would end the war if the king would only agree to banish certain of his counsellors of whose influence they disapproved. As an extra inducement to avoid further bloodshed, Simon de Montfort offered to pay the king £30,000 by way of compensation for any injuries sustained in previous fighting in other parts of the country.

These offers being rejected, the army of the barons spent the greater part of the night in prayer for victory. After every man had knelt on the turf to receive the absolution from the Bishop of Worcester, Masses were said from midnight until daybreak in Fletching's church, then an exquisite building containing many altars, built only some thirty years previously in the then popular Early English style.

Shortly before sunrise this army—every man of which wore a white cross both on his breast and back—began their march on Lewes, arriving at Plumpton Plain so early that the king's men were either asleep or caught unawares.

Here, after kneeling again in prayer, Earl Simon mustered his forces into four divisions. The van he gave to the Earl of Gloucester, the left wing to Lord Seagrave, and the right to his own two sons, Henry and Guido. The rear he commanded himself. Henry III, on the other hand, divided his army into three, commanding the centre himself and giving the right wing to his son, Prince Edward, and the left to his brother, Richard, Earl of Cornwall and King of the Romans.

The barons quickly gained an initial success by swooping down from the crest of the hill on the surprised forces of the king. Whereupon the impetuous Prince Edward hotly pursued the men under Lord Seagrave's command. Though the latter were severely routed, Prince Edward's daring soon proved to be ill-conceived. Perceiving with delight the king's best seasoned troops pursuing the least accomplished of his own, Simon de Montfort at once threw in the full weight of his army, with complete success.

While Richard, Earl of Cornwall, fled to a windmill where he surrendered that evening to Sir John Bevis, the king himself retreated to his headquarters in St. Pancras Priory, and the disillusioned Prince Edward sought shelter in the castle. Meanwhile the barons continued their ' mopping up ' operations in and around the town so thoroughly that the battlefield was ' covered with dead bodies, and gasping and groaning was heard on every side '.

It is said that above 5,000 fell in this bitter conflict, many of them dying under the weight of their armour as they lay wounded; some sinking in the surrounding marshes, too weak to rise again; some drowned in the Ouse. Many of Earl Simon's men were interred under the nave at Fletching, but those of the king's army were buried where they fell. Indeed, when the railway was cut through the hills here in 1845 some fifteen wagon-loads of the bones of these victims were unearthed, thus fulfilling the prophecy of George Sotheby:

There, after length of time, the peaceful swain,
Who ploughs the turf that swells o'er armies slain,
Shall cast, half gnaw'd with rust, high pikes in air
And hollow helms that clash beneath the share :
And, 'mid their yawning graves, amazed behold,
Large bones of warriors of gigantic mould.

The following day Henry III signed the *Mise of Lewes* in his priory retreat, in which he again promised to respect the *Provisions of Oxford*, the treaty having been negotiated by two friars of the Lewes Grey Friars, acting for the barons, and two monks of St. Pancras Priory for the king.

Henceforth Simon de Montfort, the Earl of Gloucester and the Bishop of Hereford were to appoint nine councillors to nominate the various ministers of state, and parliament was to include a number of barons, bishops and abbots together with four knights from each shire and two representatives of each of a number of named towns.

Thus, at the conclusion of one of the most important battles in English history, the seeds of our democratic parliamentary system were sown at Lewes with the victorious Earl Simon its first principal administrator.

v

All that remains of St. Pancras Priory on the slopes of Southover, where Henry III signed this historic deed, are some fragments of the church, some stones of the great gate of Sussex marble, part of the hospitium, which now serves as the parish church of Southover, the south wall of the refectory with its ' double-splayed ' windows and winding stairway, and sections of the dormitory and its annexe, the rere-dorter, as well as the infirmary chapel.

The priory was dissolved by Henry VIII in 1538, but it was Cromwell who brought about its almost complete destruction. His original reports, still extant, reveal that he intended to preserve the prior's lodgings as a residence for his son, Gregory,

who had married Jane Seymour's daughter, and that he employed an Italian engineer to destroy the rest of the buildings
by undermining the walls with wooden props which were then
ignited.

Alas that this should have come about, for St. Pancras Priory
was part of the history not only of Lewes but of Monastic
England. The first Cluniac house in the country, it was
founded in about 1077 or 1078 by William de Warenne—who,
as one of the faithful followers of William the Conqueror, was
awarded the Rape of Lewes—and his wife, Gundrada, still
believed by many to have been the Conqueror's daughter.

After some ten years energetic work organizing their rape,
William and Gundrada decided to take a holiday in Rome,
partly by way of a rest and partly, as was the custom of the
noblemen of those times, to receive the blessing of the Pope and
thereby become absolved of any past sins. Since, however,
conditions on the Continent were then somewhat disturbed,
they failed to reach their destination, but, instead, stayed in
Burgundy where they visited the famous Abbey of Cluny, then
the great European centre of religion and art and the headquarters of a movement for monastic reform.

De Warenne and his wife were so impressed by all they heard
and saw there that they decided to found a Cluniac house at
Lewes, and obtained the consent of the abbot to bring back
with them a number of monks. Upon their return home they
then proceeded to build their church at Southover on the plan
of the Cluny abbey—a splendid building containing twin
western towers, no less than thirty-two pillars, double transepts,
each with its chapel, and a ring of seven further chapels at the
apsidal eastern end. In addition to this church, which is
believed to have been of greater length and altogether more
splendid than Chichester Cathedral, they built a chapter-house,
frater, dorter, rere-dorter and warming-house, all complete
with cellars, kitchens and such like.

In 1098 the church was consecrated by Ralph, Bishop of

Chichester, in the presence of a number of other bishops. Thus the Cluniac order was established in England for the first time, and this, its first house, soon became the parent of six daughter houses at Castle Acre, Clifford, Farley, Monks Horton, Prittle-well and Stanesgate.

Unhappily, neither of the founders lived to see their great work completed. Gundrada died in child-bed in 1085, and her husband followed her to the grave three years afterwards. But both were later buried in the priory. When the railway was cut through the valley here, their two lead coffins were discovered, and their bones are now preserved beneath the beautiful tomb-stone of Gundrada in Southover Church.

VI

Lewes Castle, which de Warenne built in so strategic a posi-tion on the hill-top guarding this river valley, protected by two artificial mounds, one to the west of the town and the other to the east, is also sadly ruined. All that is left are part of the walls (ten to thirteen feet thick at the base) of one of its two shell-keeps, the south arch of its early Norman gate, the im-posing barbican of knapped and squared flint-work—said to be one of the most perfect examples in the country—which the eighth and last Earl de Warenne built in the early fourteenth century, and the tilt-yard, now one of the few bowling greens where ' crown bowls ' is still played.

This castle, whose ruins are still remarkably impressive con-sidering how little is left, was numbered among the greatest strongholds of feudalism in the country, and its lords—who enjoyed the titles of Baron of Lewes and Earl of Surrey—were among the most influential.

One of the de Warennes commanded King Stephen's army at the Battle of Lincoln and later went on a crusade to the Holy Land; another, who was instrumental in forcing King John to seal the *Magna Carta*, also played a prominent part in the great baronial struggles in the Welsh border country, and was cup-bearer at the coronation of Queen Eleanor in 1236. John de Warenne was one of the barons who opposed Simon de Mont-fort at the Battle of Lewes, and for his loyalty to Henry III became a favourite of his impetuous son, Edward.

Each generation saw Lewes Castle increase from strength to strength. Yet, with the death of the last de Warenne in 1347, it ceased to be even a residence, and the two titles passed to other families. While the Howards, as we have seen, later inherited that of Earl of Surrey, the Barony of Lewes is now shared by the Duke of Norfolk, Earl de la Warr and the Marquess of Abergavenny.

Worse still, in 1620, the greater part of the castle was dis-mantled and the materials sold to the people of Lewes at four-pence a load.

VII

Fortunately the barbican was preserved almost intact, and a near-by building—a lovely sixteenth-century building, timber framed with Georgian front and containing such varied archi-tectural features as a stone fireplace dated 1579, a Georgian stairway, and a Charles II ceiling and landing—is now the museum of the Sussex Archæological Society.

One of the most interesting museums in the country, it con-tains an extraordinarily wide variety of links with the county's past. Prehistoric flint implements and antler picks from Ciss-bury, Blackpatch and Harrow Hill; pottery and worked chalk from Whitehawk, above Brighton; and early Iron Age metal from the hill-forts of the Trundle and Mount Caburn; a Roman helmet salvaged from Chichester Harbour; grave ornaments from the Saxon cemeteries at Winton Street, near Alfriston, and Saxonbury, near by; two Ancient British canoes, both of which were found near the Arun, one by South Stoke and the other by Burpham; medieval domestic implements in pewter, brass and glass, together with a number of ornaments and steelyard weights of the same period; and a remarkable collection of Sussex iron-work, including some of the railings made for St. Paul's and the hammer and anvil from the old iron works at Etchingham; these and countless other relics every bit as interesting may be seen in the Barbican Museum to help tell the story of Sussex.

Nor is this the town's only museum of importance. The hall of Anne of Cleves House—once the property of Henry VIII's consort and believed to have been built out of the materials from the ruined priory—is hung with the heraldic shields and arms of the principal Sussex families, and contains a fine series of tapestries from Halland, near Uckfield, which were made in Lambeth as copies of Brussels work.

Here, too, is a map showing the sites of all the Sussex furnaces and bloomeries. And there are further links with the iron industry in the form of firebacks, irons, spits, cranes, keys and so on.

VIII

With Celtic fields and the long barrows and tumuli of the prehistoric dead riddling the downs to east and west, Lewes may well claim to be one of the oldest towns in England. On Plumpton Plain, to the west, near the scene of the great Battle of Lewes, the men of the Late Bronze Age had their settlements, and, as deduced from the discoveries there, may well have been the first in Sussex to use the plough; on Mount Caburn, to the east, those of the Iron Age built a hill fort.

Mount Caburn, Mr. Curwen tells us, appears to have dominated the whole downland area east of the Adur at one time, and is peculiar in having double defences on the north side, the outer one of which is apparently of a slightly later period than the inner one. Though not so large as some of the other Sussex hill settlements, it was, nevertheless, the last to be abandoned.

In this hill city of something like three-and-a-half acres some 200 to 300 people are believed to have lived in a little over 50 huts of wattle-and-daub, and from the objects found in the pits, Mr. Curwen is able to give an impression of the life of the inhabitants.

Well prepared for attack, they were lucky, it seems, to be able to live in peace. They were particular about their appearance, the women wearing ornate brooches with bronze clasps and the men shaving with iron razors. They kept horses and dogs and delighted to hunt both the red deer and the wild boar which then frequented the Wealden forests. Beef, mutton and pork formed the principal feature of their diet, and they did their cooking by means of heated stones.

Unlike the settlers on Plumpton Plain, these hill folk were not farmers. Thus, they had to buy their corn, milk, and such of their meat as they did not kill themselves from their neighbours. To pay for such commodities they would smelt bronze in crucibles, and make ploughshares, sickles, billhooks and other tools of iron, fitting them with handles fashioned out of the antlers of the deer. In addition, they spun wool, wove cloths and turned pottery. In short, they established, like the men on the Trundle, a recognized manufacturing centre, and had no difficulty in finding a ready market for their goods.

Just how early Lewes itself was first inhabited is impossible to say, but it was certainly a place of considerable importance long before the landing of the Conqueror and the arrival of William de Warenne. By the time of Athelstan it already boasted two mints, and in the reign of Edward the Confessor, when Earl Godwin was lord of the manor, its citizens were required to pay £1 towards the cost of munitions whenever the king's fleet put to sea. Moreover, the *Domesday Book* shows that towards the end of Saxon times the people were subject to a number of unusual customs and dues. If a man committed murder, for instance, he was set free on the payment of a fine of seven shillings and fourpence; on the other hand, where adultery was committed both parties were expected to forfeit eight shillings and fourpence, the man paying his fine to the king and the woman hers to the archbishop.

Even though its military significance waned with the departure of the de Warennes, this lovely old-world, still partially walled-in market town on the hill-top—once the scene of many fairs and still boasting a Monday cattle market—has the proud distinction of being the chosen one of the six rape capitals to become the county town, governed by a town council whose roots lie in the Merchant Guild of early Norman, or perhaps even Saxon, times.

IX

Lewes, with its seven churches, is one of those towns whose streets and alleys speak of age. Almost every corner has its little bit of local history. There is Juggs' Borstal, the pathway across the downs along which the Brighton fishwives, known always as 'Juggs', used to make their way to the market in Fisher Street in the days when they were forbidden to sell their fish in their own town. There is Pipe Passage, named after a clay pipe factory that used to be sited here, and Fair Place in Cliffe where, every year on the feasts of St. Matthew and St. Mark, they held their three days' fair. Then, too, there is Keere Hill, an incredibly steep cobbled way leading to Southover, down which the Prince Regent, as Prince of Wales, once drove a coach at full speed for a wager and was lucky not to have broken his neck!

As we wander through Lewes, in and out of the labyrinth of old houses—some of them particularly fine examples of Elizabethan architecture, as, for instance, Bull House, Southover Grange, Shelleys and Pelham House—we think of some of the famous people who have been associated with the town at various times—Lord Howard of Effingham who lived in High Street, and Dr. Gideon Mantell, one of the greatest authorities on prehistory, who was born in Castle Place in 1790; the diarist, John Evelyn, who, as a boy, lived with his grandparents in Southover Grange at the foot of Keere Hill; Richard Cromwell, who beat a hasty retreat from the town by boat as soon as he heard of the Restoration; ' Sea Water ' Russell, who first made Brighton; Tom Paine, the Radical son of a Quaker stay-maker and author of *The Rights of Man* and *The Age of Reason*, who, while living at Bull House, formed his political ' Headstrong Club ' at the Elizabethan inn, *The White Hart*; and the Duke of Newcastle, head of the Pelham family, who led a similar Whig group in the New Coffee House, now called Newcastle House after him. . . .

We think of the Nonconformists of the seventeenth century, who conducted their clandestine meetings in the town, supported by the principal tradespeople; and of the Georgian dandies, Sir John Lade among them, who turned Lewes into a minor fashion centre and refronted so many of the houses, particularly those in High Street, replacing the original casement windows with sash ones.

First and foremost, though, we remember the Marian martyrs who, after being confined in the cellars of *The Star*, upon whose site the town hall now stands, were burnt at the stake in this High Street. Seventeen men died for their Protestant faith here between the years 1555 and 1557, and in the last of the four martyrdoms no fewer than ten were consumed in the same fire.

A monument stands to their memory on Cliffe Hill, but the people of Lewes remember them in a more sensational fashion by displaying ' No Popery ' banners at their famous November Bonfire Ceremony.

x

Though, as elsewhere, both the Gunpowder Plot and the landing of William of Orange are commemorated on November 5, it is the martyrs and the thought of Pope Paul IV—who, encouraged by Bloody Mary, sent them to their doom—who have helped to make this night of nights at Lewes the most elaborate of the kind in England.

At one time feeling ran so high that Lewes became the scene of serious rioting on such occasions. To-day it is a well-organized affair, guided by a Bonfire Council and arranged by no less than five societies, the Lewes Borough, Commercial Square, the Cliffe, Landport and South Street. Yet the ceremony has lost none of its significance, nor its splendour, and draws people from miles around.

Each society arranges five or six processions and tableaux, and it is an unforgettable sight to watch these men, women and children—perhaps three hundred and more of them—in their strangely varied costumes threading their way through the streets by various routes, all carrying their torches of burning tow, to the chosen spot for the burning of their effigies. For hour after hour, from somewhere about 6 p.m. until close on midnight, the bands will play them on their way.

In the old days a lighted tar barrel used to be rolled through the streets to the common danger of all; to-day they keep alive this old tradition in less harmful fashion by hurling a similar barrel into the River Ouse.

While each society naturally carries its effigies of Guy Fawkes, two of these bodies still choose to burn a likeness of Pope Paul as well, and another also burns Catesby. As each of these fires is lit in various corners of the town, some at the hill-top, others down below, at the end of the ' Grand Procession ', Lewes is literally aglow.

But Bonfire Night at Lewes has not lost its semi-religious flavour. Each society has a number of clergy in its procession, and one or two appoint their ' Archbishop '. The Suffragan Bishop of Lewes himself sometimes takes part, and as the fires burn brightly the proceedings are invariably brought to a close with the chanting of special Bonfire prayers and the singing of

The Barbican, Lewes Castle

The Gatehouse, Battle Abbey

the National Anthem and such songs as *Rule Britannia, Auld Lang Syne* and *Sussex by the Sea.*

XI

Like Chichester to the west, Lewes is an excellent centre for exploring the surrounding countryside, and before we continue southward to Newhaven there are three villages to the east of the Ouse that are well worth a visit if only for their interesting associations—South Malling, now a northern suburb of Lewes, Ringmer and Glynde.

It was at the deanery which Archbishop Theobald founded at South Malling in 1150 as a college for a dean and six prebendaries in place of a Saxon monastery that the murderers of Thomas à Becket are said to have sought shelter after the assassination in Canterbury Cathedral. Though all too little is known of their activities here, a curious legend has survived that tells how, as they flung their armour on to the table with an air of contentment, the table bounced into the air and flung everything to the ground.

The deanery, like the priory of St. Pancras, was dissolved by Henry VIII, but South Malling still has the church which Evelyn's grandfather, John Stansfield, built in 1628. The diarist was a boy of eight at the time, and he relates in his diary that he helped the masons to lay some of the first stones. According to the registers one of the first men to be married in this church—where, incidentally, there is a memorial to Dr. Richard Russell—was John Harvard, who set sail for America in 1637 to found the famous college that bears his name.

Harvard's wife, Anne Sadler, hailed from Ringmer, but a few miles to the east, and by a strange coincidence this pleasant wide open village, clustered round a green—the green where Gilbert White discovered the tortoise whose activites he described in his *Selbourne Notes*—was also the birthplace of

Gulielma Springett, wife of William Penn, the founder of Pennsylvania. Though Anne Sadler had left for America before Gulielma was born, it is more than likely that their respective fathers were well acquainted, since John Sadler was Ringmer's rector at about the same time as Sir William Springett was its squire.

As Penn's father was an admiral, so was Gulielma's a soldier. A staunch Puritan, Sir William was killed at the Siege of Arundel a few months before his famous daughter was born, and in Ringmer Church—where there are many seventeenth-century monuments and brasses to the Springetts—may be seen his bust.

According to E. V. Lucas, Sir William's father, Sir Herbert Springett, was one of the Sussex squires who used to go to church in a carriage drawn by a team of oxen. At the time he wrote his *Highways and Byways* volume (1904) these beasts were still used for ploughing the fields around here, and Lucas records the dangers that beset the blacksmiths whose job it was to shoe the oxen—' to protect the smith from their horns they have to be thrown down: their necks are held by a pitchfork, and their feet tied together '.

The third village, Glynde, is of note as having been the home of Henry Brand, first Viscount Hampden, who was Speaker of the House of Commons from 1872 to 1884, of Lord Wolseley, and of John Ellman, the greatest of all the South Down flock masters. It is also of interest on account of the unique opera house of Glyndebourne near by.

Born at Hartfield in 1753, John Ellman was the Robert Bakewell of the South Downs. He moved to Glynde in 1780 where, on 580 acres, he kept 700 ewes, rams and wethers in winter and more than double that number in summer, and in the next 49 years probably did more than any other man to improve both the meat and wool value of this breed. Arthur Young, who often inspected his flocks, was generous in his praises, while to-day the Southdown Sheep Society acknowledge him as the

'Father' of the Southdown, a breed long popular in New Zealand, the United States, and all the other sheep-breeding countries.

But Ellman did more than develop the 'Speckle-legged heath breed' into the full-faced sheep with well-set shoulders, wide and deep chest, and fleece of remarkably fine texture, that graze the hills to-day. His flocks won such widespread admiration that his Glynde rams were soon much sought after. As time went on and Ellman won more and more prizes at the various sheep fairs of Sussex and elsewhere, farmers came from all over the country to consult him. Likewise, Ellman himself travelled far and wide. Among the notable breeders whom he was able to influence was no less a person than Coke of Holkham, the Norfolk squire who was created Earl of Leicester, and in 1791 he sold his lordship 500 ewes and lambs together with four of his finest rams.

Like Coke of Holkham, Ellman's chief interest lay in trying to advance his particular branch of agriculture, and he always did his utmost to help others to profit by his experiences—even when to give such help proved to his personal disadvantage. For instance, when any sheep that had been bred from his rams were entered at the fairs he would often withdraw his own entries rather than risk winning prizes at the expense of those with whom he had done business.

Like Coke, too, he was a kindly man and remarkably considerate to his employees. He lodged all his unmarried labourers under his own roof, and when any of them married he would provide them with sufficient pasture land for the grazing of one sheep and one cow and a certain amount of arable. Moreover, he built a school at Glynde for the education of his employees' children, and always saw to it that a plenteous supply of ale was brewed on his farm for those who worked for him.

Glyndebourne Opera House stands in a delightful parkland setting of woods, lakes and rolling lawns less than a mile to the north of the village of Glynde, and has been built on to the old manor-house of Glyndebourne. This fine house of mellow red brick—almost entirely rebuilt in Elizabethan times—still contains part of its medieval structure, including a certain amount of contemporary panelling.

In a most informative article in *Everybody's*, a few years ago, Lady Dunn gave an interesting account of how this unique opera house first came into being.

When Mr. John Christie inherited the property from his father, Glyndebourne already possessed a splendid music-room, an organ, and a musical library that was second to none in a private house. The Christies were undoubtedly musical; Mr. John Christie particularly so. He had enjoyed opera on the Continent, and was already anxious to see it developed in this country to a pitch where it could challenge that of the European centres, when he married ' a young opera singer with a beautiful voice and much personal grace, for whom the operas of Mozart seemed admirably suited '.

Remembering that Mozart wrote most of his leading roles for young singers, his marriage to Miss Audrey Mildmay largely inspired Mr. Christie to embark upon his venture, and when, in 1934, he produced his first ' Festival of Mozart Operas ' his wife naturally figured among the principal singers.

Mr. Christie did nothing by half measure. He engaged the services of Fritz Busch as conductor and Carl Ebert as producer, and he selected the finest singers in the world. ' These artists,' Lady Dunn says, ' came as guests to Glyndebourne, where they were able to have the many rehearsals without which no excellent opera is ever achieved. . . . They had the run and use of the old Manor and beautiful grounds with tennis and other sports for their leisure hours and they grew into an almost perfect ensemble.'

How successful was the venture can be seen in the fact that whereas the first festival lasted only a fortnight and comprised but two operas, the second extended over five weeks during which time four operas were produced. Before the third festival the opera house had to be enlarged to accommodate 600, and in 1938 two Italian operas—Verdi's *Macbeth* and Doni-zert's *Don Pasquale*—were included in the programme.

Though the last war caused Mr. Christie to close down on his enterprise, Glyndebourne is open again—a fashionable centre to which music lovers from far and wide will journey in the season to hear opera at its best in an opera house that is both acoustically perfect and delightfully situated, and whose stage is the largest and best equipped in the British Empire.

XII

As the Ouse widens out to the south of Lewes it pursues a lonely course once more, passing only a few scattered villages and hamlets on its passage to Newhaven. Near the east bank are Beddingham, below Mount Caburn, Tarring Neville and South Heighton, each of them pleasant in their way but of no special interest: near the west bank, Kingston, whose four-teenth-century church is dedicated to St. Pancras, the patron saint of the Lewes priory, and near-by Swanborough where there is a farm-house that was originally a grange of this priory; Rodmell, formerly the property of Anne Boleyn, where Queen Elizabeth delighted to walk along the river valley at a point known after her as Princess Gap; Southease whose enchanting little church contains a round tower surmounted by a cross; and the two villages of Telscombe and Piddinghoe.

These last two were once the haunt of smugglers, and at Piddinghoe the story is still told how once a band of smugglers, caught in the act of trying to haul a cask out of its hiding-place in the Ouse, tried to convince a Preventive Man that they were fishing for a cheese, which, however, proved to be none other than the reflection of the moon! But this story is by no means the copyright of Sussex, for I have also heard it in

Wiltshire where the menfolk are sometimes known as ' Moon-Rakers '.

These two villages are in the same parish, but Telscombe now belongs to Brighton. It was left to the ' Queen of Watering Places ' in the early years of this century by Squire Ambrose Gorham, who, in return for his generosity, stipulated that whenever the living falls vacant a broad-minded rector—one fond of sport and neither a non-smoker nor a teetotaller—must always be appointed.

XIII

Newhaven is both ancient and modern. Once known as ' Meeching ', Roman discoveries on the cliffs have led to the belief that it formed the terminal point of a Roman road from London. Besides this, it still has an old church whose chancel, a twelfth-century tower with an eastern apse, is one of the most remarkable in England.

As a port, however, it is comparatively modern, and in character extremely so.

Originally the Ouse entered the sea at Seaford, a little to the east, and it was not until somewhere about the time of Elizabeth, when the river changed its course to form a ' New Haven ' for shipping caught in the Channel gales, that we hear of it as a place of any maritime importance.

In its four hundred years since then Newhaven has steadily grown from a trading port, used principally for the export of oak from the Wealden forests and the import of wines and spirits from the Continent, into one of the leading cross-Channel passenger ports linking England with France. Yet its history has been entirely uneventful, and its only charm to-day lies in the romance of ships and the memories of the famous men and women who have embarked or disembarked here at various times.

Of all the travellers who have ever come to Newhaven

perhaps the two who created the greatest stir were plain Mr. and Mrs. Smith, who landed here on March 2, 1848. This couple, whose name was so very English yet whose accent was so unmistakably French, spent the night at the old inn, now known as *The Bridge*, and took train the following morning for Croydon, where one of Queen Victoria's own carriages awaited them.

Probably the people of Newhaven were no more than mildly puzzled by their accent at the time. For it was not until a little while afterwards that it was learned that this couple had, only a short time before their arrival, fled from the Tuileries Palace in Paris, and that ' Mr. and Mrs. Smith ' were, in fact, none other than Louis-Philippe and his wife, Marie Amélie, the fallen Emperor and Empress of France, seeking asylum in England, where they were to spend the rest of their days at Esher as the Count and Countess of Neuilly.

CHAPTER ELEVEN: *The East Sussex Downs*

I

EAST of the Ouse the South Downs drop down to the sea to end their long journey through the greater part of the county some twelve miles farther on by Eastbourne. In parts even more bare and lonely than the Middle Downs, they possess a pastoral beauty such as can only be appreciated by exploring them by river valley and dene as well as by the main roads that more or less encircle them.

A mile or so along the coast road out of Newhaven we come to the old tide mill of Bishopstone—so called because the hamlet once belonged to the Bishops of Chichester—where William Catt used to grind his corn. The son of a small Sussex farmer, Catt, who was born in 1780, became, through his industry, one of the most prosperous of the Sussex millers. Like the shepherd, John Dudeney, he educated himself, and was not afraid of hard work. He married at the age of nineteen, and every morning he and his young wife would rise at 3 a.m., he to thrash his corn by candlelight and she to feed the poultry. Their holding was far too small to offer much scope, but, by scrimping and scraping and working themselves to the bone, the couple were able to save enough money to lease an area of waste land, together with the tide mill, from the Earl of Sheffield.

Much of this land Catt brought to heart by his own labour, and in his first year he grew so excellent a crop of oats that he earned sufficient to allow him to extend the mill into the largest of the kind in the county. Later, he increased the power of his mill by converting the rest of the scrub land into a reservoir.

As, year by year, William Catt—who brought up a family

of twelve—increased in wealth, so his reputation as a miller was enhanced. At close on seventy, he was sent to Paris to advise Louis-Philippe upon his flour mills, and when, two years later, the French emperor landed at Newhaven as 'Mr. Smith', the old miller was one of the first to welcome him in his exile.

William Catt is buried in the graveyard of Bishopstone's flint-built church—an enchanting little church, tucked away in a fold of the hills and boasting many interesting architectural features from Saxon to Early English, including a square Norman tower and a Saxon porch of 'long-and-short' work with a sundial bearing the name Eadric. There is also a curious slab stone with a cross on which the lamb and two doves are seen amidst entwining circles.

Beyond the tide mills of Bishopstone is a rather desolate stretch of country, badly developed and sadly lacking in charm. Indeed, it is not until we have passed Seaford—historic as one of the Corporate Members of the Cinque Ports Confederation and the site of a Roman cemetery—and its suburb, East Blatchington—burial-place of Henry Tracey Coxwell, who, with Dr. James Glaisher, made aerial history in 1862 by ascending seven miles in a balloon—and reach the River Cuckmere at Exceat that we really see the beauty of these eastern downs.

II

One of the smallest of the Sussex rivers, the Cuckmere is, nevertheless, considered by many to be the prettiest, and at Exceat—where they were still ploughing with oxen as recently as 1926—we are greeted by an unforgettable picture of the river winding its extremely leisured way across the Saltings in a series of noble loops to flow—or one might even say trickle—into the sea at Cuckmere Haven.

This district, from the Cuckmere to Birling Gap, a little to the east, was a famous haunt for smugglers, who followed a

definite technique. As the news was received that a ' run ' was
to be made at a certain spot on a certain night, all those not
averse to ' a present from the gentlemen along o' being good '
would be informed, either directly or in a roundabout way, so
that they could leave the doors of their stables and cart lodges
' accidentally ' unlocked. Later, when the owners had gone to
bed, their horses and carts would find themselves on the beach
with the ' gang ', who stood anxiously peering seawards for the
tail light of the smuggler's craft.

If the Preventive Men or Revenue Cutters were about, a little
light would be flashed from the beach warning the approaching
craft to stand out of danger. As soon as the coast was clear the
craft would come ashore, when all would be transformed into
stir and bustle as the cargo was hastily loaded into the carts
and on to the pack-horses for transport to the up-country hide-
outs. Speed was the keynote of their success, and Kipling gives
an excellent picture of the scene in his *Smugglers' Song* when
he tells of the

> Five and twenty ponies,
> Trotting through the dark,
> Brandy for the parson,
> Baccy for the clerk,
> Laces for a lady,
> Letters for a spy.
> And watch the wall my darling
> While the Gentlemen go by.

By the morning all would be seemingly normal again—the
' gentlemen ' making their way to work as usual; the horses
safely returned to their stables along with a keg or some other
present for the borrowing.

It was, of course, understood that those who were ' good '
would be suitably rewarded. Thus, as an early nineteenth-
century writer says, ' Every now and then a fisherman's great
boots were found to be stuffed with French lace, gloves and
jewellery, or a lady's petticoat to be quilted all through with
silk stockings and lace. Here and there a nice-looking loaf of

bread was found to have a curious kernel of lace and gloves; and a roll of sail-cloth turned out to be a package of gay lute string.'

Though men of all walks of life were in 'the trade', the smugglers were by no means romantic. To each other they were loyal, but to those who hindered them, and especially to 'informers' they could be entirely ruthless, and, as Kipling's warning might suggest, those who did not actually connive were wise to keep silent:

> If you wake at midnight and hear a horse's feet
> Don't go drawing back the blind, or looking in the street.
> Them that asks no questions
> Isn't told a lie.
> Watch the wall my darling
> While the Gentlemen go by.

The coastguards and Excise officers needed to be both daring and spry. For as well as being 'tough' the smugglers were wily. Even the 'lieutenants' in charge of the coastguards were sometimes deceived. At one village, for instance, the older inhabitants still tell of a fair-sized house with a remarkably concealed roof valley. The occupants became friendly with the lieutenant in their district and used to invite him to spend the long winter evenings with them. No sooner were they all comfortably seated round the fire, however, than the word was passed to the smugglers outside who at once proceeded to stow their contraband in the secluded valley, literally over his head!

The coastguards, too, could be wily, for when they seized contraband it was customary for an Excise officer to come over and condemn it by broaching the kegs into a 'French drain'. Before sending for him, however, they would sometimes see fit to cleanse the drain thoroughly and bung it up so that after his departure they could recover the condemned spirits for their own inward comfort!

III

Northwards along the Cuckmere Valley the scene is very peaceful with the cattle grazing in the lush meadows by the river and the downs rising stark, but friendly, on either side. Following the by-lane along the east bank from Exceat, we are soon within near reach of Westdean, where, tradition has it, Alfred the Great met his biographer, Asser, the monk who later became Bishop of Sherborne. A hamlet set in an oasis of elms and beeches, Westdean is really little more than a cluster of lovely old farm buildings, one of which contains in its fabric part of the flint walls with dressings of Caen stone of the twelfth-century manor-house of Charlston, which is thought to have been inhabited by one of the sons of William the Conqueror's half-brother.

Beyond Westdean the lane takes us through Litlington, another enchanting little hamlet of flint cottages with roofs of thatch, to Lullington, whose diminutive church with white weatherboarded tower surmounted by a cross stands in a field on the hill-side, lost in the trees, in one of the prettiest settings imaginable. Measuring only some sixteen feet square, and with seating accommodation for no more than twenty, Lullington's church has been described as the smallest in the country. It should be realized, however, that although services are still held here every third Sunday, the church we see to-day is merely the chancel of a considerably larger building the rest of which fell to ruin long years ago.

Lullington is now in the parish of the old glove-making centre of Alfriston on the farther bank of the river—haunt of one of the most notorious of all the smugglers' ' gangs ' who, under the leadership of Stanton Collins, had their headquarters in what is now the *Market Cross Inn*, where some of their secret hiding-places may still be seen.

IV

With its many mellow old houses and cottages, its stump of a market-cross sheltering under the branches of a spreading chestnut tree, its late fourteenth-century church impressively situated on a mound by the village green with, near by, a unique thatched clergy house of the same period—a humble, one-storeyed building with original roof rafters and clay floor, now the property of the National Trust—and its peeps of the placid Cuckmere flowing through the meadows, Alfriston is unquestionably one of the prettiest of all the Sussex villages.

Some consider it to be the oldest too. The site of a Saxon cemetery where some of the treasures in the Barbican Museum were found, it is named after a Saxon nobleman, Alfric, to whom Alfred the Great awarded the manor as a fief (land granted in return for military service). Alfred himself probably knew the place well, and, indeed, there is a local tradition that it was at *The Star* here, and not in Somerset, that he burnt the cakes. That, however, could never have been, for the oldest part of this fascinating little half-timbered, partly tile-hung inn, boasting many unusual carvings, goes back no further than the thirteenth century, while the greater portion of the building is dated about 1450.

Yet this little gem of medieval architecture—a section of whose roof is composed of solid blocks of stone, some of which weigh as much as two hundredweight—is not without its history. Originally the property of Battle Abbey, it is one of the last of the old pilgrims' hostels now left to us, and though smaller, comes into the same category as the famous *George Inn* at Glastonbury. Its walls have given shelter and hospitality to many a footsore pilgrim as he trudged eastwards across Sussex to worship at the shrine of St. Thomas à Becket at Canterbury, or westwards to leave his offering on the tomb of St. Richard at Chichester. They have given shelter to others, too, for when pilgrimages grew less fashionable, *The Star* became a recognized Sanctuary House, and, as such, afforded protection to criminals fleeing from justice.

But Alfriston itself was a pilgrimage centre once. Nearly two centuries before Alfred gave the manor to Alfric, the small monastery church of St. Andrew stood on that mound by the green where is now the village church, and here, in the closing years of the seventh century, they laid St. Lewinna, a Sussex woman and virgin martyr, to rest. For 300 years after her death people came to Alfriston from far and near to pray for her soul, and many miracles are said to have been performed at her tomb.

How or when the monastery fell to ruin is not known, but it was in the closing years of the fourteenth century that the present church began to arise in its place, and an interesting story has been handed down concerning the choosing of its site. It seems that the Prior of Michelham, who undertook the work, was anxious to build in a field known as the Seven Crofts. But each night the stones that had been laid by the masons with such care by day were hurled by some unknown hand over the roofs of the village to the field called the Tye where the old monastery church had stood. At last one wiser than the rest, seeing four cows lying together in the form of a cross in the field to which the stones had been removed, suggested that this must be a portent that the new church should be built to the cruciform design on the very spot where the cattle were resting.

So, Alfriston's imposing cruciform church arose in its present splendid position—a wonderfully proportioned edifice, referred to as 'The Cathedral of the Downs', containing some of the finest flint work in England of the period of transition from Decorated to Perpendicular and with a graceful shingled spire that stands out as a landmark from all directions.

Every Rogationtide a special service is held in this church and afterwards the neighbouring fields, folds and orchards are blessed.

It is perhaps particularly appropriate that the orchards

should be blessed, for the fame of Alfriston's apples has spread afar. From one raised in this village in 1800 a number of grafts were stuck in potatoes to keep them moist on the long voyage, and sent to New Zealand. Since when the growing of apples has developed into one of New Zealand's major industries, and, ironically, we are now pleased to import ' Alfriston ' apples from that country!

V

If, on leaving Alfriston, we keep to the west bank of the Cuckmere we soon join the main road to the north of the downs by Berwick—pronounced ' Ber-wick '—whose church contains a most interesting series of murals by three modern artists, Vanessa Bell, Quentin Bell and Duncan Grant.

Executed on canvas in their individual styles without any slavish copying of the medieval, these paintings are really splendid works of art. Many of the subjects portrayed by the artists of the Middle Ages—*The Nativity, The Annunciation, Christ in Glory* and *The Parable of the Wise and Foolish Virgins*—are all to be seen, and it is interesting to contrast them with the somewhat crude works of those earlier crafts-men who, of course, painted direct on to the stonework, adopting very often, as at Hardham, the media of tempora and oil painting.

Indeed, one of the most unusual features is the combination of the ancient and modern. For whereas the subjects are all traditional, many of the figures are likenesses of living people. Two shepherds from neighbouring farms are seen in *The Nativity*, for instance, while the Bishop of Chichester and the Rector of Berwick both figure in *Christ in Glory*.

This is the first Sussex church to be redecorated in this fashion and, as an experiment in brightening an otherwise rather uninteresting interior, has been adjudged favourably—and rightly so.

VI

The way westwards to Lewes from Berwick leads past Alciston, where there is a magnificent tithe barn and a farmhouse with a dovecote that once was a grange of Battle Abbey, to Firle Beacon, another link in the chain of downland warning-points. The views from this 700-foot eminence are so extensive that Augustus Hare, describing them in 1896, gave what must be one of the best expressions of the atmosphere of the downs ever written:

> We know not a more tranquillizing scene for the overwrought brain to rest upon than the prospect from the Downs on a fine summer's day—the true Copley Fielding landscape: here the many twinkling smiles of the ocean always a feast to look upon; there the slow-yoked oxen, with their peaceful pace and low-bent necks, teaching us in these fevered days of steam and electricity, a very lesson of patience and humility; there the bleating flocks browsing the sweet short pasture with their minutest wants cared for, and their least wanderings restrained, by that ever-watchful and sagacious guardian, the English sheep dog.

The horse has replaced the ox, and, in large measure, the tractor has succeeded the horse since then, yet otherwise the scene remains as tranquil and lovely as ever.

West Firle, home of the Gage family from the reign of Henry VI down to the present day, is in the shadow of the beacon. The Gages are descended from one of the Normans who fought at Hastings, and though they were never rewarded by the Conqueror to the same extent as the Montgomeries, the de Warennes or the de Braoses, two of them, at least, held important posts in Tudor times.

Sir John Gage was appointed Constable of the Tower of London by Henry VIII, and, in the reign of Mary, had as two of his prisoners the luckless Lady Jane Grey, and, while still a princess, Queen Elizabeth. Since Lady Jane was related to him by marriage, his unhappiest task as Constable must have been to preside over her execution.

His son, Sir Edward Gage, when a magistrate for the county, had the almost equally distasteful duty of apprehending the martyrs—a duty which, by all accounts, he performed with the utmost courtesy.

Sir Edward's son, also Sir John, married the famous Lady Penelope D'Arcy who, as a girl, loved three men, and, since she could not choose between them, promised to marry each in turn—and proved herself as good as her word! Widowed the first time at seventeen by Sir George Trenchard, she married Sir John, to whom she bore nine children; widowed again, she turned to her third suitor, Sir William Hervey, who outlived her.

But of all the members of this illustrious Sussex family the one likely to be remembered the longest is Sir Thomas Gage, who is said to have brought back a plum from abroad, planted it in the gardens of Firle Place, and so given us the greengage, which is named after him.

Sir Thomas Gage died in 1590, and in the church of West Firle, where there are several monuments and brasses to the family, he is seen in full armour with his wife and two daughters.

VII

Eastwards from Berwick a rather ugly, and often extremely busy main road takes us past a side lane leading to Wilmington and the famous 'Long Man'. This extraordinary chalk outline of a giant on the hill-side, measuring 240 feet from head to feet and carrying in each hand a stave taller than himself, is the only ancient carving of the kind in the county, and is seen on a sheer drop of the barren hills as a kind of menacing guardian over the ploughlands below.

Who cut this figure nobody knows. Since the downs hereabouts contain a large number of prehistoric sites, some believe that it may have been carved by the superstitious hill folk of the pre-Christian era in connection with some fertility practice; others, considering it to be less old, credit it to the monks of the near-by thirteenth-century Benedictine priory, whose impressive ruins—including part of the great hall, one of the largest barns in the county, and some lovely old doorways, one or two with carved fourteenth-century bosses—may still be seen.

This priory was originally a cell of the Grestain Abbey, founded in France by Herluin de Conteville, who married Arlette, mother of William the Conqueror. Wilmington's rather plain but pleasing church once belonged to it, and still boasts a monks' chancel with Norman windows. In the graveyard of this church is a yew tree which is said to have been planted more than 1,000 years ago over the tomb of a Saxon chief.

Wilmington has one other pleasing feature—a green where the privilege of 'ancient lights' is so carefully protected that to this day the tenant of one cottage is still called upon to pay a tax of a shilling a year for the right to have a window overlooking it!

VIII

Polegate, beyond Wilmington, marks the north-eastern terminal point of the South Downs, and from here we can either drop down to Eastbourne by a main road, or, which is infinitely preferable, cut through the hills along a dene, or dry valley, that takes us through Jevington down to Friston, home of the Selwyns whose Tudor mansion is now a farm-house, where we rejoin the road from Newhaven.

This dene is very lonely—just one quiet track passing through the hills, now climbing, now dropping, with hardly ever a house, let alone a hamlet—except, of course, Jevington—in sight. The only signs of life, very often, are the song of the birds and the purring of the tractors that draw the ploughs

across the downland slopes. There are no hedges; only occasional short lines of trees that stand out as gaunt silhouettes
against the skyline. And since there are no hedges, there are
no divided fields either, but just one immeasurably long and
wide stretch of down. Yet there is beauty in plenty—the
beauty of graceful contours, and no one can claim to have
seen Sussex in all her moods until they have journeyed through
this dene.

IX

Friston, headquarters of the Southdown Gliding Club, leads
into Eastdean, another extremely pretty village with a line of
flint cottages overlooking a sloping triangular green and a
partly Norman church set in a hollow, the latter approached
by a special kind of revolving gate, known in Sussex as a
' tapsell gate '.

There are a number of interesting pieces of craftsmanship
in Eastdean Church, including a Norman font which, though
restored, is one of the best in the country; a thirteenth-century
lead chalice and paten, found in the grave of a priest during
the restoration of the chancel; a fourteenth-century coffin slab;
a foliated stoup of the same period; and a seventeenth-century
oak pulpit.

But it is for one of its incumbents—Parson Darby—that
Eastdean is most noted. Distressed by the tales of the wrecks
that so often took place along the coast, one of Jonathan
Darby's first acts on taking up the living here in 1715 was to
hollow a cave out of the face of the cliffs between Birling Gap
and the old Belle Tout lighthouse, a little to the south of the
village. Here, above high-water mark—approached by a stairway carved out of the cliffs—he became the friend and saviour
of mariners in distress. There was no lighthouse in those days,
so each night when the seas raged, the parson would trudge
across the fields, set up a lamp in his cave so that it was well

visible at sea, and then wait inside lest his help be needed. In time ' Parson Darby's Hole ' became a familiar landmark to those at sea, and it is said that hundreds who might otherwise have drowned were saved by the humane venture of East-dean's vicar.

It has been suggested that he had other motives for building his cave. Some say that he was in league with the smugglers and used it as a hide-out; some that he welcomed it as a retreat from his wife who nagged him from morn until night, though this is difficult to reconcile with another story that the vicar and his wife are thought to have been the original ' Darby and Joan '. In any case it seems certain that he was essentially a good man, and it is kindest to think of him as the first to help sailors along this treacherous coast before the establishment of the lightship at Beachy Head.

The coast from Birling Gap to Eastbourne and beyond is quite different from anything we have seen hitherto. Where-as to the west of the county it is flat and sometimes inclined to be a little monotonous, from Brighton eastwards the land suddenly rises. From Birling Gap the great white chalk cliffs known as the ' Seven Sisters '—Went Hill Brow, Baily's Brow, Flagstaff Point, Rough Brow, Short Brow and Raven Brow— appear in a series of seven graceful folds to reach a height of 575 feet at Beachy Head and give the South Coast its tallest headland. These cliffs may be seen as far away as the by-pass road by Sompting on a clear day, and they constitute one of the best known of the Sussex landmarks.

The views from Beachy Head are very fine, but the magni-ficence of these cliffs—where the peregrine falcon nests and occasionally the raven is seen—can only really be appreciated by walking in their shadow along the foreshore at low tide when the many little jagged rocks at their foot—rocks that have caused so many wrecks and the loss of so many lives— are exposed.

Undoubtedly, the coastline here with the downs rising

behinds the cliffs is some of the best in Sussex. Fortunately neither cliffs nor downs are likely to be spoilt, for the greater part of this area is owned either by the National Trust or Eastbourne Corporation.

Eastbourne—famed alike for its schools and excellent sporting facilities—is a young town with only a few interesting old features or associations. Until a hundred years ago it boasted no more than a few houses on what is now Marine Parade, and it is only since 1860 that it has gradually grown into the third largest town in Sussex. Thanks, largely, to the good taste of the former Dukes of Devonshire, upon whose land much of Eastbourne is built, it is however, an extremely well-laid-out town, and its Corporation are keenly appreciative of the beauty which lies to their west, and are zealous to safeguard it.

CHAPTER TWELVE: *Around the Pevensey Levels*

I

AT Eastbourne we bid farewell to the South Downs, and as we journey north-eastwards to the low-lying plain and marshes of the Pevensey Levels we see Sussex once more in an entirely different light.

Few will take kindly to the Pevensey Levels. Bleaker and more barren than the Hundred of Manhood, and in parts no more than four feet above sea-level, they extend for several miles almost to the outskirts of Bexhill to the east and Hailsham and Herstmonceux to the north, their vast acres relieved only by a series of rifes and ditches—or ' dicks ', as they say in Sussex—designed to carry away the flood waters.

To the bird lover, however, they are of much interest, the shingly beach between Eastbourne and Pevensey affording an excellent observation post for studying not only the whimbrel and the oyster catcher—known respectively in Sussex as the ' titterel ' and the ' olive '—but also many species of plover and tern.

The surface of this beach, both here and farther east, is so rough that rather than plod wearily along it in the usual way, the coastguards attach pieces of wood, known as ' racksters ', to the soles of their boots to act as sledges, which allow them to skate smoothly over the loose shingle in a fraction of the time and with far less tedium.

Because of its low-lying nature this part of the coast has always been regarded as one of the county's greatest danger points whenever invasion has threatened. During the Napoleonic scares, when 103 Martello towers were set up along the shore from Sussex right round the East Coast to Suffolk, all but one of the 47 guarding Sussex were erected between East-bourne and Rye. Such towers, which were Spanish in origin, were designed to accommodate as many as twenty men and were claimed at the time to be capable of resisting the heaviest gunfire then known. Some of them cost as much as £15,000 to £20,000 to build, and when no longer required for defence purposes they served as outposts from which to spy upon the activities of the smugglers. A few of these towers still survive along this stretch, one or two of the less dilapidated being put to various uses.

II

It was at Pevensey, of course, that William the Conqueror, accompanied by his army of Normans in black chain armour, first set foot on English soil, and, on stumbling, grasped a handful of sand and made the well-known comment: ' See, I have seized the land with my hands! '

But Pevensey was already more than nine centuries old when William arrived that September day of 1066. As early as the third century the Romans enclosed ten acres of what had been an Ancient British stronghold, and built their great castle of Anderida here as one of a chain of about a dozen forts designed to protect the ' Saxon Shore ' between Southampton Water and The Wash against Saxon pirates and other would-be invaders.

After the departure of the Romans, Anderida was occupied by the Britons once more, but in 490, according to the *Anglo-Saxon Chronicle*, Aella and Cissa, the Saxon conquerors of Chichester, who took eight years to subjugate the country between the cathedral city and Pevensey, besieged the fort with such fury, we are told, that not a Briton within survived the slaughter.

When, in their turn, the Saxons were driven out by the Normans, William the Conqueror awarded Anderida to his half-brother, Earl Robert de Mortain, who built a new castle within the Roman walls and made Pevensey the capital of another of the county's rapes.

Thereafter the tide of fortune was to turn many times, and the castle pass through numerous hands. On four occasions it was besieged before at last it was deserted—in 1088 by William Rufus when Odo, Bishop of Bayeux, was plotting with Robert de Mortain to put Robert of Normandy on the throne; in 1147 by King Stephen when his rival claimant, Matilda, was in residence; in 1265 by Simon de Montfort; and, finally, during the Wars of the Roses when the White Rose of York tried to capture it from the Red Rose of Lancaster.

Pevensey was occupied by the Pelhams during the last siege, and, in the absence of her husband, Sir John Pelham, the castle was heroically and successfully defended by Lady Joan Pelham, who, in one of the earliest letters extant, gives her husband an inkling of some of the hardships she must have suffered and, by the nature of the wording, reveals something of the cool courage with which she endured them: ' And, my dear Lord, if it like you to know *my* fare I am here laid by in manner of a siege with the county of Sussex, Surrey and a great parcel of Kent so that I may not go out nor no victuals get me, but with much hard . . . Farewell, my dear Lord, the Holy Trinity keep you from your enemies, and soon send me good tidings of you. Written at Pevensey in the Castle by your own poor J. PELHAM.'

During those centuries of strife and stress many State prisoners were detained at Pevensey, one of the most notable being Joan of Navarre, who was detained here for nine years —on a charge of practising witchcraft on her stepson, Henry V.

Just when Pevensey was deserted nobody knows, but by the time of the Armada, when Drake gave the warning ' Look ye well to the defence of Sussex ', it was already in so ruinous a state that an order was given for it to be either razed or rebuilt. The ruins were actually sold for building materials, but, fortunately, demolition work was never started. So that Pevensey still possesses its proud monument to the past.

It lies a mile or so from the shore, beautifully set in the marshes—a ruined medieval castle with twelfth-century stone keep containing apsidal projections, part of the gatehouse, the dungeon in which prisoners were detained, the old well, and a number of other interesting features, the whole still enclosed in great part by the oval wall which the Romans built, together with ten of the bastions they provided for its protection. Some twelve-feet thick and twenty-eight-feet high, this wall is built of flint rubble, faced with sandstone and bonded with red bricks, and is set on a framework of wooden beams, which, in turn, are packed with flints and embedded in well-puddled clay.

A number of Roman relics in the form of tiles and coins and some five hundred catapult balls were found here in the early years of this century.

Sussex has few buildings older than Pevensey Castle. Yet the dangers that prompted the Romans to build Anderida have not lessened the need for a fortification at this vulnerable stretch of the coast, and in 1940, when invasion fears were uppermost once more, the castle was refortified and manned by the Home Guard.

III

Though the dangers remain, Pevensey itself has changed. Now only a small village a mile from the shore, enriched by a good Early English church and one or two fascinating old buildings such as the mint-house and the home of Andrew Boorde, whom we met at Cuckfield, and, of course, the castle ruins, it was once an island lapped by the sea. Never very large, it then possessed a reasonably good harbour, and was attached to Hastings as a Corporate Member of the Cinque Ports Confederation. The freemen of its port were styled 'Barons', but were apparently so simple-minded that Andrew Boorde—whose brother, Dr. Richard Boorde, held the livings of Pevensey and neighbouring Westham, an enchanting spot with the square tower of the church peeping over a half-timbered cottage with overhanging upper storey—wrote many jokes concerning them, sarcastically describing them as 'the Wise Men of Gotham', Gotham being then a manor in Pevensey.

Yet, for all their simplicity, they enjoyed the many privileges granted to the other Cinque Ports towns. As Pevensey was also capital of the rape, its people were exceptionally well favoured, and quite early in the Middle Ages were holding a seven-days' fair and a Sunday market.

The whole of the Pevensey Levels were then more or less under the sea, and it is reasonable to suppose that many of the neighbouring place names ending in 'ey' or 'eye'—Chilley, Manxey, Horse Eye, Whelpley, and so on—denote the positions of other islands. As the sea probably went almost as far inland as Herstmonceux, the Levels are virtually reclaimed land.

IV

Herstmonceux also has a castle, whose particular interest lies in the fact that it was one of the earliest to be constructed of brick and was the largest house in Sussex to be owned by a commoner. It was built in 1440 near the site of the manor-house belonging to the de Monceux family who married into the de Hersts—after whom the village is jointly named—by Sir Roger de Fiennes, Henry VI's treasurer and a hero of Agincourt, whose son, Richard, married Joan, heiress of Lord Dacre.

A fortified manor rather than a castle, it was constructed in the form of a square with its four walls—each over two hundred feet in length—enclosing four courtyards. It had a moat, with a drawbridge, and was protected by a machicolated gatehouse and a series of towers which were evenly spaced along the battlemented walls, with one at each corner and two by the picturesque entrance gateway, one of the latter being used as a watch tower and the other as a signalling post.

While the domestic quarters included—besides the fine galleried living apartments—dairies, brew-house, cellars, distilleries, kitchens, and so on, and while the occupants could normally enjoy every comfort, in time of disturbance they could also offer some defence.

Unhappily, Herstmonceux also fell to ruin—not in battle but through the jealousy and greed of the wife of one of its later occupants. In 1708 one of the Dacres—who, on his marriage to Lady Ann Fitzroy, a natural daughter of Charles II, was created Earl of Sussex—sold the property to George Naylor, who left it to his nephew Francis. On the latter's death in 1775 it passed to his half-brother, the Rev. Robert Hare, whose father was Bishop of Chichester from 1731 until 1740. The trouble occurred when Robert Hare, who already had a son, married for the second time. His second wife, Henrietta Henckell, anticipating that on his death the castle would pass to his heir, and not to any child of hers, persuaded him to dismantle a great part of the house and to build another place in the beautiful deer park out of the materials. Thus Herstmonceux became a shell—and all in vain. For no sooner had her wish been fulfilled than Henrietta was disappointed to learn that the entire park was entailed land so that this new house had also to pass to her stepson!

The Hares appear to have been somewhat unfortunate in their choice of wives, for the bishop's grandson, Francis Hare-

Naylor, over whom the trouble arose, eloped with the daughter —one Georgiana—of another bishop, and she, in later years, appears to have behaved in the most extraordinary fashion.

Every day she used to dress herself in white and ride round the grounds of Herstmonceux on a white ass, accompanied by a white doe. She was so attached to the doe that it is said she even took it to church, and when at last the animal was killed by some dogs she went out of her mind and persuaded her husband to sell the estate. Whereupon the castle gradually fell to even greater ruin, until in 1933 it was carefully restored by Mr. Walter Godfrey. Now, with its moat filled once more, it is the home of the Greenwich Observatory.

The castle stands in a pleasant valley along which the smugglers used to bring their contraband from Pevensey Bay. As the cargoes were landed one of the Herstmonceux gardeners, a Frenchman called Tarte, used to hurry to a secret chamber and as ' the Gentlemen ' lumbered by on their pack-horses he beat a drum so loudly and furiously that people believed the valley haunted . . . which was as he intended. The monotonous roll, rising to a terrible crescendo, was heard so often that at the sound of the drum the villagers kept to their homes, fearful to venture out into the dark. And so the way was cleared of ' informers ' and often, no doubt, of Preventive Men as well.

In 1738 a chest, together with two large hammers, was discovered in the castle, and when beaten it was found to make a noise very similar to that of a drum. Though it was lost again almost as soon as it was found—having mysteriously vanished when the finders went off to report their discovery— it is said that the strange drumming can still be heard now and again coming from the ' Drummer's Hall '. Many stories are told to account for this strange happening, the most popular being that the noise is made by the spirit of a woman who was walled in here.

The church to which Georgiana Hare used to take her doe

is in the same valley, opposite one of the entrances to the castle grounds. Partially built of brick, it contains a splendid Dacre chapel that is contemporary with Herstmonceux Castle and several monuments to those who occupied the castle during the four centuries of its prosperity. One rather pleasing detail is that each pew is fitted with its own candle-light, contained in an iron holder.

v

One of the most popular kinds of gardening basket—the Sussex trug—is made at Herstmonceux. Though it is now favoured by farmers and private gardeners all over the country, and is exported to many parts of the world, it is peculiar to Sussex, and is fashioned in only two other villages, East Hoathly and Robertsbridge.

It appears that the trug first achieved fame as the result of a joke. A number of villagers were discussing the forthcoming Great Exhibition of 1851 over a tankard of beer in the local inn when one of the company mockingly suggested that even the old trug might find its way to Hyde Park. Thomas Smith, who made these baskets in his little village workshop, took the remark seriously, and without a word set off on foot for London a few days later, carrying a number of specimens on his back. When later he returned home by the same slow method he surprised his fellow drinkers with the news that he had made arrangements for the trug to be displayed.

'Trugging' is an interesting craft. After splitting his ash or chestnut rods, the craftsman steams them for about ten minutes in a long wooden trough. While still hot, he sets his rods between two horizontal poles, and curves them, afterwards shaping them round a rectangular frame, and fastening the two ends together to form an oblong.

The 'trugger' then pushes one frame through another to

intersect at right angles and fixes them at their two points of juncture. One of these frames forms the rim of the trug while the other acts as a one-piece base and handle. He now cuts a number of thin, widish strips of willow, which he smooths on a 'horse' by draw-knife, steams into gentle curves, and tapers at each end. Working from the centre, he then nails his strips lengthways both to his base and rim until he has completely filled in one half of his frame. All that is now left is to trim up, and the boat-like wooden basket—so renowned for its strength and durability—is complete.

VI

Hailsham, which marks the western limit of the Pevensey Levels, is also the centre of an interesting traditional industry.

Once renowned for its hats, it used to be said that no well-dressed woman ever attended a hunt unless she wore a Hailsham hat, a Lewes costume, and gloves that had been made either at Alfriston or Newick.

The hat-makers have long departed, but the hangman's rope is still made at Hailsham. In the old days the hemp would be 'scutted' and 'retted' by hand over teeth combs, and the craftsmen used to 'spin' their thread by walking backwards along a 'rope walk' that stretched for 800 to 1,000 yards. After spinning their lengths of yarn, they would harden, size and twist and, finally, 'lay up' into rope by means of a circular rope jack. Though the old methods are still practised in some parts—notably in Yorkshire—most of the work is now done by machinery at Hailsham.

The remnants of Michelham Priory, whose prior experienced such difficulty in choosing a site for the building of Alfriston's church, stands on the edge of a large common about two miles to the west of Hailsham. Founded as an Augustinian house in the time of Henry III, it is now a private house, and, though much reduced in size, still has its three-

Pevensey Castle from the air

Beachy Head

storeyed medieval gateway and remains of its refectory, with the beautiful prior's room over a crypt, while the moat—beautified by lilies and overhanging trees—and the fish stews—so important to monkish life—also remain.

Standing on the banks of the Cuckmere, its moat actually fed by the stream, the priory is beautifully situated, while the countryside around, though rather open, provides a pleasant contrast to Hailsham, which is extremely drab.

VII

Just across the river is further common land, known as The Dicker—rather flat, nondescript country encompassed by the villages of Upper and Lower Dicker, Ripe, Chalvington and Selmeston.

At Lower Dicker—where Horatio Bottomley was once squire —is the pottery where the famous ' Dicker Ware ' has been made from local clay for the last century or more. The pottery was closed during the war but has since opened under new management, and most of the traditional pieces—seed pans, bread crocks, milk pans and various types of decorative ware —are being made here once more.

The Dickers are in the parish of Hellingly, a village clustered about a Saxon burial mound, still boasting a water-mill of Henry III's time and an imposing half-timbered moated manor-house, with five restored gables and many carved oak beams, that was built in the days of Edward IV by the Devenish family.

This manor of Horselunges has a link with Herstmonceux Castle as the scene of a tragedy that sent one of the owners of the fortified manor to the gallows. One night in 1541 the third Lord Dacre, who, only the year before, had welcomed Anne of Cleves on her arrival in England, set off from Herstmonceux with three of his friends to poach deer in the demesne of Horselunges. Here they were accosted by three keepers, one of whom was killed in the hand-to-hand fighting that ensued.

Whether or not Lord Dacre played any part greater than trespassing on forbidden territory has never been definitely proved, but he and his companions paid the penalty at Tyburn.

Hellingly has another sad memory, one of its rectors, John Milles, having been one of the martyrs burnt at Lewes in 1557.

CHAPTER THIRTEEN: *In the Eastern Weald*

I

ONE of the charms of Sussex is that her scenery is so extremely varied. Where the South Downs drop down to the rather dreary Pevensey Levels, the Levels, in turn, open northwards into perhaps the most glorious part of the Weald.

So long the most important centre of the iron-workers and charcoal burners, this still well-wooded country with lovely distant views of gently undulating fields and hedgerows, studded with copses of oak—kin of the 'hearts of oak' the shipwrights used for the 'wooden walls of England'—was once as much part of the Forest of Anderida as St. Leonard's or Ashdown. The woods may be thin by comparison with those of St. Leonard's, the hills mere mounds against those of downland Sussex, but the two together, hills and woods, afford a splendid set-piece.

Neighboured to north and east by Kent, the eastern end of the Weald might well be part of the 'Garden of England'. Here the village architecture assumes the Kentish style, and is at its best. While the villages in other parts, though attractive, lack any individual style, here there are cottages with fresh white weatherboarding, and comfortable yeomen's farm-houses, usually hung with tiles of Wealden clay and often possessing fascinating outside chimney breasts—all so typical of Kent. And the difference seems the more pronounced with every mile we journey eastwards, until we see for the first time oast-houses of mellow red and grey bricks, their white swinging cowls peeping through the trees and reminding us that hops have been grown in Sussex for more than four cen-

233

turies and that once this county was even more productive in this respect than Kent.

II

The Uckfield road out of Hellingly takes us within easy reach of Chiddingly, birthplace in 1813 of Mark Anthony Lower, schoolmaster, antiquary and one of the founders of the Sussex Archæological Society.

This village was once a seat of the Pelhams and the Jefferays, both of which families are remembered in the church. Above one of the doorways is a replica of the famous Pelham Buckle which the King of France gave to his captor at Poictiers, while there are also a number of monuments to the Jefferays, the most elaborate being the eighteen-feet high marble tomb of Sir John Jefferay, Chief Baron of the Exchequer, who died in 1578.

It is said that Sir John and his lady were so proud that every Sunday a series of cheeses was laid on the ground between their stately home and the church to serve as stepping-stones and so save their feet from touching the ground as they went to worship. Sir John, in his ermine robes, lying in splendour with his wife, daughter, son-in-law and grandchild, certainly looks very proud in this rather grandiose tomb.

A number of slightly eccentric characters seem to have lived in this part from time to time. In his *Sussex Folk and Sussex Ways* the Rev. John Coker Egerton, Rector of Burwash from 1867 to 1888, tells of one Chiddingly couple who made a pact that when either was not in the best of humour, he or she was to arrange an article of clothing in a particular way as a kind of danger signal. Thus, when the husband saw his wife's shawl draped over her left shoulder or the wife her husband's hat on the back of his head, the other would take the hint and maintain strict silence rather than risk a ' scene '.

Then at East Hoathly, near by—where a little colony of

craftsmen make trug baskets, hay rakes, ladders and tool handles—there was Thomas Turner, who worked as schoolmaster, haberdasher, grocer and undertaker, and who divided his spare time between drinking, quarrelling with his mother-in-law, reading sermons to his friends, and keeping a diary. He began his diary in 1754, and, in as candid a fashion as Pepys told of happenings in more fashionable circles, gave a delightful picture of the life of the times in a quiet Sussex village. His house still stands.

At East Hoathly the main road swings sharp left by the church, past the drive to a magnificent Queen Anne house, known as 'Old Whyly', for Halland, a hamlet at the foot of Terrible Down, named, it is said, after a gruesome battle in which the soldiery waded up to their knees in blood. Halland was also a seat of the Pelhams.

Uckfield, a rather overgrown place, is only three miles away, and if we follow the main road through this town and turn right at Coopers Green we soon come to Buxted—whose church stands in a beautiful old deer park, famous for its avenue of trees—where the first iron cannon ever made in England was cast.

III

It was in 1543 that Ralph Hogge, a man extremely competent at working a furnace and furnishing molten iron, and Peter Baude, a Frenchman with an equally sound knowledge of bronze guns, cast their iron cannon at the furnace of Parson William Levett, a former rector of Buxted who was deprived of his living by Henry VIII because he favoured the Papists and who was later reinstated by Queen Mary for the same good reason.

Thereafter the making of guns became an important feature of the Sussex iron industry. Further gun furnaces were established at various parts of the Weald, and in them many of the cannons used to fight the Spanish Armada were cast. Probably there were never at any one time more than ten such furnaces, yet the Sussex craftsmen—whose pieces proved to be the cheapest as well as the most efficient—enjoyed world-wide fame for close on two centuries.

Like most craftsmen, they kept their methods secret, but Mr. Straker paints an interesting picture as to how they probably set about their work:

> A spindle of light wood . . . about the length of the finished gun, tapered to the same degree, was furnished with pins at each end so that it could be revolved by hand in bearings on a rigid frame. Round this twisted bands of hay were wound spirally . . . The hay bands were then coated with hair and manure. When the desired diameter was attained the final coat was turned by means of a board or strickle carefully cut to the exact external shape of the finished gun, with the various rings and thickenings.
>
> When thoroughly dry the model was dressed with a preparation of ashes to prevent adhesion, and the mound coated round it in the same manner . . . After several coats iron hoops were secured with wire round the mould and again buried in further coats of clay. When quite dry, the wooden spindle was knocked out and the hay bands with the clay coating were withdrawn, leaving the mould hollow. Moulds of the breech end, and of the ' gun head ', having been prepared in like manner, were attached to the gun mould by means of wire. . . . All being prepared, the mould was lowered, breech downward, into a pit in front of the furnace, the space between the mould and the sides of the pit being tightly packed with earth, and the molten metal run into it.

Ralph Hogge's home, over whose door is a model of a hog, is in the park, not far from the church where William Words-worth's brother, Christopher, was rector for something like fifty years. Of the furnace where he and the Frenchman cast their cannon, however, less is known. Some authorities believe that it was sited at Huggett's Furnace by Hadlow Down; others that it was at near-by Oldlands Furnace. In any case, there is little left to see at either place other than slag, broken bits of a bay, and perhaps a few rusty relics.

IV

The charming little town of Mayfield—' the sweetest village in England ', Coventry Patmore considered it—with its lovely old houses, its convent which was once a palace of the Archbishops of Canterbury, and its shingled spired church, with iron slabs cast by Ralph Hogge, beautifully set near the centre of the High Street, lies a little to the north-east of Hadlow Down.

Standing on a mound in one of the most soothing corners of the Weald, Mayfield owes its origin to St. Dunstan, one of the greatest of all the Archbishops of Canterbury, and has grown up around its church and palace, both of which, though since rebuilt, were founded by the saint.

As early as 838 a long strip of Northern Sussex had been transferred at a ' witenagemot ' held at Kingston-on-Thames from the See of Selsey to the Church of Canterbury. When St. Dunstan was archbishop this land was wild and densely wooded, and, since there was no other convenient place where he could rest on his journeyings through this part of his diocese, he built a palace at Mayfield. At the same time he erected a wooden church as a place wherein to convert the swineherds of the forest.

Gifted as an artist, painter, architect, and musician and a skilled craftsman who was as much at ease building organs or founding bells as at following the trade of a smith, he also taught them how to work the rich iron deposits in the district, and many stories are told of his being visited by the Devil while at work in his little forge here.

On one of these visits the saint lost his patience, it seems, and gripped the Devil's nose with his red-hot tongs, causing him such pain that when at last he broke free, he took one mighty leap to Tunbridge Wells where he plunged his nose into the spring, which thereafter was found to possess chalybeate properties.

The Devil turned up again at the smithy some time later, this time as a weary and footsore traveller begging for a steel shoe to help him on his journey. Seeing that the saint recognized him, the Devil became apologetic on this occasion, promising that if St. Dunstan would but grant the favour he would never again enter a house where a horseshoe was hung! And that is why country folk so often hang horseshoes over their cottage doors with the two ends uppermost to prevent the good luck flowing out!

A number of pleasing legends are centred around the life of St. Dunstan. One of the simplest but most charming concerns the dedication of his church at Mayfield. As the saint was leading a procession round the outside during his ceremony he noticed to his sorrow that it was slightly out of the Line of Sanctity, and so quietly leant his shoulder against one wall and set it right.

Many other Archbishops, from St. Thomas à Becket, who, as at Tarring, is believed to have planted the original fig trees in the palace grounds, and Boniface, who endowed the vicarage and obtained the first charter to hold fairs and markets, to Cranmer, who eventually surrendered the manor to Henry VIII, have been associated with Mayfield, and many important deeds were signed here.

From Henry VIII the palace passed into private ownership, one of the most notable owners being Sir Thomas Gresham, founder of the Royal Exchange and favourite of Queen Elizabeth whom he is believed to have entertained in great style in a room in the palace now known as the ' Queen's Chamber ' when the queen made a six days' stay with Lord Abergavenny at Eridge.

In course of time the palace, once surrounded by a noble park, gradually fell to ruin, until in 1863 it was opened as a Roman Catholic convent, and so returned to the Church after being divorced from it for three centuries and completely neglected for more than one hundred years.

Though its condition, with roofs staved in and ivy destroy-·
ing the walls, was such that it had to be heavily restored, the
Great Hall of about 1350—notable for the Kentish tracery in
its windows—together with a number of other fourteenth-
century features, have been left almost undisturbed.

A number of interesting relics are housed at the palace,
including an anvil and pair of tongs said to have been used
by St. Dunstan for fashioning sacred vessels, and a Spanish
rapier with which Queen Elizabeth is believed to have
knighted Sir Thomas Gresham during her visit.

Mayfield is reputed to have given birth to the Californian
seedless raisin when, many years ago, three cuttings from a
local grape vine were sent out to a settler in California. Two
of these cuttings were tended with every care, but were destroyed by flood. Whereupon the settler turned to the hitherto
neglected third cutting, which, to his amazement, was found
to bear seedless fruit.

v

A quiet by-way leads from Mayfield along the valley of the
Rother to the Kentish border, but the whole of this stretch of
the Weald is so lovely that the best way to appreciate it is to
follow a more devious course that will take us right round the
north, then westwards again through its heart, and, finally,
eastwards along its southern edge.

The northern half is almost entirely woodland and farmland, the only village between Mayfield and Frant, some six
miles distant, being Rotherfield, where both the Ouse and
the Rother find their source. Rotherfield, with its slender
spire a landmark for many miles, also stands on a mound,
and is renowned alike for its cowslips, adjudged to be the
largest in the county, and for the fact that its womenfolk are
born, they say, with two ribs more than the men!

Frant, with its old cottages clustered around a green on the hill-top enjoying extensive views across the wooded Weald, is only three miles from Tunbridge Wells, and from here we can complete our northern circuit by hugging the Kentish border on a south-easterly course down to Hurst Green. Though this road, like the one from Mayfield to Frant, is a main one, it passes only two villages—the old iron centre of Wadhurst, whose spire rises above a labyrinth of weather-boarded and tile-hung cottages and whose churchyard contains not only the graves of many of the seventeenth- and eighteenth-century iron-masters but also a pavement of iron grave slabs; and Tice-hurst, whose Women's Institute have, in recent years, earned more than local fame for reviving the dying art of making the old round frocks with their intricate traditional embroidery and smocking.

These smocks used to be embroidered on the cuffs and yokes with recognized designs showing whether the wearer was a carter, a woodman, or a shepherd, so that at the hiring fairs a man's calling was proclaimed by the design on his smock.

VI

At Etchingham, a mile or so west of Hurst Green, the little Dudwell joins the Rother. If we follow this peaceful stream to its source by Heathfield we pass through the heart of the Weald along a road whose views of the rolling country to either side are lovely all the way, especially on a sunny summer's evening when there are woolly clouds in the sky and the lights are seen to perfection.

Kipling's Burwash is on this road. Once a royal manor whose inhabitants were expected to supply Edward I with a sack of flour, a pound of pepper, three hens, a cock and a pair of spurs each year, Burwash is, if anything, even prettier than Mayfield—a fresh little place with a row of old cottages hiding behind a line of pollarded trees on one side of the main street, and, on the other, some splendid seventeenth- and eighteenth-century houses, most of them tile-hung but one or two weather-boarded, standing back behind a wide and well-kept grass verge. One of these houses, Rampyndene, is a particularly fine example of William and Mary architecture, and must rank among the most splendid of all the houses built by the Sussex iron-masters.

Burwash's church—a thirteenth-century building with a Norman tower and containing another of the Pelham Buckles, an iron grave slab with Lombardic lettering which is believed to be the oldest in Sussex, and a brass to Kipling's son, who was killed in the first world war, stands at the eastern end of the village by a lane that drops down to the Dudwell.

Bateman's, where Kipling lived and worked from 1903 until his death in 1936, is just by the Dudwell. Indeed, the stream passes through the grounds. Built in the first half of the seventeenth century, or perhaps a little earlier, Bateman's was later enlarged by John Britain, a local iron-master who died in 1707 and whose derelict forge is still to be seen in the woods.

When Kipling bought the property it was used as a farm-house, and the gardens—where the double oast-house of 1730 remains—were simply a hop yard. To-day the house, now owned by the National Trust, stands in 300 acres of farm and parkland in the midst of beautiful gardens of well-kept lawns, with a pond, rose garden, an avenue of limes and one of the most enormous willow trees in the country, and, beyond, the little Dudwell trickling past the old watermill, the general lay-out having been designed by Kipling himself.

Kipling dearly loved this old stone house with its noble chimney stacks, its three-storeyed gabled porch and its panel-ling—' no shadow of ancient regrets, stifled miseries, nor any other menace ' did he ever experience in this, ' The Very Own House '. Kipling and Burwash became indivisible, and at Mrs. Kipling's request his study at Bateman's has been pre-served just as he left it, his books still lining the walls, his elbow chair before the long oak table at which he wrote, and.

conveniently at hand, his waste-paper basket and two map-globes of the world. It was here that he wrote his *Puck of Pook's Hill* and *Rewards and Fairies*, and many other books and poems, including, no doubt, his *Smugglers' Song* and *Sussex*.

Certainly no writer of such fertile imagination could have chosen a better spot than Burwash for his home, for the whole district is steeped in tradition. Nearly every house is linked either with the iron-workers or the smugglers; the 'five and twenty ponies' must often have trotted through the dark to Burwash where the contraband used to be concealed not only in the cellars of the inns and cottages but even in a vault of the church! While leading from ' Pook's Hill ', an eminence with lovely views, is ' the Gunway ' along which the locally cast cannons that were to help defeat the Armada were brought.

Just as some of the cottage folk still living here are assuredly the descendants of those smugglers, so a few can show documents to prove that, though they themselves are now humble, their ancestors were once wealthy iron-masters of the district. It was, no doubt, through talking to such folk as these that Kipling obtained much of his material, and many of the characters he portrayed so well must have been the people of the countryside about him.

When Richard Jefferies visited Burwash he found the people to be remarkably superstitious. As he tells in his *Field and Hedgerow*, no man ever put on new boots on a Saturday lest some disaster should befall him. Dandelion leaves, served between slices of toast, constituted a favourite dish, while the curative and health-giving properties of herbs were widely and wisely appreciated. Nor could any be convinced that a frog would die before sunset, whatever misfortune befell it.

Though no longer quite so firm in their beliefs, perhaps, Burwash folk are still inclined to be superstitious.

It is said that many of them are of Huguenot extraction, and they still sing the popular folk song, *The Old Sow*, a corruption of a twelfth-century Troubadour song, first introduced by the foreign refugees.

Another tune very popular in these parts until quite recent times was *Twanky-dillo*, the song of the blacksmiths who, within living memory, used to celebrate St. Clement's Day (November 23) by setting a model of ' Old Clem '—the patron saint of the blacksmiths—above the door of one of the local inns to guard the place while they went inside to feast on leg of pork with sage and onions—a dish known in Burwash as ' way-goose '.

VII

Beyond Burwash the road cuts across a lovely common and on past Tottingworth Park to Heathfield and Cross-in-Hand, the latter possessing a particularly fine windmill.

It used to be said that the first cuckoo of summer was released from a basket by an old woman at Heathfield's ' Hefful Fair ', and to this day Sussex folk, no matter where they are, still reckon to hear the cuckoo for the first time on April 14, the traditional date of that fair. On that day many still sing the famous song (the earliest secular song known) *Sumer Is Icumen In* exactly as it was written by John of Fornsette, a monk of Reading, more than seven hundred years ago:

> Sumer is icumen in
> Llude sing cuccu!
> Groweth sed and bloweth med
> And springeth the wude nu
> Ewe bleteth after lamb
> Llouth after calve cu
> Bulluc sterteth, buck verteth
> Murie sing cuccu
> Cuccu, cuccu
> Wel singes thu, cuccu
> Ne swik thu naver nu.

There are two unusual memorials at Heathfield—a column

to the Sussex martyrs who were burnt at the stake, and the Gibraltar Tower in Heathfield Park to George Augustus Eliott, whose long defence of Gibraltar (1779 to 1783) during hostilities with Spain ranks high in the annals of British arms.

After his heroic stand in the face of almost continual bombardment and blockade, Eliott was awarded prize money by a grateful nation. Out of this he bought Heathfield Park, whose Tudor mansion had been rebuilt about one hundred years previously, and when honoured with a peerage became the first Lord Heathfield. He now lies buried in the village of his adoption.

In the National Gallery there is a portrait of Lord Heathfield by Sir Joshua Reynolds, while in the Tate Gallery there is one by Turner of Heathfield itself. Though it is no longer possible to see what Turner portrayed, the views from the Gibraltar Tower are extensive, and on a clear day it is supposed to be possible to pick out the spires of something like forty churches.

Heathfield is also noted for its spring chicken, known locally as 'hucksters', and for its natural gas, discovered at great depth towards the end of last century when a party of workmen were sinking a well.

VIII

It was at Cade Street, a hamlet adjoining Heathfield, that Jack Cade, the callous champion of the lower orders of society, met his death on July 13, 1450, while attempting to flee the country after his abortive insurrection.

Some ten days previously he had left Kent, where he practised as a leach, to march on London with 40,000 followers. There Cade and his men met with certain initial successes and remained masters of the situation for three days, during which time they executed Lord Say, a detested favourite of the king, and plundered and pillaged the homes of many noblemen, often murdering the occupants.

At the end of the third day, however, their power was broken when the citizens of the capital gained command of London Bridge, and offered pardon to the insurgents if they agreed to disperse. Whereupon many of his followers deserted Cade, who, with a price upon his head, then tried to reach the coast, only to meet his death at the hands of Alexander Iden at Cade Street where, in a cottage garden, a monument commemorates the incident.

IX

Cade Street is almost due east of Heathfield, and from here we can thread our way back towards the Kentish border along a network of side roads and lanes that lead us through many pleasant little villages.

Warbleton, home of the iron-master, agriculturist and last of the Lewes martyrs, Richard Woodman, whose house still stands, is only a short distance away, and in the churchyard here may be seen a watch-house from which they used to keep vigil against the body-snatchers. And not so very far from Warbleton is beautiful Ashburnham, where, in 1802, the last of the Sussex iron furnaces finally closed its doors. It has been claimed that the railings for Wren's St. Paul's were forged here, but this has been strongly challenged by Lamberhurst in Kent, and the general opinion now seems to be that the work was shared by the various furnaces of the two counties.

In the restored mansion of Ashburnham Place, which stands in a well-wooded park, are the blood-stained shirt and silk drawers worn by Charles I at his execution, together with his watch and the sheet, bearing the C.R. and crown, that covered his body on the way from the scaffold. They were given to John Ashburnham, whose forebears had been staunch Royalists from earliest times, one of them having stood by King Harold in the defence of Dover Castle at the time of the Conquest.

John Ashburnham was Groom of the Bedchamber to Charles I, to whom he often lent money during the Civil Wars. Through many of his trials and troubles he was one of the king's closest companions, yet, by an irony of fate, it was he who was responsible for his royal master's final capture at Carisbrooke Castle, when, hoping to enlist the aid of the governor, he went against the advice of the king in revealing certain secrets of his plans. Realizing his mistake, Ashburnham would have drawn his sword and slain the governor on the spot but for the intervention of Charles. Instead, the king, who bore no malice, went to his fate, and Ashburnham passed into ' retirement '.

Upon the Restoration John Ashburnham became Groom of the Bedchamber to the second Charles. Thus restored to riches, he rebuilt Ashburnham's church, where he now lies in an elaborate marble tomb along with his ancestors.

The fragmentary remains of Ashburnham forge, together with one or two old cottages belonging to the furnace, are to the north of this park by a quiet by-way leading northwards through Penhurst, another iron centre, to Brightling, home of the eccentric squire, Jack Fuller.

Born in 1756, the son of a parson, Fuller owned estates in various parts of the world, and was immensely rich. It is said that when he entered Parliament in the early years of the nineteenth century his election campaign cost him £50,000. Besides squandering much of his wealth, he also devoted a great deal of his money to good causes. He bought Bodiam Castle when it was in danger of being demolished, and it was he who commissioned Turner to paint not only Heathfield but also the Vale of Ashburnham, Pevensey Bay, Beachy Head and Battle Abbey.

At the same time he was, by all accounts, extremely pompous. Whenever he travelled he did so in a coach-and-four,

Eastbourne Seafront

Mermaid Street, Rye

accompanied by a bodyguard with swords and pistols, and at dinner-parties he would brag about the splendid prospects—which are still superb—he enjoyed from his home on Rose Hill. On one of these occasions he was challenged when he announced that he could see the spire of Dallington Church from his lawn. When his challenger offered to bet him any sum he liked that this was not so, Fuller, as was invariably his wont, readily accepted. On discovering to his dismay when he returned home that night that, in fact, he had exaggerated, he hastily summoned all the masons in the district and ordered them to build a replica of the church spire at a point where it would be well visible from his lawn. This they did in the space of a few hours . . . and Fuller was thereby saved the embarrassment of having to admit he was in the wrong! Or so the story goes.

This folly building—now a landmark known as ' The Sugar Loaf '—was but one of many built by Fuller. He also erected an extraordinary temple in which he is believed to have held gambling-parties, and in the churchyard he is buried in a weird pyramidal tomb which, presumably, would have pleased him greatly. Tradition has it that inside this tomb he is seated in an arm-chair, fully dressed.

x

Robertsbridge, where, as already mentioned, they also make trug baskets, is only a short distance from Brightling.

Unfortunately its Cistercian abbey has almost entirely disappeared. Once among the wealthiest and most powerful in the county, whose monks gave hospitality to both Henry III and Edward I, it became no more than a stone quarry after the Dissolution, its stones being used for building many of Robertsbridge's cottages and for road-making. Such few remains as there are have been incorporated into a farm-house and are now of little interest.

As a centre of rural craftsmanship, however, the village is once more a place of some importance.

Ever since about 1870 when the village carpenter, Mr. L. J. Nicolls, walked to the wicket carrying a bat of his own making, and was afterwards pressed by his friends to fashion similar ones for them, the making of cricket bats has steadily developed into an important local industry enjoying a wide export to Australia, South Africa, New Zealand and the West Indies.

Within little more than twenty years, in 1895, W. G. Grace scored his hundredth century and more than one thousand runs in May with a Robertsbridge bat. Since then countless other Test players—' Ranji ', Fry, Walter Hammond and Keith Miller, to mention but a few—have given the Sussex workshops their patronage.

Though some of the willows are grown by the Rother, most are imported from Essex. From the time that the willow cutting is planted it will be some twelve years before the tree is big enough for felling. Then, perhaps, it will yield some 36 bats.

The willows are felled in winter, sawn into rounds 28 inches long, and split into shapes roughly representing blades, the greatest care being taken to ensure that the splitting always follows the natural grain of the wood.

The craftsman then stacks his ' blades ' in criss-cross tiers and leaves them exposed to the wind and rain, but sheltered from the sun, for nine months, after which he will restack them indoors for a further three months.

The seasoning complete, he presses his blades, or ' clefts ', between two hand-turned rollers, capable of exerting a pressure of some two tons to the square inch, and it is remarkable to see how the timber becomes steadily thinner and thinner. The object of this is to harden the wood, and so make it less likely to split when it comes into contact with the hard cricket ball. This done, he takes his draw-knife and sets to work shaping the back of his blade before cutting the splice for the handles.

The handles are made of East Indies cane. This the crafts-man saws into handle lengths which, in turn, he planes into rounds. The rounds he glues together to form ' slips '; strips of rubber to provide the springing are introduced between the slips, which likewise are glued together. When the handle has set it is shaped by draw-knife and let into the splice—a process requiring the keenest accuracy and a critically sharp tool.

The handle fixed, the craftsman proceeds to give the whole bat a final shaping with his draw-knife and spoke-shave. Many declare that this is the most difficult of all the branches of the craft, since one shave too much can well alter the entire balance of the bat—and balance is everything.

All that remains now is to smooth the bat with sandpaper, burnish it, and then string the handle.

Robertsbridge boasts yet another unusual industry. About the same time as Mr. Nicolls was starting his bat factory a number of Cornish miners began to mine for gypsum at near-by Mountfield. Sirapite—the material used for the interior plastering of houses—was first made here, and the local gyp-sum is now quarried on a steadily increasing scale for the production of both sirapite—a name invented by spelling Paris backwards and adding ' ite '—and plaster of Paris, as well as various other materials of importance to the building industry.

XI

The old abbey of Robertsbridge—where Sir John Pelham and his wife, Lady Joan, the gallant defender of Pevensey, are believed to have been buried—stood close by the banks of the Rother.

Bodiam Castle, some of whose lords endowed the abbey, is also by this withy-lined river. Standing on a mound between

the Rother and its tributary, the Kent Ditch—the latter the
dividing line between the two counties—looking down upon a
plain and surrounded by a wide tree-fringed moat which is
beautiful for its water lilies and the joy of anglers for its roach,
Bodiam Castle is one of the most delightfully situated ruins in
England.

Its name suggests that Bodiam may originally have been the
ham of a Saxon dweller named Boda or Bode, and the *Domesday Book* shows that at the time of the Conquest one Osbert
de Bodeham lived here in a timbered hall as thegn. From the
de Bodehams the manor passed in 1250 to the de Wardeux
family, and a little more than a century later it descended
through the marriage of their heiress, Lady Elizabeth, to Sir
Edward Dalyngrigge, a knight of East Grinstead stock who
had already fought with honour in France.

Hitherto Bodiam had served merely as a private dwelling-
place, but under the ownership of Sir Edward Dalyngrigge it
assumed considerably more importance. By 1380 both the
Cinque Ports of Rye and Winchelsea had been sacked and
burnt by the French, and since the Rother, which formed part
of the port of Winchelsea, was then navigable as far as Bodiam
Bridge, there was nothing to prevent future invaders pene-
trating well inland.

Thus, in 1385, Sir Edward was granted a special licence to
build Bodiam Castle as an inland defence post commanding
the Rother valley.

As it happened, the castle was never required for the purposes for which it had been built. On the contrary, it seems
that the only time it was ever attacked was during the Wars
of the Roses when its holder, Sir Thomas Lewknor, appears to
have surrendered without offering the slightest resistance.
How it came to be gutted is a matter of speculation, the most
general belief being that it was dismantled, or ' slighted ', by
Waller during the Civil Wars.

All too little is known about the history of Bodiam after

the fifteenth century other than the fact that Squire Jack Fuller saved it from demolition in his time and that Lord Curzon performed an equally valuable service in 1917 by restoring it and then leaving it on his death in 1926 to the National Trust, together with the manor-house, inn and cottages.

Though a roofless shell, the exterior of the castle shows little signs of deliberate damage and can surely be only a little less impressive than on the day it was built. Rectangular in plan, its six-foot thick walls stand 41 feet above the water with a drum tower—29 feet in diameter—at each corner and a square tower on each flank. At both front and rear there is an imposing machicolated gate-house, the one to the north bearing three heraldic shields of the de Wardeux, Dalyngrigge and (it is believed) the Raydynden families.

This main entrance to the north, approached across an earthen causeway and comprising two massive rectangular towers, united by a lofty arch with machicolated parapet and pointed windows, is described in the official handbook as ' one of the noblest facades of medieval military architecture in Britain '. If small by comparison with many other castles, Bodiam certainly exudes an atmosphere of might, and it is a queer sensation to pass under the great portal with its spiked portcullis still in position, and on through the vaulted passage into a grass-floored shell.

Inside the walls are so very fragmentary that, though the Lord's hall, chapel, great chamber, kitchen, buttery, and many other interesting features in the way of spiral staircases, tiled fireplaces, the old dungeon, well, and so on, remain in varying degrees of preservation, it is only with the aid of a ground plan that we can obtain anything approaching a true picture of their original design and of the life of the occupants.

XII

Bodiam is in the heart of the Sussex hop country. In this

rather heavy loamy soil, drained by the Rother, the popular 'Fuggle' hop thrives well, and men and women labour hard. No sooner is one crop finished than preparations are made for the next. In the months of winter the hoppers are busy skinning and pickling their poles and setting them in position in their hop-yards. March sees the stilt-walkers arranging their strings from the overhead wires to pegs in the ground, using as much as 10,000 miles of string in the process. Then, as the plants shoot up eight bines from each are entwined in pairs round each of four strings, and the rest are cut off. From then on all will be at work with their ploughs, 'kufs', 'spanes', 'becks', and such like, harrowing and hoeing and spraying against the dreaded red spider. Finally, in September, the pickers arrive from the East End of London.

As I describe in *A Breath of England*, the hops are picked into canvas-covered wooden frames, known as 'bins', and carried to the oast-houses in 'pokes', where they are spread out on a platform of battens that has previously been covered with horse-hair mats. There, above a charcoal (locally produced in the woods) and anthracite furnace, they are left to dry under the care of two men who move them about with their enormous wooden shovels for twelve hours or more to ensure that they are evenly baked throughout and do not scorch.

In the old days practically every farmer of importance in the eastern Weald grew his hops, while many brewed their beer for their labourers on the spot. To-day by far the greatest acreage is in the hands of the famous firm of Guinness who grow something like 750,000 hop plants in these Sussex fields and use machinery for some of the processes.

Mechanical pickers are now beginning to appear on the scene, and Messrs. Guinness have built an enormous modern oast-house with nearly 20,000 square feet of drying floors. Yet, even here, the traditional methods are still greatly in evidence, and the employees are mostly men whose forebears have worked in the Sussex hop-yards for generations.

XIII

Some of the prettiest villages of all are to be found in this hop country, three of particular interest being Sedlescombe, Ewhurst and Northiam.

Sedlescombe, with its many timbered houses of the sixteenth and seventeenth centuries and its picturesque pump on the large village green, was voted some years ago the most perfect village in East Sussex, and its charm has not lessened since.

Ewhurst, on a hill looking across to Bodiam Castle, can claim what must be the unique distinction of having had the electric light installed in its parish church primarily by the Methodists as a memorial to the Rev. John Richardson, who was curate here from 1759 to 1762.

During the three years of the latter's curacy here, John Wesley several times preached in this district, and Richardson used to attend the Wesleyan meetings after concluding his own services. When a number of the parishioners objected to this, Richardson was relieved of his post by the rector, the Rev. Thomas Nairn. Whereupon John Wesley, who was always on the look-out for ordained priests, appointed Richardson to the Foundry Meeting House, Moorfields, where he remained until his death.

The third village—Northiam—was the home of many generations of the Frewen family to whom there is a mausoleum in the church. One of the Frewens, who was born in the rectory here in 1588 and given the extraordinary name of Accepted (his brother was called Thankful) by his father, Northiam's Puritan rector for 45 years, became Bishop of Lichfield and later Archbishop of York, having been driven out of the country with £1,000 on his head between the two appointments because he turned Royalist.

The Frewens' family seat of Brickwall House—an Elizabethan building with Stuart additions—still stands, and here may be seen a pair of high-heeled green damask shoes which Queen Elizabeth discarded when she paused at Northiam in 1573 while on her way to inspect her ships at Rye, but seven miles distant.

It is said that on her ' progress ' through Northiam the queen dined under the massive oak tree on the diminutive green at the end of the High Street, and that the fare was cooked in the heavily timbered house opposite. The queen took so kindly to this little village, and was so satisfied by the welcome afforded her, that she returned to Northiam a second time . . . as well might any one to-day who would see a really lovely corner of old England : ' O, rare Northiam ', as Michael Drayton described it.

CHAPTER FOURTEEN: *In and Around the Cinque Ports*

I

AT Rye, whither Queen Elizabeth—like other sovereigns both before and after her—journeyed from Northiam, we enter the area of the Sussex Cinque Ports.

As far back as 1050 Edward tthe Confessor granted each of the various ports a separate charter, and these towns were incorporated as the Cinque Ports by William the Conqueror. As their name implies, they were five in number—Dover, Sandwich, Romney, Hythe and Hastings—Hastings being the only one in Sussex.

After a while Rye and Winchelsea—both of which were given, as part of the Manor of Rameslie, by King Canute to the Abbey of Fécamp—were added to these five, though at first these were merged with Hastings to help the latter keep up her quota of ships, and were not granted full membership until about 1320. At the same time eight corporate members and twenty-four 'limbs', or non-corporate members, were also added. To the former group Sussex gave Pevensey and Seaford, and to the latter Guestling, Bulverhythe, Petit Shaw, Hidney, Beakesbourne and Grange, the majority of which places are now mere names.

Their main purpose was to provide a maritime defence, and under the terms of the charter granted by Edward I, they were required to maintain a fleet of at least fifty-seven ships, each of which had to be manned by a 'rector', 'constable', twenty-one men and a boy. In fact, they constituted the nucleus of the 'King's Navee', and were liable to assemble once a year at a given rendezvous for a fifteen-days' exercise at their own expense.

In the reign of Edward III Rye furnished five ships and Winchelsea ten, and together the Cinque Ports sent no less than 105 ships and over two thousand men to the Siege of Calais. At the time of the Armada they were still powerful, Hastings then sending twenty ships to serve in the fleet of Lord Howard of Effingham.

Since to build and maintain such ships caused considerable financial burden on these ports, their burgesses were granted many exceptional privileges. Though the number and scope of these privileges varied from town to town, according to the services entailed, each port was entitled to send two barons to Parliament, while collectively they could claim the right to appoint representatives to hold the canopy over the sovereign's head at the coronation and, afterwards, to sit upon his right hand at the state dinner. They had the right to sell and buy in any market in England, and their ships were excused harbour dues wherever they went. Not only were they exempt from the payment of innumerable taxes, tolls and such like, but they had the power to levy taxes themselves. If any of their ships were stranded nobody else was allowed to salve them; on the other hand, the right to wrecks and to flotsam and jetsam cast up on the foreshore within their jurisdiction was vested in them. Moreover, they maintained their own peculiar courts of justice, offenders against the law being untouchable by any other court, no matter what their offence.

The Cinque Ports have not sent a man-of-war to sea since the reign of Charles I. Even so, a few of the old privileges remain. Though the canopy is no longer used, representatives of the Cinque Ports still attend the coronation of English sovereigns—while Winchelsea—now no more than a village—continues to be governed by a ' corporation ' whose style is the ' Mayor, Jurats and Commonalty of the Antient Town of Winchelsea '.

The mayor is elected every Easter Monday at a Hundred Court by the mayor, jurats and freemen then in office. If he refuses to receive his charge, or chooses to absent himself without good reason, the people may still, by age-old law, ' go and shut in his chief tenement '. Immediately after his election the mayor appoints a number of freemen jurats to assist him during his term, the freemen being admitted at a Common Assembly.

Rye also has its mayor, and during his annual election hot pennies are thrown from the balcony of *The George* to a crowd of eager youngsters assembled in the street below.

II

Standing high up on a mound of solid rock at the mouth of the eastern Rother, Rye may well claim to be unique. The stranger, seeing its steep cobbled streets of medieval houses— most of them so narrow that those living on one side can open their windows and carry on a conversation with their neighbours on the other side without needing to raise their voices unduly—might well be excused for imagining himself to be in Brittany or Provence.

Although Rye was so often plundered and pillaged and was twice burnt by the French, it remains in essence medieval, or, at the latest, Tudor. True, several Queen Anne and Georgian fronts are also to be seen, but more often than not these conceal something far older. Every conceivable building style seems to be represented beneath those mellow wavy roofs of so many different levels. Yet there is hardly a discordant note.

Commanding the highest point in the town, its spire sticking up above the closely packed roofs, is the church. Built in the twelfth century and known as the ' Cathedral of East Sussex ', it contains many interesting features, including Perpendicular flying buttresses, a window by Burne-Jones, a chantry chapel with groined roof, and the oldest working clock in England, made by a Winchelsea man in 1568 with a pendulum of eighteen feet and four gilded ' boys ', each over four feet tall, to strike the quarter-hours. It has also an altar of Spanish mahogany which some believe was made of timber salvaged from the Spanish galleons so badly battered off the coast here during the rout of the Armada. Several of Rye's houses contain timbers from those ships.

At one time the church, like *The Star* at Alfriston, served as a sanctuary. A criminal fleeing from justice, having made his way along the king's highway to this port at grave risk, could demand to see the mayor of Rye. Upon confessing to him, his worldly goods would be forfeit to the town, and his life spared so long as he set sail to some other country within forty days. The old sanctuary knocker used by the fugitives is now in the Hastings Museum.

One of Rye's most noted clerics was Richard Fletcher, a local minister and preacher who, after attending Mary Stuart at her execution as Dean of Peterborough, later became Bishop of London, and died, it is said, through the immoderate use of tobacco. Richard's still more famous son, John Fletcher, dramatist and contemporary of Shakespeare, was born in 1579 in the original vicarage. This building was pulled down in 1699 and a magnificent timbered house, whose oak room has been described as one of the best examples of timbering extant, was built on the site, and is generally, but erroneously, associated with Fletcher.

It has also been said that it was at *The Mermaid* here that Fletcher first met his collaborator, Francis Beaumont, who hailed from Leicestershire and was seven years his junior. Since, however, this inn was then only a butcher's shop and since Fletcher left Rye before he was three, such a suggestion is obviously ridiculous.

Numbered among the leading dramatists of the Elizabethan age, these two, Fletcher and Beaumont, became such close friends that they not only shared the same house in London— where they wrote most of their works—but even wore identical costume. Among their best-known plays were *The*

Woman Hater, *The Maid's Tragedy*, *Philaster* and *A King and No King*. After Beaumont's premature death in 1616 Fletcher wrote many plays on his own—producing no less than eleven in the last four years of his life—before falling a victim to the plague of 1625.

After Fletcher's time *The Mermaid*, like *The Flushing Inn*, became a mecca of smugglers, some of whose hidden contraband was found during recent structural alterations to the former inn. The near-by Walland Marshes afforded a happy landing-ground for ' the Gentlemen ' and the cellars of many of Rye's houses—standing, as they do, upon the cliffs—proved unusually convenient. *The Flushing*, for instance, has two medieval cellars with a suitable approach up the cliffs.

Though *The Mermaid* has been considerably restored, and *The Flushing* reduced in size, both these inns are rich in unusual architectural features, one of the most interesting being a Tudor wall-painting, some sixteen feet long by eight feet wide, in an old building that used to belong to *The Flushing*.

Discovered by a workman behind some Jacobean panelling, it is believed to represent either the Garden of Eden or a hunting scene. Three oblong tablets—each held by a pair of cherubs and containing in Old English lettering some of the words of *The Magnificat*—are seen on a broad frieze of fleur-de-lys. Between the tablets are two shields, one bearing the Royal Arms, and the other, it is thought (it is too damaged to identify for certain), those of Jane Seymour, mother of Edward VI. While at each end there is a Tudor rose charged upon the sun in splendour with rays shooting from it—the heraldic badge of that king. Beneath this is a woodland scene with peacocks and fallow deer, and many other beasts and birds in a setting of trees, creepers and brightly coloured flowers.

Considering their age, the paintings are well preserved. What prompted so elaborate a work is, however, a mystery, and it can only be assumed that it was executed by some one of artistic temperament in commemoration of Edward VI's visit to Sussex.

Another interesting old inn is *The George*, which, though its front is Georgian, goes back at least three hundred and fifty years and contains a magnificent assembly room with a musicians' gallery.

Rye is so rich in lovely old buildings that it is impossible to do more than list just a few of the more outstanding. Among these must be numbered the Old Friary, erected in 1379 as a chapel for the Friars of St. Augustine and later used by the Huguenot refugees who settled in Rye in such numbers that once the little town gave shelter to no less than 1,500 of them; the grammar school (built as a private house in 1636 by Thomas Peacock, a jurat of Rye, and founded as a school in his will three years later), the school to which Thackeray sent ' Denis Duval '; the Oak House, containing many frescoes and carved beams of the sixteenth century; the Old Hospital, so called because wounded soldiers were treated here during the Napoleonic wars; Lamb House, where James Lamb, who came of a long line of mayors, entertained George I in 1725, and where the author, E. F. Benson, another mayor, spent the last years of his life; and the early Georgian town hall in which are preserved the silver maces of 1767, said to be the finest in England and held in such high esteem that the Canadian Government have a replica of one of them in their House of Commons.

Besides the houses, there are such individual landmarks as the Land Gate with its two massive drum towers, each over forty feet high, and the Ypres Tower, an extraordinary fortification on the cliff-side which was built about 1250 by Henry III when the sea lapped the rock on which Rye stands and the town had no other defences. The tower is named after John Ypres who bought it in 1430. Then there is the Gun Garden, where the guns were mounted at the time of the Armada and again during the Napoleonic scares; and Queen Elizabeth's well, whose waters the queen is supposed to have drunk when, delighted by her visit, she christened the place 'Rye Royal', an appellation that has stuck to this day.

With its ancient fortifications and old houses, its little cobbled streets bearing such fascinating names as Mermaid and Watchbell (the latter dating back to the time when a bell used to be rung here to warn the inhabitants of any impending danger), its small hand pottery where traditional pieces are fashioned of local clay, its windmill and the old warehouses by the quay; with these and so many other pleasing features, Rye is one of those places where one can poke about for hours —perhaps even days—and still feel that there may be some unsuspected nook or cranny one has missed.

Then a mile or so to the south, beyond the marshes, is the harbour, which, though shrunk in size, is still an important fishing cove whence the fishermen, or 'tan-frocks'—so many of whom are of Huguenot extraction—put out to Rye Bay to fish for turbot, plaice and other trawl fish, to say nothing of mackerel, which they catch by means of 'keddle-nets' set up on poles, or 'stands' of floating nets. Indeed, Rye Bay is still considered so good a fishing-ground that French fishermen frequently risk the heavy penalties and encroach upon the 'three-mile limit'.

The harbour, and all that it has meant to Rye in its long, long history, still figures in the local Bonfire Ceremony, which, with its 'mammoth fires' and 'grand processions' is only a little less elaborate than that of Lewes. Every year on that bright November night Rye still 'burns its boats' in memory of those days in the fourteenth century when it was customary to draw any French raiding vessel captured by the Cinque Ports Fleet through the town and then burn it in a prominent position as a warning to others who might be marauding near the coast: so, too, do they still eat bloaters—'cured to perfection, cooked to perfection'—around their fires in honour, presumably, of the local fishing fleets that have put to sea for so many centuries.

The views from across the marshes are very lovely, with Rye sparkling in the sun like a toy on its pinnacle of rock in the north, and the Rother flowing between groyned banks to join Rye Bay beyond those velvet-like Camber Sands. To the east we can look across the river to the sheep-grazed Walland and Romney Marshes and Dungeness; to the west is Camber Castle—one of a chain of fortifications, boasting a tall central circular tower surrounded by four shorter ones, which Henry VIII built at a cost of £23,000 out of materials from the dissolved monasteries—with Winchelsea, on its high hill beyond, and, to the south of Winchelsea, Fairlight Cove, meeting-place of the Atlantic and North Sea tides and another smugglers' haunt.

III

For the last one hundred and fifty years or so romantic Fairlight has also been a traditional meeting-place of lovers. The story goes that in 1785 the daughter of a well-to-do Kentish family named Boys fell in love with Lt. Lamb, R.N., of Rye. Strongly disapproving of the match, the girl's parents sent their daughter to a farm-house at Fairlight. The girl, however, not to be put off so easily, used to steal from this house night after night to the cliff-side of Fairlight Glen, a little farther west towards Hastings, where she would flash a lantern seawards. Needless to say, her lover always happened to be cruising in the vicinity at such times, and as soon as he saw the light would come ashore. Eventually, after many such nocturnal trystings, the two were secretly married at St. Clements Danes in London, and all ended happily.

In memory of this romance a seat—known as ' Lovers' Seat '—was set up at their meeting-place, and for generations lovers have gone there to plight their troth, confident that to do so at this spot would ensure their future happiness. During the last war some unromantic soldier, out of patience with such tales, hurled the seat over the cliff into the sea. However, another now takes its place, so that the stage is set for future lovers!

IV

Rye and Winchelsea are but two miles distant from one another. Once they were closer still. The original Winchelsea—a place of about 300 houses with at least 50 inns to serve a population of some 700—is thought to have stood about a mile from the spot now occupied by Camber Castle. But in 1287 'the moon was at its prime, the sea passed her accustomed bounds, flowing twice without ebbing', and swept away most of the town together with its harbour and important shipbuilding yards—yards even more productive than those of Rye.

After visiting the scene of the disaster, Edward I, who was Lord Warden of the Cinque Ports, appointed John Kirkeby, Bishop of Ely and Treasurer of England, to choose a suitable site for a new town. Thus a second Winchelsea—laid out in thirty-nine squares according to the king's own plan—arose on its present high hill, then a sea-washed promontory.

Alas, the tides that had submerged the first Winchelsea were later to recede again, leaving the second high and dry as an inland village whose port gradually grew so shallow that by the middle of the fifteenth century it had become entirely useless. But not before Winchelsea had been sacked several times by the French in both the fourteenth and fifteenth centuries and had witnessed the defeat of a Spanish fleet by Edward III off the coast here.

Though Rye and Winchelsea have, as it were, 'flowed and ebbed' together and are regarded to this day as twin towns, Winchelsea is as different from Rye as is possible to imagine. For whereas the latter is so very French, Winchelsea has the appearance and atmosphere of a perfectly planned Georgian village. It is on a plateau, spacious and airy, with roads of prim Georgian fronts, both large and small, running at right angles to one another, and nearly every house exceptionally well cared for and obviously loved.

Yet the strange part is that, despite its outward appearance, Winchelsea, though now about a fifth of its original size, is still very much as Edward I planned it, with its roads now dividing the village into eight definite squares. Also, most of the houses are infinitely older than their eighteenth-century fronts would lead one to suppose. While Winchelsea also boasts three of its original gates, Strand Gate, Pipewell and New Gate.

Turner once painted New Gate, and in a field by Strand Gate—a field with lovely views across Pett Level to the sea beyond—Sir John Millais portrayed his famous ' Blind Girl ', using his sister-in-law as his model. Millais stayed at Glebe House on that occasion.

As is only to be expected, the enchanting little hill-top village has attracted many famous people in its time—Rossetti, Ruskin, William Morris, John Wesley, Thackeray and Dame Ellen Terry, to name but a few.

Before moving to her last home in Kent, Ellen Terry lived for many years in a cottage with a Georgian front and a medieval back close by Strand Gate on the steep hill leading in from Rye. She was here at the time of Edward VII's accession, and went to the sister town of Rye to hear his proclamation. Beloved wherever she went, they still tell how the star of the Lyceum used to enter wholeheartedly into the life of Winchelsea, being never too proud to take part in the local amateur dramatics when a show was to be produced in aid of some charity.

Many years before her time the Duke of Wellington stayed in this same cottage when he visited Winchelsea during the Napoleonic scares to inspect his troops on Pett Level. These troops were then stationed in the extensive cellars of the houses in Barrack Square, some of which are so large that it is claimed that they could still accommodate ' a regiment of foot '. A house called ' Periteau ' then served as the officers' mess, while the munitions and such like were stored in ' Magazine House '.

Two of Winchelsea's most interesting old buildings are the medieval Court House, where the mayor-making ceremony takes place, and the ruined chapel with imposing choir arch and lancet windows used by the Greyfriars. Their old friary, built in 1320 but since rebuilt out of the original materials, was the home of the Weston brothers whom Thackeray has immortalized in his *Denis Duval*. These two brothers were after the style of Jekyll and Hyde, living in the Friary the lives of respectable country gentlemen but at other times menacing the surrounding countryside as highwaymen, for which exploits they eventually met their doom at Tyburn.

But the pride of Winchelsea is its three-gabled church, which occupies one of the village's eight squares. When it is remembered that this church—which is dedicated to St. Thomas à Becket—now stands at one end of the village, whereas once it was in the centre, it can be seen how greatly Winchelsea has shrunk since Edward I's time when it was so often being attacked by the French, and, by way of reprisal, was continually sending out its own sons to raid the French coast.

Though the church itself—which was one of the first buildings to be erected in the new Winchelsea—lost its nave during one of those attacks, its remaining chancel and two chapels are of such noble proportions that it would seem that the original building must have assumed the stature of a small cathedral. Indeed, the ruins of the tower piers and transepts and the still visible foundations of the vanished portions of the structure only strengthen that impression.

Winchelsea Church contains the finest Decorated work in the county, and the mouldings on the dividing arches have even been adjudged the best in the world. Among the many other pleasing features are two sedilia with open flower diaper work, a number of roof timbers from old ships wrecked off the coast here, and some splendid Kentish tracery in the windows.

The Perpendicular porch appropriately displays the arms of the Cinque Ports to the first of whose ' admirals ', Gervase Alard, who held the post at the turn of the thirteenth and fourteenth centuries, is a restored but still splendid Decorated canopied tomb which Thackeray introduced into *Denis Duval* and which Millais used as a background for one of his paintings. There is a similar tomb to Stephen Alard, who, like his grandfather, was also a Cinque Ports admiral.

It was by the west wall of Winchelsea's church that John Wesley, standing under the shade of an ash tree, delivered his last outdoor sermon, and in the square to the north is the Methodist Chapel which he opened, with the high pulpit from which he preached.

v

Udimore—the site of whose church is said to have been selected by the angels, who moved the stones by night to a more suitable spot than the marsh originally chosen by the masons—is only some two miles or so to the north of Winchel-. sea. And not far westwards of Udimore is Brede, with its Tudor mansion and Early English church in which may be seen Dean Swift's cradle.

These two villages are near the infant River Brede, approached through the Pipewell Gate, or Land Gate as it is sometimes called.

To complete our tour of the Cinque Ports, however, we must keep to the main road through Winchelsea, which takes us past Icklesham and Guestling—birthplace of Gregory Martin, author of the Douai version of the Bible—and so down to Hastings, so named after a Danish sea rover.

Hastings, the most important of the Sussex Cinque Ports, is

very much a place of two expressions in that, although it has developed into one of the largest of all our southern resorts, the old ways of life still linger.

The town crier, in silver-braided top hat and morning coat with silver buttons bearing the Cinque Ports arms, still parades the streets proclaiming his ' Oyez! Oyez! ' even though he sometimes experiences difficulty in vieing with the noise of the traffic. And in the little shipyards skilled crafts-men may be found constructing trawlers, or ' luggers ', of Sussex oak as did their forebears who built the ships for the Cinque Ports Fleet nearly one thousand years ago and later at the time of the Armada.

In their quaint tarred wooden worksheds on the beach the fishermen themselves—many of whom, like those of Rye, are of Huguenot extraction—are to be found making nets and shopping-bags in between putting to sea.

The fishermen have their own church, and every Rogation-tide their boats and nets and the sea are all blessed, when two processions, each led by the clergy and choir—one from the fishermen's church and the other from All Saints'—meet on the beach to join in prayers by the water's edge in a simple but arresting scene.

The Hastings fishermen have long forsaken their ' Hocking ' custom when on the Tuesday after Easter they would close all the streets in the town and exact tolls from any who wished to pass through; but in their Winkle Club they have started another which brings happiness to hundreds of children every Christmas.

This curious club came into being in an unusual way shortly before the Boer War. It is always said that the reason so many of the Hastings fishermen have patched seats to their trousers is that they have not sufficient work to do and so sit down too much! It would seem that in the closing years of the last century there may have been some truth in this, for some fifteen of their number were then so very much ' at a loose end ' that to help pass the time, so a fisherman once told me, they formed this society with a subscription of a penny a week and the one rule that each member was to carry on his person a fresh winkle. When one member met another he was to challenge him to ' winkle up ', and if the latter failed to do so he was required to forfeit the sum of twopence. Their object was to raise sufficient funds to provide an annual supper of bread and cheese with a pint of beer per head.

From such humble beginnings the Winkle Club grew until to-day many famous men and women all over the world, including at least one member of the Royal Family, now number among its members, and the club is able to give a Christmas tea to more than two thousand children in addition to holding their own dinner.

The members' wives do most of the catering, and the children march through the streets to the accompaniment of the club's own band. After their tea they are entertained and given presents. As for the fishermen, in normal times, they have been known to consume at their dinner as much as twelve legs of pork and 140 lb. of beef, while the quantity of beer served is not mentioned!

VI

The old fishing quarters in the shade of the high rugged cliffs with Old Town and the three-acre St. Clement's Caves where the smugglers of yore hid their contraband and where the people of Hastings sought shelter during the last war, can have changed but little with the centuries. Hastings, with its sister town of St. Leonards, has developed into the second resort in Sussex, surpassed only by Brighton and Hove, yet the Fish Market and Old Town remain much the same as when Turner came to paint the scene, finding here subjects for some of his greatest masterpieces.

Though Hastings, like Brighton, is now in essence modern,

many old buildings have survived. In All Saints Street and High Street in Old Town, as in George Street and West Street, are many half-timbered houses of the sixteenth century. Some of these have been stuccoed over, but, bit by bit, the stucco is being removed. Here and there are others equally pleasing, while on the promenade a number of late Georgian or Regency façades are to be found among the Victorian.

Writers, poets and artists of all ages have loved Hastings for its old corners. Charles Lamb, Byron, Kingsley, Thomas Hood, Coventry Patmore, 'Mark Rutherford' (W. H. White) and Edward Capel, Shakespearian commentator and friend of Garrick, and, in our time, Rider Haggard, Britten Austen and Sheila Kaye-Smith, these and many others have all lived or stayed in Hastings for lengthy periods.

Here, too, at Clements Church in Old Town, Dante Gabriel Rossetti married his famous model, Elizabeth Siddall, a beautiful Hastings girl.

This splendid Perpendicular Church of St. Clements dates back to 1380, its predecessor having been almost totally destroyed by the French. For Hastings, like Rye and Winchelsea, has also been plundered and sacked not once but many times. Indeed, two cannon balls may still be seen embedded in a wall of the tower of the church. Only one of them, however, is the scar of battle. The first was fired from a Dutch or French raiding vessel in the eighteenth century; the second was placed there to even things up from the artistic point of view.

All Saints, too, another fine example of the Perpendicular style, whose choir and clergy, as already mentioned, take part in the Blessing of the Sea ceremony, is also a fifteenth-century successor to one destroyed by the French.

But then, of course, Hastings has always been associated with war. The Saxons had a primitive earthwork here, and on the cliff-top are the sad but romantic fragmentary remains of the castle which William the Conqueror built.

The first Norman castle in England, it is said that he ferried the Caen stone across the Channel in boats like ' cockle shells ' and that once it was a mighty fortification occupying many acres. But so much has disappeared, not only of the building but also of the very ground on which it stood, that it is impossible to obtain anything like a true picture of its past magnificence. To-day all that remains are an archway, one or two bits of walls, the dungeons and the ruins of a church where St. Thomas à Becket served as dean and to which the Roman Catholics make an annual pilgrimage on the Wednesday following August Bank Holiday.

Though it was not until after his great victory of 1066 that the Conqueror built his castle, he previously raised a temporary structure here, and it was at Hastings that he mustered his forces before engaging King Harold in battle on lonely Senlac Moor, but six miles to the north-west.

VII

' If victory is granted to me in this battle I will found an abbey here for the salvation of the souls of all who fall in the engagement.' So said William of Normandy on reaching Telham Hill by Senlac Moor that 13th day of October, 1066.

Every one knows the carnage that followed when, throughout the next day, Saxon with bill, club or axe, fought Norman with lance, sword or mace, and victory hung in the balance for a full twelve hours. At last the undaunted King Harold received the fatal arrow in his eye, and Battle Abbey was soon to be built in all its splendour—a massive quadrangular edifice enclosed by a circular wall nine miles long. The monks whom William brought with him from Normandy would have raised it in the near-by valley where a more plenteous water supply was available, but William was adamant that it must stand on the hill-top where his hard-pressed victory had been won.

The first abbot was appointed in 1076 and sixty Benedictine

monks from the Abbey of Marmoutier in Normandy formed its nucleus. The Conqueror died before the building was completed, but when William Rufus presided over the consecration in 1095 he presented the abbey with his father's coronation robes and the sword he had carried in battle, together with the battle roll of the knights who had fought by his side.

Soon Battle became one of the wealthiest abbeys in England, possessed of many prosperous manors in various parts of the county with its abbots above episcopal authority and privileged to sit in Parliament. Its church, some 315 feet long, was considered second only to the Cathedral of Canterbury, and on its high altar—set up on the very spot where Harold fell— many kings made offerings.

At the Dissolution Battle passed to Sir Anthony Browne whom we met at Midhurst and who now lies in a sculptured tomb in the parish church of Battle. (Edmund Cartwright, the inventor of the power loom, is also buried here.) Whether it was at Battle or at Cowdray that the lasting curse was pronounced upon Sir Anthony and his descendants will always remain a matter for dispute, but not long after Battle came into private ownership the historic abbey gradually fell to decay, its ruined state being rendered the more complete by fire in our own time.

The great church has almost disappeared, leaving only a fragment of the altar to lie in the open like some milestone, while such as is left of the rest of the abbey—notably the medieval half-timbered Abbots' Lodge (now used as a girls' school) and the refectory with lancet windows, buttressed walls and vaulted ceilings—has been considerably, though sympathetically, restored. Thus it can no longer be considered contemporary with the Conqueror so much as a worthy memorial marking the site of the greatest battle in English history—a memorial of many crumbling Norman walls and foundations framed in well-mown green swards and approached through a magnificent three-storeyed gateway with octagonal towers of 1388, which, in the centre of a long, castellated wall of yellow sandstone, stands sentinel over Battle's High Street.

To visit Battle to-day it is hard to realize that the tide of English history was turned on the green fields where this ruined abbey and the little weather-boarded cottages now stand. For life goes on here much the same as in any other Sussex village.

BIBLIOGRAPHY

HARE, AUGUSTUS J. C.: *Sussex.* (1896.)
Sussex. (1777.)
WILLIS, T. G.: *Records of Chichester.* (1928.)
Jubilee of Brighton Corporation. (1904.)
LUCAS, E. V.: *Highways and Byways in Sussex.* (1904.)
MEE, ARTHUR: *Sussex.* (1937.)
HORSFIELD, THOMAS WALKER: *The History, Antiquities, and Topo-
    graphy of the County of Sussex.* (1835.)
YOUNG, GERARD: *The Cottage in the Fields.*
Bognor and Arundel Guide. (1828.)
MUMBY: *Memorials of Old Sussex.* (1909.)
HARRISON: *Notes on Sussex Churches.* (1920.)
ALLEN, E. HERON: *Selsey Bill.* (1911.)
Sussex. Methuen's Little Guide Series. (1938.)
MAXSE, LADY: *Petworth in Ancient Times.*
Petworth. Official Guide.
WINBOLT, S. E.: *Wealden Glass.*
STRAKER, ERNEST: *Wealden Iron.* (1931.)
SITWELL, OSBERT, and BARTON, MARGARET: *Brighton.* (1935.)
FYFE, HAMILTON: *The A.B.C. of Brighton.*
Adams' Guide to Rye.
Ye Historie of Ye Olde Palace of Mayfield.
Bodiam Castle. National Trust Guide.
HAY, ALEXANDER: *History of Chichester.*
JESSE, EDWARD: *Gleanings in Natural History.* (1835.)
COBBETT, WILLIAM: *Rural Rides.* (1835.)
PARISH, REV. W. D.: *A Dictionary of the Sussex Dialect.* (1875.)
WOODMAN, T. C.: *The South Downs.* (1902.)
GOSSET, A. L. J.: *Shepherds of Britain.* (1911.)
EUSTACE, G. W.: *Arundel, Borough and Castle.* (1922.)
WILLS, BARCLAY: *Shepherds of Sussex.*
EGERTON, REV. JOHN COKER: *Sussex Folk and Sussex Ways.* (1892.)
BURSTOW, HENRY: *Reminiscences of Horsham.* (1911.)
FLEET, C.: *Glimpses of Our Sussex Ancestors.* (1882.)

ANDREWS, HILDA: *My Ladye Nevells Booke.* (1926.)
BECKETT, ARTHUR: *The Spirit of the Downs.* (1909.)
HARPER, C. G.: *The Brighton Road.* (1892.)
WOODWARD, A. SMITH: *The Earliest Englishman.* (1948.)
The Southdown Sheep. Ed. E. WALFORD LLOYD. (1936.)
WYMER, NORMAN: *A Breath of England.* (1948.)
—— *English Country Crafts.* (1946.)
——*English Town Crafts.* (1949.)
Sussex County Magazine. (Various Issues.)
The Antiquaries Journal. (Various Issues.)
Country Life. (Various Issues.)

INDEX

275